I0044736

PRESENTED TO:

_____

FROM:

_____

HIS PASSION

HELPING PEOPLE WORLDWIDE EXPERIENCE *the* MANIFEST PRESENCE *of* GOD

Scripture quotations are from the following sources:

The Holy Bible, New International Version (NIV), copyright ©1973, 1978, 1984, International Bible Society. Used by permission of Zondervan Bible Publishers.

The *Holy Bible*, New Living Translation (NLT), copyright ©1996. Used by permission of Tyndale House Publishers, Inc., Wheaton, Illinois 60189. All rights reserved.

THE AMPLIFIED BIBLE (Amp.), copyright ©1954, 1958, 1962, 1964, 1965, 1987 by The Lockman Foundation. All rights reserved. Used by permission. (www.Lockman.org).

The New American Standard Bible® (NASB), copyright ©1960. 1962, 1963, 1968, 1971, 1972, 1973, 1975, 1977, 1995 by the Lockman Foundation. Used by permission.

The King James Version (KJV).

The Holy Bible, New King James Version (NKJV), copyright ©1979, 1980, 1982 by Thomas Nelson, Inc. Used by permission. All rights reserved.

The New Revised Standard Version Bible (NRSV), copyright ©1989 by the Division of Christian Education of the National Council of the Churches of Christ in the USA.

Produced with the assistance of The Livingstone Corporation (www.LivingstoneCorp.com). Introductions written by Neil Wilson. Project staff includes David Veerman, Linda Taylor, Joel Bartlett, Ashley Taylor, Kirk Luttrell, Emily Malone, Sharon Wright, Carol Fielding, Elly Johnson, Rosalie Krusemark.

Cover & Interior Design: DeAnna Pierce, Brand Navigation, LLC
(The Office of Bill Chiaravalle) www.brandnavigation.com
Cover Image: Arte & Immagini srl/Corbis
Interior Images: Mike Jaroszko

ISBN 1-59145-156-6

Printed and bound in China.
04 05 06 07   7 6

DEVOTIONS *for* EVERY DAY *of the* YEAR

His
PASSION

CHRIST'S JOURNEY
to the RESURRECTION

The MOST MOVING WORDS EVER WRITTEN
ABOUT *the* LAST DAYS *of* JESUS' LIFE

INTEGRITY®
PUBLISHERS

INTRODUCTION

For many centuries, followers of Jesus have considered with awe, silence, and renewed commitment His final days. The culmination of His suffering moves us to tears and to action. We cherish His last words. We meditate on the hours leading up to the Cross. We contemplate that rugged instrument of torture as a precious object because it measures the immeasurable. No matter how large we may imagine God's love to be, the cross shows us that His love is larger still.

During His last week, Jesus taught. He argued. He cried out. He answered some questions, parried others, and challenged both enemies and friends with the truth. He stood before His accusers silent. He allowed Himself to be crucified. He died. Those who loved Him as well as they knew how buried His body and mourned.

But not for long. The new week ushered in a new world. The first day turned out to be so much more than the beginning of another week—Resurrection Sunday cast a bright new light on everything. That is why the experience of Christ's Passion did not end with the moment His heart stopped beating but continues through today and on into eternity.

For the next 365 days, enter deeply into the Passion of Jesus. See Him through the eyes, minds, and words of others who have traveled this journey.

JESUS ENTERS JERUSALEM

—

*"Blessed is He who comes
in the name of the Lord!"*

MARK 11:9 NKJV

JESUS ENTERS JERUSALEM

The Triumphal Entry got so many things right but the crucial things wrong. Jesus received a royal welcome for shortsighted reasons. Those who cut the branches and spread their coats expected a lot from Jesus. They didn't expect enough. They wanted a king; they needed so much more.

The Triumphal Entry represents all of those clear moments when humanity has expressed its strongest wishes for God to intervene, but has mistaken its own purposes for God's. This opening scene in Jesus' final week serves as a reminder of all the ways in which Jesus' entry into history was misunderstood even by those who were expecting Him. The Triumphal Entry teaches us to acknowledge Jesus Christ for who He really is.

The readings in this section will not only focus on the events immediately surrounding the Triumphal Entry, but will also explore many of the other lessons about the earlier life and ministry of Jesus that might be seen one way, but ought to be understood in another. Our understanding of Jesus Himself has much to do with the way we see and understand the Triumphal Entry.

FOR US

JOHN 3:16 KJV
*For God so loved the world, that he gave his only
begotten Son, that whosoever believeth in him should
not perish, but have everlasting life.*

Thus dear did God hold the world. How dear? That He
gave His only-begotten Son for every one in the world
who will trust in Him. And how did He give? He gave Him,
in His birth as man, in order to be for ever one with us. He
gave Him, in His death on the cross as Surety, in order to take
our sin and curse upon Himself. He gave Him on the throne
of heaven, in order to arrange for our welfare, as our Representative and Intercessor over all the powers of heaven. He
gave Him in the outpouring of the Spirit, in order to dwell
in us, to be entirely and altogether our own. . . . Yes; that is the
love of God, that He gave His Son to us, for us, in us.

Nothing less than His Son Himself. This is the love of
God; not that He gives us something, but that He gives us
some one—a living person—not one or another blessing,
but Him in whom is all life and blessing—Jesus Himself.

ANDREW MURRAY

LIFE *in* HIM

JOHN 1:1,4 NLT
In the beginning the Word already existed. . . .
Life itself was in him, and this life gives light to everyone.

The Word was with God in the beginning, and the Man was subject to the pain of death. The human nature wasn't eternal, and the divine nature wasn't mortal. All His other attributes are considered in the same way. . . . It wasn't the human nature that fed the thousands, nor was it all powerful strength that hurried to the fig tree. Who was weary from the journey and who made the world exist by His word? What is the brightness of the glory and what was pierced with the nails? What body was beaten during Passion Week, and what body is externally glorified? This much is clear: that the blows belong to the servant who was the Lord, and honor belongs to the Lord who was a servant. As a result, Christ's natures are unified and their respective attributes belong to both natures. Just as the Lord received the scars of the servant, the servant is glorified with the honor of the Lord. For this is why the cross is called the cross of the Lord of glory, and why every tongue confesses that Jesus Christ is Lord, to the glory of God the Father.

GREGORY OF NYSSA

THE WORD MADE FLESH

JOHN 1:14 KJV

And the Word was made flesh, and dwelt among us,
(and we beheld his glory, the glory as of the only
begotten of the Father) full of grace and truth.

"The Word was made flesh" so that the wisdom of God could come within the reach of human beings. For his Word—the expression of the whole truth about God—is far beyond our comprehension. No creature can ever fully understand his creator. But the Word, the Son of God, put on a humble, human form, so that infinite truth could be seen in finite terms.

He humbled himself, coming down to the lowest human level. Those who will join him there—denying themselves, taking the low place—will be raised up with him to the heights of heaven.

It is not easy for man to stoop so low, or to abandon his self-confidence. But when he sees the divine Son lying, as it were, at his feet, wrapped in the clothes of human poverty, then his heart may be moved and his pride cured. And when we grow weary of trying to prove ourselves, we may be ready to cast ourselves upon him.

When we do, he who came down to where we are raises us to where he is.

AUGUSTINE

LIKE US

HEBREWS 2:17 NLT

Therefore, it was necessary for Jesus to be in every respect like us, his brothers and sisters, so that he could be our merciful and faithful High Priest before God. He then could offer a sacrifice that would take away the sins of the people.

When God entered time and became a man, he who was boundless became bound. Imprisoned in flesh. Restricted by weary-prone muscles and eyelids. For more than three decades, his once limitless reach would be limited to the stretch of an arm, his speed checked to the pace of human feet.

I wonder, was he ever tempted to reclaim his boundlessness? In the middle of a long trip, did he ever consider transporting himself to the next city? When the rain chilled his bones, was he tempted to change the weather? When the heat parched his lips, did he give thought to popping over to the Caribbean for some refreshment?

If ever he entertained such thoughts, he never gave in to them. Not once. Stop and think about this. Not once did Christ use his supernatural powers for personal comfort. With one word he could've transformed the hard earth into a soft bed, but he didn't.

With a wave of his hand, he could've boomeranged the spit of his accusers back into their faces, but he didn't. With an arch of his brow, he could've paralyzed the hand of the soldier as he braided the crown of thorns. But he didn't.

Remarkable.

MAX LUCADO

GOD *with* US

MATTHEW 1:23 NIV
*"The virgin will be with child and will give birth
to a son, and they will call him Immanuel"—
which means, "God with us."*

We read and believe many things in light of the Incarnation. But even in our human feelings, we can observe God's greatness. For example, Jesus is wearied by His journey so that He can refresh the weary. He desires a drink when He is about to give spiritual water to the thirsty. He was hungry when He was about to supply the food of salvation to the hungry. He dies to live again. He is buried to rise again. He hangs on the dreadful cross to strengthen those in dread. He veils the heaven with thick darkness so that He can give light. He makes the earth shake so that He may make it strong. He rouses the sea so that He can calm it. He opens the tombs of the dead so that He can show that they are the homes of the living. He is born of a virgin so that people can believe He is born of God. He pretends not to know so that He can make the ignorant know. As a Jew He is said to worship so that the Son may be worshiped as the true God.

AMBROSE

A CAMEO *of* GOD

MATTHEW 1:23 KJV

Behold, a virgin shall be with child, and shall bring forth a son, and they shall call his name Emmanuel, which being interpreted is, God with us.

In the birth of Jesus, we see God coming in weak and vulnerable human form. God chooses to share our location and condition. God is with us. In the death of Jesus, we see God present in suffering human form. God chooses to take our part instead of being our enemy. God is for us. In the resurrection and ascension, we see God in victorious human form. In this form, insinuating himself into the depths of our very being, God is in us—as the Spirit of Christ. Three views of Jesus, three views of God.

Here, then, in a cameo, is the glory of God. Here is what God is really like. He is the God who is with us, the God who is for us, and the God who is in us. In short, when God shows his face, he always shows his grace; the treasure that he offers to lodge with us is nothing other than the grace of God. For when we say grace, we mean precisely this: the promise of God-with-us, the power of God-in-us, and the pardon of God-for-us.

LEWIS B. SMEDES

THE FORM *of a* SERVANT

PHILIPPIANS 2:6–8 NIV

*Who, being in very nature God, did not consider equality with
God something to be grasped, but made himself nothing, taking
the very nature of a servant, being made in human likeness.
And being found in appearance as a man, he humbled himself
and became obedient to death—even death on a cross!*

What does the Church think of Christ?

The Church's answer is categorical and uncompromising, and it is this: That Jesus Bar-Joseph, the carpenter of Nazareth, was in fact and in truth, and in the most exact and literal sense of the words, the God "by whom all things were made." . . .

Now, this is not just a pious commonplace; it is not a commonplace at all. For what it means is this, among other things: that for whatever reason God chose to make man as he is—limited and suffering and subject to sorrows and death—he [God] had the honesty and the courage to take his own medicine. Whatever game he is playing with his creation, he has kept his own rules and played fair. He can exact nothing from man that he has not exacted from himself.

He has himself gone through the whole of human experience, from the trivial irritations of family life and the cramping restrictions of hard work and lack of money to the worst horrors of pain and humiliation, defeat, despair, and death. When he was a man, he played the man. He was born in poverty and died in disgrace and thought it well worthwhile.

DOROTHY SAYERS

THE PROCESSION BEGINS

Go ye into the village over against you; in the which at your entering ye shall find a colt tied, whereon yet never man sat: loose him, and bring him hither.

It is indeed the lowliest of all memorable processions which He plans, and yet, in its very humility, it appeals to ancient prophecy, and says unto Zion that her King cometh unto her. The monarchs of the East and the captains of the West might ride upon horses as for war, but the King of Zion would come unto her meek, and sitting upon an ass, upon a colt, the foal of an ass. Yet there is fitness and dignity in the use of "a colt whereon never man sat," and it reminds us of other facts, such as that He was the firstborn of a virgin mother, and rested in a tomb which corruption had never soiled.

Thus He comes forth, the gentlest of the mighty, with no swords gleaming around to guard Him, or to smite the foreigner who tramples Israel, or the worse foes of her own household. Men who will follow such a King must lay aside their vain and earthly ambitions, and awake to the truth that spiritual powers are grander than any which violence ever grasped.

CHADWICK

YOUR KING COMES

MATTHEW 21:5 NKJV

"Tell the daughter of Zion, 'Behold, your King is coming to you, lowly, and sitting on a donkey, a colt, the foal of a donkey.'"

Christ's public Entry into Jerusalem seems so altogether different from—we had almost said, inconsistent with—His previous mode of appearance. Evidently, the time for the silence so long enjoined had passed, and that for public declaration had come. And such, indeed, this Entry was. From the moment of His sending forth the two disciples to His acceptance of the homage of the multitude, and His rebuke of the Pharisee's attempt to arrest it, all must be regarded as designed or approved by Him: not only a public assertion of His Messiahship, but a claim to its national acknowledgment. And yet, even so, it was not to be the Messiah of Israel's conception, but He of prophetic picture: "just and having salvation; lowly, and riding upon an ass." . . . There can, at least, be no question that this prophecy was intended to introduce, in contrast to earthly warfare and kingly triumph, another Kingdom, of which the just King would be the Prince of Peace, Who was meek and lowly in His Advent, Who would speak peace to the heathen, and Whose sway would yet extend to earth's utmost bounds.

ALFRED EDERSHEIM

TRULY HUMAN, TRULY GOD

MATTHEW 21:5 NIV
"See, your king comes to you . . ."

The God of all things and of His holy angels was made known beforehand through the prophets . . . As a result, all the Jewish people hung in expectation of His coming. After Jesus' arrival, however, they fell into a keen dispute with each other. A large number acknowledged Christ and believed Him to be the object of prophecy while others didn't believe in Him . . . Instead, they dared to inflict upon Jesus cruelties His disciples truthfully and candidly recorded. But both Jesus and His disciples desired that His followers wouldn't believe merely in His Godhead and miracles (as if He hadn't also taken on human nature and assumed the human flesh which "lusteth against the Spirit"), but that they would also see that He had descended into human nature and into the midst of human miseries. He assumed a human soul and body. From Him there began the union of the divine with the human nature, in order that the human, by communion with the divine, might rise to be divine . . . Everyone who lives according to Jesus' teaching rises to a friendship with God and communion with Him.

ORIGEN

LOVE URGED HIM ON

MATTHEW 21:7 NRSV
They brought the donkey and the colt,
and put their cloaks on them, and he sat on them.

The Saviour, what a noble flame was kindled in His breast,
When hasting to Jerusalem, He march'd before the rest.
Good-will to men and zeal for God His every thought
    engross;
He longs to be baptized with blood, He pants to reach the
    cross!
With all His sufferings full in view, and woes to us unknown,
Forth to the task His spirit flew; 'twas love that urged Him on.
Lord, we return Thee what we can: Our hearts shall sound
    abroad
Salvation to the dying Man, and to the rising God!
And while Thy bleeding glories here engage our wondering
    eyes,
We learn our lighter cross to bear, and hasten to the skies.

WILLIAM COWPER

A LOT *to* LEARN

MARK 11:8 NIV
Many people spread their cloaks on the road,
while others spread branches they had cut in the fields.

This was Jesus' announcement that he was indeed the long-awaited Messiah. He chose a *time* when all Israel would be gathered at Jerusalem, a *place* where huge crowds could see him, and a *way* of proclaiming his mission that was unmistakable. The people went wild. They were sure their liberation from Rome was at hand. While the crowd correctly saw Jesus as the fulfillment of these prophecies, they did not understand where Jesus' kingship would lead him. The people who were praising God for giving them a king had the wrong idea about Jesus. They expected him to be a national leader who would restore their nation to its former glory; thus, they were deaf to the words of their prophets and blind to Jesus' real mission. When it became apparent that Jesus was not going to fulfill their hopes, many people would turn against him. A similar crowd would cry out, "Crucify him!" when Jesus stood on trial only a few days later. It takes more than participation at a praise gathering to be a true friend and follower of Jesus. . . .

Like the people on the road to Jerusalem that day, we have much to learn about Jesus' death and resurrection. We must not let our personal desires catch us up in the celebration and shouting lest we miss the meaning of true discipleship.

LIFE APPLICATION BIBLE COMMENTARY—MARK

BLESSED IS HE WHO COMES

MATTHEW 21:9 NKJV
"Blessed is He who comes in the name of the Lord!"

Praise God! The world of humanity that had been separated from God and unable to approach Him except indirectly through the Jewish sacrifices and ceremonies was now invited to draw near and be reconciled directly to Him through this Baby Who had invaded time and space to be born! . . .

Real meaning to your life is found in the glorious dawn of God's story, which breaks into full revelation in the Person of Jesus Christ. What an astounding truth! What a life-changing message!

> Because He emptied Himself of all but love,
>   you can be filled.
> Because His body was broken, your life can be whole.
> Because His blood was shed, your sin can be forgiven.
> Because He submitted to injustice, you can forgive.
> Because He finished His Father's work, your life has worth.
> Because He was forsaken, you will never be alone.
> Because He was buried, you can be raised.
> Because He lives, you don't have to be afraid.
> Because He reached down to you, you don't have to
>   work your way up to Him.
> Because His promises are always true, you can have hope!

ANNE GRAHAM LOTZ

HOSANNA!

MATTHEW 21:9 NKJV

*"Hosanna to the Son of David! 'Blessed is He who comes
in the name of the Lord!' Hosanna in the highest!"*

Let shouts of gladness rise
Triumphant to the skies.
Now comes the King most glorious
To reign o'er all victorious:
Hosanna, praise, and glory!
Our King, we bow before Thee.

He wears no kingly crown,
Yet as a King is known;
Though not arrayed in splendor,
Hosanna, praise, and glory!
Our King, we bow before Thee.

Thy heart now open wide,
Bid Christ with thee abide.
He graciously will hear thee
And be forever near thee.
Hosanna, praise, and glory!
Our King, we bow before Thee.

AUTHOR UNKNOWN

IN *the* NAME *of the* LORD

JOHN 12:13 NKJV
"Blessed is He who comes in the name of the Lord."

The Son of God was made the Son of Man for our salvation. Nine months He waited for His birth in the womb. . . . He who encloses the world in His fist was contained in the narrow walls of a manger. . . . When He was whipped, He remained calm. When He was crucified, He prayed for His crucifiers. . . . The only fitting response we can make toward Him is to give blood for blood. Because we are redeemed by the blood of Christ, we should gladly desire to lay down our lives for our Redeemer. What saints have ever won their crowns without competing first? . . . You will find that all holy people have suffered persecution. . . . Which is best—to fight for a short time, to carry stakes for the stockade, to bear arms, and to faint under heavy battles in order to rejoice as victors forever, or to become slaves forever because we can't endure for a single hour?

JEROME

THE STONES WILL CRY OUT

LUKE 19:39–40 NASB
And some of the Pharisees in the multitude said to Him,
"Teacher, rebuke Your disciples." And He answered and said,
"I tell you, if these become silent, the stones will cry out!"

But could the stones cry out? Assuredly they could if He who opens the mouth of the dumb should bid them lift up their voice. Certainly if they were to speak, they would have much to testify in praise of Him who created them by the word of His power; they could extol the wisdom and power of their Maker who called them into being. Shall not we speak well of Him who made us anew, and out of stones raised up children unto Abraham? . . . If the stones were to speak, they could tell of their breaker, how he took them from the quarry, and made them fit for the temple, and cannot we tell of our glorious Breaker, who broke our hearts with the hammer of His word, that He might build us into His temple? If the stones should cry out they would magnify their builder, who polished them and fashioned them after the similitude of a palace; and shall not we talk of our Architect and Builder, who has put us in our place in the temple of the living God?

CHARLES HADDON SPURGEON

JESUS CLEARS *the* TEMPLE

---

*He taught them, "The Scriptures
declare, 'My Temple will be called a place
of prayer for all nations,' but you have
turned it into a den of thieves."*

MARK 11:17 NLT

JESUS CLEARS *the* TEMPLE

To some people, Jesus was a dangerous man. His passion had a fierce edge to it. He was as unpredictable in His actions as He was in His words. So, on the day of the Triumphal Entry, Mark tells us, Jesus went into the temple and looked carefully at the activities. He came back the next day and cleaned the house of God. He passed through the temple courts like a righteous, unstoppable fire. In fact, this was the second time Jesus had tried to clean house. The first time Jesus cleared the temple, early in His ministry, His disciples were reminded of an ancient phrase from the psalms, "Passion for God's house burns within me" (John 2:17 NLT; see also Psalm 69:9).

On the way into Jerusalem the next day, Jesus cursed a fig tree. The disciples wondered what it meant. Jesus told them that the withering of the fig tree pictured power in prayer. With faith, they too would be able to do anything.

This section includes readings on the central place of worship in the life of a believer. Radical action must sometimes be taken in order to keep the clutter and distractions out of our fellowship with God and our intentions to bring glory to Him.

TEARS *for the* CITY

LUKE 19:41 NLT
*But as they came closer to Jerusalem and Jesus
saw the city ahead, he began to cry.*

Jesus crested the shoulder of the last hill on the way from Bethany. The road dropped suddenly as a familiar scene stunned the travelers. For a moment, the silent stones offered the most eloquent commentary on the view.

The early morning sun warmed Jesus' shoulders. It bathed the walls and towers of Jerusalem, glowing on the far side of the valley. Tall and proud in the distance, the conquered city hid her shame behind massive stones and strong gates.

The colt stopped and those close by caught an unexpected sound. Jesus was weeping. The words that flowed with his tears explained his sorrow. He saw what others could not see. He felt the horror of the city's fate, with enemies attacking from every side. Instead of the invincible fortress before him, Jesus viewed the city leveled and her children gone.

Jesus also whispered his sorrow over the condition of Jerusalem, oblivious of "the things which make for peace." Even as he heard the welcoming crowds, Jesus knew that he walked among so many who "did not recognize the time of your visitation."

How often does Jesus get welcomed with ignorant fanfare? How often do we give him loud but uncommitted praise? How often do we recognize the time of our visitation?

NEIL WILSON

COMING JUDGMENT

LUKE 19:42–43 NIV

"If you, even you, had only known on this day what would bring you peace—but now it is hidden from your eyes. The days will come upon you when your enemies will build an embankment against you and encircle you and hem you in on every side."

Who can behold the holy Jesus, looking forward to the miseries that awaited his murderers, weeping over the city where his precious blood was about to be shed, without seeing that the likeness of God in the believer, consists much in good will and compassion? Surely those cannot be right who take up any doctrines of truth, so as to be hardened towards their fellow sinners. But let every one remember, that though Jesus wept over Jerusalem, he executed awful vengeance upon it. Though he delights not in the death of a sinner, yet he will surely bring to pass his awful threatenings on those who neglect his salvation. The Son of God did not weep vain and causeless tears, nor for a light matter, nor for himself. He knows the value of souls, the weight of guilt, and how low it will press and sink mankind. May he then come and cleanse our hearts by his Spirit, from all that defiles. May sinners, on every side, become attentive to the words of truth and salvation.

MATTHEW HENRY

MEEKNESS ISN'T WEAKNESS

*Jesus made a whip from some ropes and chased them all out
of the Temple. He drove out the sheep and oxen, scattered the
money changers' coins over the floor, and turned over their tables.*

Whenever you and I hear the word *meek,* our minds
tend to think *weak.* But meek is not weak. Not even
close. . . .

Strength under control.

Power under discipline.

Jesus is the prime example of a meek person. Was Jesus
weak? Well, go back and watch Him as He cleans out the
temple. With a whip made out of cords, He drove everyone
out of the temple courtyard in extremely short order. No
one struggled with Him. No one challenged Him. I find it
hard to believe some wimp could have accomplished this.
No one wanted to mess with the Man from Nazareth. He
was very strong and had great authority . . . but He also
characterized Himself as a meek person. . . .

Jesus was meek. He had the greatest possible strength
under the greatest possible control. While He was on the
cross, He could have called ten legions of angels to come to
His aid. But He stayed on that cross and held His vast power
in check . . . out of love for you and me.

DAVID JEREMIAH

A GOOD CLEANING

LUKE 19:45 NLT

Then Jesus entered the Temple and began to drive out the merchants from their stalls.

Jesus' outburst in the temple shows us what righteous indignation looks like. He grew furious because the priests and their associates were keeping people away from God— and that always makes God *very* angry. . . .

We should also remember that Jesus twice cleansed the temple, once at the beginning of His ministry and once toward the end (see John 2:13–17). For a while after the first cleansing, things at the temple ran well. But soon one man set up his table, the prices soared, and another joined him. In time, things got as bad as ever, so Jesus came back and did it again right before his death.

In a similar way, when we first come to Christ, Jesus "cleanses our temple." The Lord banishes filthy habits and gives us a new purpose. In time, however, some of the old things find their way back in, and soon we find our lives cluttered with junk that shouldn't be there. That's when Jesus needs to return for another "house cleaning."

What does your "temple" look like today? Could it use a little cleansing?

GREG LAURIE

ZEAL *for* GOD'S HOUSE

JOHN 2:16–17 KJV

*And said unto them that sold doves, Take these things hence;
make not my Father's house an house of merchandise. And his
disciples remembered that it was written, The zeal of thine
house hath eaten me up.*

"T hen the disciples remembered that it was written, The
zeal of Thine house hath eaten me up": because by this
zeal of God's house, the Lord cast these men out of the temple. Brethren, let every Christian among the members of
Christ be eaten up with zeal of God's house. Who is eaten
up with zeal of God's house? He who exerts himself to have
all that he may happen to see wrong there corrected, desires
it to be mended, does not rest idle: who if he cannot mend
it, endures it, laments it. . . . Therefore, let the zeal of God's
house eat thee up: let the zeal of God's house eat up every
Christian, zeal of that house of God of which he is a mem-
ber. For thy own house is not more important than that
wherein thou hast everlasting rest. Thou goest into thine
own house for temporal rest, thou enterest God's house for
everlasting rest. If, then, thou busiest thyself to see that nothing wrong be done in thine own house, is it fit that thou suffer, so far as thou canst help, if thou shouldst chance to see
aught wrong in the house of God, where salvation is set
before thee, and rest without end?

AUGUSTINE

LOVE *for* GOD'S HOUSE

JOHN 2:16–17 NLT

Then, going over to the people who sold doves, he told them,
"Get these things out of here. Don't turn my Father's house
into a marketplace!" Then his disciples remembered this prophecy
from the Scriptures: "Passion for God's house burns within me."

Jesus watched and listened for a few moments. Then he filled
his lungs, and in a voice which carried above the bleating
and lowing, shouts of sellers, and arguments of the cheated, he
called out texts from the prophets Isaiah and Jeremiah: "It is
written: 'My house shall be called a house of prayer for all
nations' But you are making it a 'den of robbers'!"

With set face, he walked up to the nearest row of money
changers' tables and pushed them over, one after another.
Coins clattered on the paving stones and rolled away. He upset
the seats of the sellers of doves and drove flocks and herds
toward the gate, calling out repeatedly the texts by which buying and selling in the Temple stood condemned. . . .

As the Twelve helped Jesus, John was impressed beyond
all else by the expression on his face: not of moral force only
but of love. John could feel the love which drove Jesus: love
for God and his Temple, love for the cheated, love for the
merchants and herdsmen who had been trapped into sacri-
lege by greed and custom, even love for the Temple authorities who had betrayed their trust.

JOHN POLLOCK

HEARTS STOLEN AWAY *from* GOD

MATTHEW 21:12–13 NKJV

*Then Jesus went into the temple of God and drove out all those
who bought and sold in the temple, and overturned the tables of
the money changers and the seats of those who sold doves. And
He said to them, "It is written, 'My house shall be called a
house of prayer,' but you have made it a 'den of thieves.'"*

Shall those who are temples of the living God, suffer themselves to be dens of thieves and cages of unclean birds?
Shall vain unchaste thoughts be suffered to dwell within
them? Much less shall any thing that is impure be conceived
or acted by them? . . . We all know with what distinguished
ardor our blessed Redeemer purged an earthly temple; a zeal
for his father's house even eat him up: with what a holy vehe-
mence did he overturn the tables of the money-changers, and
scourge the buyers and sellers out before him! Why? They
made his father's house a house of merchandise: they had
turned the house of prayer into a den of thieves.

O my brethren, how often have you and I been guilty
of this great evil? How often have the lust of the flesh, the
lust of the eye, and the pride of life, insensibly stolen away
our hearts from God? Once they were indeed houses of
prayer; faith, hope, love, peace, joy, and all the other fruits of
the blessed Spirit lodged within them; but now, O now, it
may be, thieves and robbers. . . . Cleanse thou therefore the
thoughts of our hearts by the inspiration of thy blessed
Spirit, that henceforward we may more perfectly love thee
and more worthily magnify thy holy name!

GEORGE WHITEFIELD

HOUSE *of* PRAYER

MATTHEW 21:12 NIV
Jesus entered the temple area and drove out all who were buying and selling there. He overturned the tables of the money changers and the benches of those selling doves.

Thy mansion is the Christian's heart, O Lord, Thy dwelling-place secure!
Bid the unruly throng depart, and leave the consecrated door.
Devoted as it is to Thee, a thievish swarm frequents the place;
They steal away my joys from me, and rob my Saviour of His praise.
There, too, a sharp designing trade sin, Satan, and the world maintain;
Nor cease to press me, and persuade to part with ease, and purchase pain.
I know them, and I hate their din, am weary of the bustling crowd;
But while their voice is heard within, I cannot serve Thee as I would.
Oh for the joy Thy presence gives, what peace shall reign when Thou art here!
Thy presence makes this den of thieves a calm delightful house of prayer.
And if Thou make Thy temple shine, yet self-abased, will I adore;
The gold and silver are not mine, I give Thee what was Thine before.

WILLIAM COWPER

CHOOSE YOUR SIDE

MATTHEW 21:15 NIV
*But when the chief priests and the teachers of the
law saw the wonderful things he did and the children
shouting in the temple area, "Hosanna to the Son
of David," they were indignant.*

After this episode, people could not ignore Jesus or be indifferent to him. They had to take sides. Either Jesus was a subversive radical who must be restrained (death is an effective restraint), or he was someone to be listened to, believed, and followed.

Today, indifference is common because people are not listening to Jesus' words. When Christians tell the real story, there is no middle ground. Either Jesus is God's Son, the world's Savior, or he is a befuddled, perhaps demented, imposter.

Today listen, believe, and follow—while there's time—before Jesus comes to clean the area of false religion one last time.

LIFE APPLICATION BIBLE COMMENTARY—MARK

SWEET FELLOWSHIP *and* REST

MATTHEW 21:17 NLT
*Then he returned to Bethany,
where he stayed overnight.*

Jesus knew and practiced the discipline of rest, and he honored his friends by allowing them to host him throughout this final week. Between days of intense public pressure in Jerusalem, Jesus found fellowship in Bethany. Jesus balanced stress with friendship and quietness. His example reminds us to make time for rest.

A life intent on serving God will meet resistance. Others may reject or misunderstand our efforts. Evil doesn't give ground without a fight. Even God's work leads to tired workers. The fourth commandment has not been canceled. Jesus put it in its proper context (Mark 2:27) by reminding us that God ordered us to rest for our benefit, not just to obey a command. Like Jesus, we may have to leave the place of conflict and stress in order to rest. Bethany was no escape or retreat; it was refreshment. How often do you rest? Do you plan times of withdrawal for reflection and renewal? Discipleship will be weary work without the component of rest. We are under orders to include it.

LIFE APPLICATION BIBLE COMMENTARY—MATTHEW

JESUS TELLS PARABLES *and* ANSWERS QUESTIONS

*"Now my soul is troubled.
And what should I say—'Father,
save me from this hour'? No, it
is for this reason that I have
come to this hour."*

JOHN 12:27 NRSV

JESUS TELLS PARABLES *and*
ANSWERS QUESTIONS

Jesus hid the truth in stories; His enemies concealed their weapons in questions. The parables breached defenses and destroyed arguments while sounding like little more than practical tales to those who listened carelessly. Many of the questions thrust at Jesus had a public covering of curiosity or desire to know, but they also carried a poisonous barb of self-incrimination. Verbal swordsman that He was, Jesus demonstrated His mastery of people's hearts by His counterthrusts, disarming comments, and unexpected jabs.

Even when Jesus spoke the truth plainly, it remained hidden by people's misunderstanding. This section follows Jesus during the intense days of public exposure and scrutiny as the tide of opinion shifted from the exuberant political cheering of the Triumphal Entry to the bloodthirsty calls for crucifixion that ended the week. The stories and dialogues remain as a witness to Jesus' keen awareness of the underlying sequence of events in which He had a central role.

PREPARED *for the* KINGDOM

MATTHEW 21:43 NIV

"Therefore I tell you that the kingdom of God will be taken away from you and given to a people who will produce its fruit."

One who delights in the world, who is enticed by flattering and deceiving earthly pleasures wants to remain in the world a long time. . . . Since the world hates Christians, why do you love that which hates you? And why don't you follow Christ instead, who both redeemed you and loves you? John, in his epistle, cries and urges us not to follow fleshly desires and love the world. "Love not the world," he says, "neither the things which are in the world. If any man love the world, the love of the Father is not in him. . . . And the world shall pass away, and the lust thereof; but he who doeth the will of God abideth for ever, even as God abideth for ever." Instead, beloved, let us be prepared for the will of God with a sound mind, a firm faith, and strong virtue. Laying aside the fear of death, let us think on the eternal life to come. Through this knowledge, let us demonstrate that we are what we believe . . . Then we won't delay or resist the Lord on the day He calls us to Himself.

CYPRIAN

WORTHY *of the* FEAST

MATTHEW 22:11–12 NLT

"But when the king came in to meet the guests, he noticed a man who wasn't wearing the proper clothes for a wedding. 'Friend,' he asked, 'how is it that you are here without wedding clothes?' And the man had no reply."

A certain man in the Gospels went to a marriage feast. He put on unbecoming clothes, came in, sat down, and ate—for the bridegroom allowed it. However, when he saw everyone dressed in white, he should have found the same kind of clothes for himself. While he ate food like them, he wasn't like them in his fashion and purpose. . . . [The master] saw a stranger who wasn't wearing wedding clothes and said to him, "Friend, how did you get in here? With what conscience? It wasn't because the doorkeeper didn't stop you, but because of the host's generosity. Were you ignorant of what clothes to wear to the banquet? You came in and saw the glittering style of the guests—shouldn't you have learned by what was right before your eyes? Shouldn't you have tactfully excused yourself so that you could come back again dressed appropriately?" . . . So he commands the servants, "Bind his feet which have boldly intruded. Bind his hands which didn't know how to put on bright clothes. And cast him into the outer darkness, for he is unworthy of the wedding celebration." You see what happened to that man, so be worthy of the feast.

CYRIL OF JERUSALEM

HIS PASSION

THEY SHOULD HAVE KNOWN

MATTHEW 22:15 KJV
*Then went the Pharisees, and took counsel
how they might entangle him in his talk.*

THEN. When? When most of all they ought to have been moved to compunction, when they should have been amazed at His love to man, when they should have feared the things to come, when from the past they ought to have believed touching the future also. For indeed the things that had been said cried aloud in actual fulfillment I mean, that publicans and harlots believed, and prophets and righteous men were slain, and from these things they ought not to have gainsaid touching their own destruction, but even to believe and to be sobered. But nevertheless not even so do their wicked acts cease, but travail and proceed further. And forasmuch as they could not lay hands on Him (for they feared the multitude), they took another way with the intention of bringing Him into danger, and making Him guilty of crimes against the state.

CHRYSOSTOM

THE QUESTION *of* TAXES

MATTHEW 22:17 NIV
"Tell us then, what is your opinion?
Is it right to pay taxes to Caesar or not?"

What but divine wisdom could escape from so cunningly devised a dilemma! Thus, before answering, Jesus exposes the meanness and hypocrisy in their question, thereby emphasizing the important fact that he did not dodge, but answered it. . . .

Each nation uses its own coin. Had the Jews not been under Roman sovereignty, they would not have been using Roman money; but the coin which they brought to Jesus bore witness against them that the Roman sovereignty was established in their land, and that tribute to it was therefore justly due; for whoso uses Caesar's coin must pay Caesar's tribute. This part of the answer satisfied the Herodians; and the last part "and unto God," etc., satisfied the people, for it asserted, in a manner which carried conviction with it, that the payment of enforced tribute was not inconsistent with maintaining complete allegiance of God. God was no longer, as of old, the civil ruler of his people, and hence the payment of tribute to a temporal sovereign is in no sense incompatible with his service, but is enjoined as a Christian duty. They were amazed to find how far his wisdom transcended that of the teachers in whom they had such supreme confidence.

J. W. MCGARVEY AND PHILIP Y. PENDLETON

THE QUESTION *of the* RESURRECTION

MARK 12:23 NKJV
*"Therefore, in the resurrection, when they rise,
whose wife will she be? For all seven had her as wife."*

In His argument against the Sadducees Christ first appealed
to the *power* of God. What God would work was quite
other than they imagined: not a mere re-awakening, but a
transformation. The world to come was not to be a repro-
duction of that which had passed away—else why should it
have passed away—but a regeneration and renovation. . . .

Our Lord would not merely reply, He would answer
the Sadducees; and more grand or noble evidence of the
Resurrection has never been offered than that which He
gave. Of course, as speaking to the Sadducees, He remained
on the ground of the Pentateuch; and yet it was not only to
the Law but to the whole Bible that He appealed, nay, to that
which underlay Revelation itself: the relation between God
and man. . . . He Who, not only historically but in the fullest
sense, calls Himself the God of Abraham, of Isaac, and of
Jacob, cannot leave them dead. . . . "He is not the God of the
dead, but of the living, for all live unto Him."

The Sadducees were silenced, the multitude was astonished, and even from some of the Scribes the admission was
involuntarily wrung: "Teacher, Thou has beautifully said."

ALFRED EDERSHEIM

WRONG ASSUMPTIONS

MARK 12:24 NRSV

Jesus said to them, "Is not this the reason you are wrong,
that you know neither the scriptures nor the power of God?"

The doctrines of Christ displeased the infidel Sadducees, as well as the Pharisees and Herodians. He carried the great truths of the resurrection and a future state, further than they had yet been revealed. There is no arguing from the state of things in this world, as to what will take place hereafter. Let truth be set in a clear light, and it appears in full strength. Having thus silenced them, our Lord proceeded to show the truth of the doctrine of the resurrection from the books of Moses. God declared to Moses that he was the God of the patriarchs, who had died long before; this shows that they were then in a state of being, capable of enjoying his favour, and proves that the doctrine of the resurrection is clearly taught in the Old Testament as well as in the New. But this doctrine was kept for a more full revelation, after the resurrection of Christ, who was the firstfruits of them that slept. All errors arise from not knowing the Scriptures and the power of God.

MATTHEW HENRY

THE GREATEST COMMANDMENT

MATTHEW 22:36 NRSV
"Teacher, which commandment in the law is the greatest?"

An interpreter of the law asked our Lord a question, to try, not so much his knowledge, as his judgment. The love of God is the first and great commandment, and the sum of all the commands of the first table. Our love of God must be sincere, not in word and tongue only. All our love is too little to bestow upon him, therefore all the powers of the soul must be engaged for him, and carried out toward him. To love our neighbour as ourselves, is the second great commandment. There is a self-love which is corrupt, and the root of the greatest sins, and it must be put off and mortified; but there is a self-love which is the rule of the greatest duty: we must have a due concern for the welfare of our own souls and bodies. And we must love our neighbour as truly and sincerely as we love ourselves; in many cases we must deny ourselves for the good of others. By these two commandments let our hearts be formed as by a mould.

MATTHEW HENRY

NOT FAR *from the* KINGDOM

MARK 12:34 NRSV
When Jesus saw that he answered wisely,
he said to him, "You are not far from the kingdom of God."
After that no one dared to ask him any question.

If the first thought of your spirit has been, How can I honour Jesus? If the daily desire of your soul has been, "O that
I knew where I might find Him!" I tell you that you may
have a thousand infirmities, and even scarcely know whether
you are a child of God at all, and yet I am persuaded, beyond
a doubt, that you are safe, since Jesus is great in your esteem.
I care not for thy rags, what thinkest thou of His royal appar-
el? I care not for thy wounds, though they bleed in torrents,
what thinkest thou of His wounds? Are they like glittering
rubies in thine esteem? I think none the less of thee, though
thou liest like Lazarus on the dunghill, and the dogs do lick
thee—I judge thee not by thy poverty: what thinkest thou of
the King in His beauty? Has He a glorious high throne in
thy heart? Wouldst thou set Him higher if thou couldst?
Wouldst thou be willing to die if thou couldst but add
another trumpet to the strain which proclaims His praise?
Ah! then it is well with thee.

CHARLES HADDON SPURGEON

WHAT THINK WE *of* CHRIST?

MATTHEW 22:45 NRSV
"If David thus calls him Lord, how can he be his son?"

When Christ baffled his enemies, he asked what thoughts they had of the promised Messiah. How he could be the Son of David and yet his Lord? He quotes Psalm 110:1. If the Christ was to be a mere man, who would not exist till many ages after David's death, how could his forefather call him Lord? The Pharisees could not answer it. Nor can any solve the difficulty except he allows the Messiah to be the Son of God, and David's Lord equally with the Father. He took upon him human nature, and so became God manifested in the flesh; in this sense he is the Son of man and the Son of David. It behooves us above all things seriously to inquire, "What think we of Christ?" Is he altogether glorious in our eyes, and precious to our hearts? May Christ be our joy, our confidence, our all. May we daily be made more like to him, and more devoted to his service.

MATTHEW HENRY

GLORIFY THY NAME

JOHN 12:27–28 NIV

"Now my heart is troubled, and what shall I say? 'Father, save me from this hour'? No, it was for this very reason I came to this hour. Father, glorify your name!" Then a voice came from heaven, "I have glorified it, and will glorify it again."

What does it mean to glorify God? It may get a dangerous twist if we are not careful. *Glorify* is like the word *beautify*. But *beautify* usually means "make something more beautiful than it is," improve its beauty. That is emphatically *not* what we mean by *glorify* in relation to God. God cannot be made more glorious or more beautiful than he is. He cannot be improved, "nor is he served by human hands, as though he needed anything" (Acts 17:25). *Glorify* does not mean add more glory to God.

It is more like the word *magnify*. But here too we can go wrong. *Magnify* has two distinct meanings. In relation to God, one is worship and one is wickedness. You can magnify like a telescope or like a microscope. When you magnify like a microscope, you make something tiny look bigger than it is. A dust mite can look like a monster. Pretending to magnify God like that is wickedness. But when you magnify like a telescope, you make something unimaginably great look like what it really is. With the Hubble Space Telescope, pin-prick galaxies in the sky are revealed for the billion-star giants that they are. Magnifying God like that is worship.

JOHN PIPER

JESUS WARNS AGAINST HYPOCRISY

*The greatest among you must be a servant.
But those who exalt themselves will be
humbled, and those who humble
themselves will be exalted.*

MATTHEW 23:11–12 NLT

JESUS WARNS AGAINST HYPOCRISY

Jesus read people like books. He was never impressed by covers but eagerly examined the contents of people's lives. He pointed out that fancy covers and elaborate facades often mask shameful stories. He gave those volumes scathing reviews. But He cherished ragged covers that enclosed hearts of gold. His comparisons between lives had a masterful way of leaving the righteous with little reason for pride and the unrighteous with every reason for repentance and improvement.

As we follow Jesus through personal encounters, we are invariably drawn into His audiences. Depending on the state of our continuously wandering souls, we recognize at times our need for His corrections, confrontations, or comforts. We see in His words the wise application of tone and truth that flow from someone who really cares. Our elaborate covers don't protect us, and keeping them closed before God doesn't prevent His awareness of who we are. But willingly flinging them open before our heavenly Father allows us to experience the intimacy of His fingers tracing the lines written on our lives.

NOBODY SAID IT WOULD BE EASY

MATTHEW 23:11–12 NRSV
*"The greatest among you will be your servant.
All who exalt themselves will be humbled, and all
who humble themselves will be exalted."*

We can only achieve perfect liberty and enjoy fellowship with Jesus when his command, his call to absolute discipleship, is appreciated in its entirety. Only the man who follows the command of Jesus single-mindedly, and unresistingly lets his yoke rest upon him, finds his burden easy, and under its gentle pressure receives the power to persevere in the right way. The command of Jesus is hard, unutterably hard, for those who try to resist it. But for those who willingly submit, the yoke is easy, and the burden is light. "His commandments are not grievous" (I John 5:3). The commandment of Jesus is not a sort of spiritual shock treatment. Jesus asks nothing of us without giving us the strength to perform it. His commandment never seeks to destroy life, but to foster, strengthen and heal it.

DIETRICH BONHOEFFER

NOT EXACTLY SUBTLE

MATTHEW 23:16 NLT
"Blind guides! How terrible it will be for you!"

The religious of his day were offended because he did not follow their rules and traditions. He was bold and outspoken. He favored extreme change and valued what they felt was insignificant, which was largely the "unlovely." Jesus knew the power and prestige of the Pharisees, a key group of Jewish leaders. And he knew they expected people to show deference to them. But he loved the Pharisees and wanted them to see plainly who they were and how far many of them were from God's kingdom.

What did he say to them? . . . To say he was not the master of subtlety would be to put it mildly. Imagine a scene in which you would gather all the powerful leaders and religious elite so they could hear Jesus give a talk. . . . When they are seated, Jesus comes out and his opening words are "You bunch of snakes. You smell bad. You remind me of decomposed bodies walking around. You're hypocrites and blind guides. And I want to thank you very much for coming." It was not exactly a speech that endeared Jesus to the Pharisees, which was what the disciples pointed out when they told him with a sudden flash of insight, "We think you might have offended them."

REBECCA MANLEY PIPPERT

TOUGH TALK

MATTHEW 23:16 NRSV
"Woe to you, blind guides."

True, he was tender to the unfortunate, patient with honest inquirers, and humble before heaven; but he insulted respectable clergymen by calling them hypocrites. He referred to King Herod as "that fox"; he went to parties in disreputable company and was looked upon as a "gluttonous man and a winebibber, a friend of publicans and sinners"; he assaulted indignant tradesmen and threw them and their belongings out of the temple; he drove a coach and horses through a number of sacrosanct and hoary regulations; he cured diseases by any means that came handy, with a shocking casualness in the matter of other people's pigs and property; he showed no proper deference for wealth or social position; when confronted with neat dialectical traps, he displayed a paradoxical humor that affronted serious-minded people, and he retorted by asking disagreeably searching questions that could not be answered by rule of thumb. He was emphatically not a dull man in his human lifetime, and if he was God, there can be nothing dull about God either. But he had "a daily beauty in his life that made us ugly," and officialdom felt that the established order of things would be more secure without him. So they did away with God in the name of peace and quietness.

DOROTHY SAYERS

GOD'S DRESS CODE

MARK 12:38–39 NRSV

*As he taught, he said, "Beware of the scribes,
who like to walk around in long robes, and to be greeted
with respect in the marketplaces, and to have the best seats
in the synagogues and places of honor at banquets!"*

Don't fish for compliments, lest you defy God while you are applauded. . . . For Christ's soldiers march on through good talk on the right hand and evil talk on the left. No praise excites them. No criticism crushes them. They aren't puffed up by riches nor do they withdraw because of poverty. They despise both joy and sorrow. The sun doesn't burn them during the day nor the moon by night. Don't pray on the street corners for fear that human applause would interrupt the straight course of your prayers. Don't flaunt your fringes, wear phylacteries for show, or wrap yourself up in the self-interest of Pharisees. Do you know what kind of dress the Lord requires? Wisdom, justice, self-control, courage. Let these be the four edges of your horizon. Let them be a four-horse team to carry you, Christ's charioteer, to your goal at full speed. No necklace can be more precious than these. No gems can form a brighter galaxy. You are decorated by them, you are fastened in, you are protected on every side. They are your defense as well as your glory. For every gem is turned into a shield.

JEROME

INCARNATE HOLINESS

LUKE 20:46 NLT

*"Beware of these teachers of religious law! For they love
to parade in flowing robes and to have everyone bow to them
as they walk in the marketplaces. And how they love the
seats of honor in the synagogues and at banquets."*

We might argue that the Pharisees hated Jesus because
He was so critical of them. No one likes to be criti-
cized, especially people who are accustomed to praise. But
the venom of the Pharisees went deeper than that. It is safe
to assume that had Jesus said nothing to them they still
would have despised Him. His mere presence was enough to
cause them to recoil from Him.

It has been said that nothing dispels a lie faster than the
truth; nothing exposes the counterfeit faster than the genuine. . . . The presence of Jesus represented the presence of the
genuine in the midst of the bogus. Here authentic holiness
appeared; the counterfeiters of holiness were not pleased . . .

The Incarnate Christ is no longer walking the earth.
He has ascended into heaven. No one sees Him or speaks
audibly with him in the flesh today. Yet the threatening
power of His holiness is still felt. Sometimes it is transferred
to His people. As the Jews at the foot of Mt. Sinai fled in terror from the dazzling face of Moses, so people today get
uncomfortable in the mere presence of Christians.

R. C. SPROUL

THE PROBLEM *with* LEGALISTS

MATTHEW 23:23 NIV

"Woe to you, teachers of the law and Pharisees, you hypocrites! You give a tenth of your spices—mint, dill and cummin. But you have neglected the more important matters of the law—justice, mercy and faithfulness. You should have practiced the latter, without neglecting the former."

The Pharisees became so fond of being good that they kept inventing new traditions and codes to obey. In the process they became stricter than God. In fact, Jesus reproved them for placing spiritual burdens on people that God never intended. Godliness means to be like God. Any addition to or subtraction from who He is, what He is like and what He requires is a move away from Him. Ungodliness is not always about the really bad people. Sometimes it is about the really good people who are more restrictive than God. . . .

Jesus wasn't impressed with the Pharisees' brand of righteousness. The better they had become on the outside, the worse they had become on the inside. That's why Jesus came down so hard on them. They misrepresented Truth. . . .

If we're not careful, we too will equate being good with loving Jesus.

JOSEPH M. STOWELL

WHAT'S *in* YOUR HEART?

MATTHEW 23:27 NIV
"Woe to you, teachers of the law and Pharisees,
you hypocrites! You are like whitewashed tombs, which
look beautiful on the outside but on the inside are
full of dead men's bones and everything unclean."

Above all else, the Christian life is a love affair of the heart. It cannot be lived primarily as a set of principles or ethics. It cannot be managed with steps and programs. It cannot be lived exclusively as a moral code leading to righteousness.

The truth of the gospel is intended to free us to love God and others with our whole heart. When we ignore this heart aspect of our faith and try to live out our religion sole- ly as correct doctrine or ethics, our passion is crippled, or perverted, and the divorce of our soul from the heart pur- poses of God toward us is deepened.

The religious technocrats of Jesus' day confronted him with what they believed were the standards of a life pleasing to God. The external life, they argued, the life of ought and duty and service, was what mattered. "You're dead wrong," Jesus said. "In fact, you're just plain dead [whitewashed tombs]. What God cares about is the inner life, the life of the heart" (Matthew 23:25–28). Throughout the Old and New Testaments, the life of the heart is clearly God's central concern. . . .

Our heart is the key to the Christian life.

BRENT CURTIS AND JOHN ELDREDGE

GOOD GIFTS

LUKE 21:3–4 NLT
*"I assure you," he said, "this poor widow has given
more than all the rest of them. For they have given
a tiny part of their surplus, but she, poor as she is,
has given everything she has."*

The poor widow only put two mites into the treasury.
However, because she put in everything that she had,
Scripture says her gifts to God were much more valuable than
what the wealthy offered. For such gifts aren't evaluated by
their weight, but by the willingness of the giver....Therefore,
I wouldn't want you to offer to the Lord only what a thief
can steal from you or an enemy can capture. Don't give Him
what a law could confiscate or what is liable to fluctuate in
value. Don't offer what belongs to a long line of owners who
follow each other as fast as wave follows wave in the sea. To
sum this all up, don't offer what you must leave behind when
you die. Instead, offer to God that which no enemy can carry
off and no tyrant can take from you. Give Him that which
will go down to the grave—rather, will go with you to the
kingdom of heaven and the enchantments of Paradise.

JEROME

JESUS TELLS ABOUT *the* FUTURE

———

*"Therefore be on the alert, for you do not
know which day your Lord is coming."*

MATTHEW 24:42 NASB

JESUS TELLS ABOUT *the* FUTURE

Several times during His final week Jesus took special care to prepare His disciples for the future. He also left numerous guidelines for future disciples. Having repeatedly told about His departure, He now spoke of what conditions would be like in His absence. But the lessons and parables always included a note of temporary-ness. False prophets would come before He came. The bridegroom would eventually return. The landowner might be gone for a long time, but He would appear unexpectedly. Jesus told His followers to be ready for hardship, ready for waiting, and ready for His return.

This section will focus on Jesus' extended teaching about the "in-between" times during which He would be absent in body, but present in His Body, the church. His commands to stand ready with anticipation remain in force. No one ever has to wait longer than a lifetime to meet Jesus face-to-face.

HIS TENDER HEART

MATTHEW 23:37 NKJV
*"O Jerusalem, Jerusalem, the one who kills the prophets
and stones those who are sent to her! How often I wanted to
gather your children together, as a hen gathers her chicks
under her wings, but you were not willing!"*

Jesus Christ had a remarkably tender and affectionate heart. He is the shepherd whom the flock should follow. His virtue is expressed much in the exercise of holy affections. His is the most wonderful example of ardor, vigor, and strength of love, both to God and man, that ever was. These affections gave Him the victory in the mighty struggle and conflict of His agonies when "He prayed more earnestly, and offered strong crying and tears" and wrestled in tears and in blood. The power of the exercises of His holy love was stronger than death. In His great struggle He overcame the natural affections of fear and grief, even when He was so amazed and His soul was exceedingly sorrowful even unto death.

During the course of His life, He also appeared to be full of affection. Fulfilling Psalm 69, He had great zeal: "The zeal of your house has eaten me up" (John 2:17). He felt grief for man's sins. "He looked round about on them with anger, being grieved for the hardness of their hearts" (Mark 3:5). He cried when he thought of the sin and misery of ungodly man. When he was viewing the city of Jerusalem and all its inhabitants, He cried: "O Jerusalem, Jerusalem…!"

JONATHAN EDWARDS

THINGS *to* COME

MATTHEW 24:7–8 NLT

*"The nations and kingdoms will proclaim war against
each other, and there will be famines and earthquakes
in many parts of the world. But all this will be only
the beginning of the horrors to come."*

Those who fight for God, having been placed in the heavenly army, should hope for the things prophesied. Since the Lord told us these things would come, we won't tremble at the storms and whirlwinds of the world and will have no cause for alarm. The encouragement of His foreseeing Word instructs, teaches, prepares, and strengthens the people of His church to endure the things to come. He predicted that wars, famines, earthquakes, and plagues would arise everywhere. For fear that an unexpected and new evil should shake us, He previously warned us that suffering would increase more and more in the last times. The kingdom of God, beloved, is almost at hand. The reward of life, the rejoicing of eternal salvation, and the eternal joy and obtaining of Paradise are coming now with the passing away of the world. Already, heavenly things are taking the place of earthly, great things of small, and eternal things of things that fade away. What room is there here for anxiety and concern? Who, in the midst of these things, is trembling and sad except those without hope and faith? For it is those who aren't willing to go to Christ who fear death. It is those who don't believe that they are about to reign with Christ who aren't willing to go to Christ.

CYPRIAN

FALSE TEACHERS

MARK 13:22 NKJV
*For false christs and false prophets will rise and show signs
and wonders to deceive, if possible, even the elect.*

The most dangerous characteristic of false prophets is that they claim to be from God and to speak for Him. "The prophets prophesy falsely, and the priests rule by their own power; and My people love to have it so" (Jeremiah 5:31).

Such leaders nearly always appear pleasant and positive. They like to be with Christians, and they know how to talk and act like believers.

False prophets usually exude sincerity and thereby more easily deceive others (see 2 Timothy 3:13). But you identify false teachers' true colors by noting what they do not talk much about. They usually *don't deny* basic doctrines such as Christ's deity and substitutionary atonement, the sinfulness of humanity, or unbelievers' going to hell. They simply *ignore* such "controversial" truths.

But whenever a false prophet is in your midst, you must not ignore his presence or the harmful effects of his heretical teaching.

JOHN MACARTHUR

No Oil *in* Their Lamps

MATTHEW 25:3–4 NRSV

"When the foolish took their lamps, they took no oil with them; but the wise took flasks of oil with their lamps."

They that were foolish took their lamps of an outward profession. They would go to church, say over several manuals of prayers, come perhaps into a field to hear a sermon, give at a collection, and receive the sacrament constantly, nay, oftener than once a month. But then here lay the mistake; they had no oil in their lamps, no principle of grace, no living faith in their hearts. . . . In one word, they never effectually felt the power of the world to come. They thought they might be Christians without so much inward feeling. . . .

Whilst I have been drawing, though in miniature, the character of these foolish virgins, have not many of your consciences made the application, and with a small, still, though articulate voice, said, *Thou man, thou woman, art one of those foolish virgins, for thy sentiments and practice agree thereto?* Stifle not, but rather encourage these convictions; and who knows, but that Lord who is rich in mercy to all that call upon him faithfully, may so work upon you even by this foolishness of preaching, as to make you wise virgins before you return home?

GEORGE WHITEFIELD

THE WISE TOOK OIL

MATTHEW 25:3-4 NRSV
"When the foolish took their lamps, they took no oil with them; but the wise took flasks of oil with their lamps."

The wise virgins had their lamps; herein did not lie the difference between them and the foolish, that one worshipped God with a form, and the other did not: No: as the Pharisee and Publican went up to the temple to pray, so these wise and foolish virgins might go to the same place of worship, and sit under the same ministry; but then the wise took oil in their vessels with their lamps; they kept up the form, but did not rest in it; their words in prayer were the language of their hearts, and they were no strangers to inward feelings; they were not afraid of searching doctrines, nor affronted when ministers told them they deserved to be damned; they were not self-righteous, but were willing that Jesus Christ should have all the glory of their salvation; they were convinced that the merits of Jesus Christ were to be apprehended only by faith; but yet were they as careful to maintain good works, as though they were to be justified by them: in short, their obedience flowed from love and gratitude, and was cheerful, constant, uniform, universal, like that obedience which the holy angels pay our Father in heaven.

GEORGE WHITEFIELD

BE PREPARED

MATTHEW 25:13 NLT
*"So stay awake and be prepared, because you do
not know the day or hour of my return."*

Every generation of Christians has expected Christ to
return in their lifetime. And they have had one thing in
common: They have all been wrong. . . .

Supposing Jesus had said, "I'll give you three millennia
to evangelize the world, and then, on January 1, A.D. 3001, I
will return at precisely 9:00 GMT." What would the promise of his return have meant to generations of believers who
lived in the preceding centuries? In the midst of their sufferings, exiles, and martyrdom, what comfort would they have
derived from his promise, knowing that he would not come
soon? And what would have been the effect on the church
if they had known that they still had a little time to do what
they wanted to do before getting around to doing what he
had told them to do? Where would have been the sense of
urgency, the challenge to holiness, and the keen sense of tip-
toe anticipation?

Jesus' point was that all his disciples should be living in
a sense of anticipation, actively on the job, working hard to
bring about the consummation of his purposes and living
consistent lives so they would not be ashamed at his coming.

STUART BRISCOE

HIS PASSION

JESUS IS
BETRAYED

Then one of the Twelve—the one called
Judas Iscariot—went to the chief priests and
asked, "What are you willing to give me if
I hand him over to you?" So they counted
out for him thirty silver coins.

MATTHEW 26:14–15 NIV

JESUS IS BETRAYED

While all of us had a share in the betrayal of Christ, the plan required a point man. Jesus' betrayal was an inside job. The plan also required a supporting cast, and the human landscape held many candidates: corrupt religious leaders, corrupt and fearful political leaders, and radical religious elements. It has been historically popular to assign special blame to Judas or the Jewish leaders, but such efforts tend to deflect the point that all of us are ultimately responsible for the cross. The Bible describes specific roles in the dark side of salvation, but the gospel also makes it clear that we're all accessories to the deed. Jesus was betrayed and crucified on our behalf.

The following reflections will focus on the events and people involved in the details of Jesus' betrayal. Here we have one of the clearest examples in history of the way in which God transforms the angry and sinful efforts of human beings into components of His eternal plans.

ACT *of* BETRAYAL

MATTHEW 26:14–15 NLT
Then Judas Iscariot, one of the twelve disciples,
went to the leading priests and asked, "How much
will you pay me to betray Jesus to you?"
And they gave him thirty pieces of silver.

Human feelings toward Judas have always been mixed. Some have fervently hated him for his betrayal. Others have pitied him for not realizing what he was doing. A few have tried to make him a hero for his part in ending Jesus' earthly mission. Some have questioned God's fairness in allowing one man to bear such guilt. . . .

In betraying Jesus, Judas made the greatest mistake in history. But the fact that Jesus knew Judas would betray him doesn't mean that Judas was a puppet of God's will. Judas made the choice. God knew what that choice would be and confirmed it. Judas didn't lose his relationship with Jesus; rather he never found Jesus in the first place. He is called "the one headed for destruction" (John 17:12) because he was never saved.

Judas does us a favor if he makes us think a second time about our commitment to God and the presence of God's Spirit within us. Are we true disciples and followers, or uncommitted pretenders? We can choose despair and death, or we can choose repentance, forgiveness, hope, and eternal life. Judas's betrayal sent Jesus to the cross to guarantee that second choice, our only chance. Will we accept Jesus' free gift, or, like Judas, betray him?

LIFE APPLICATION BIBLE

POWER PLAY

MATTHEW 26:16 NRSV
*And from that moment he began to look
for an opportunity to betray him.*

Jesus really did abandon power when He lived among us. He wasn't simply holding back and pretending to possess our physical limitations—He truly was one of us. We don't like that fact and do our best to suppress it. We want to think of Him disguising Himself as a sophisticated Rotarian who could step into a phone booth, rip off His robes, and show us who He is—a first-century Clark Kent/Superman.

Judas was one who refused to accept such a limited Messiah. On Palm Sunday, power had been within the Master's grasp. It was the logical time to take over. It was the opportunity to rally the masses to the cause, the hour when He should claim power. And Jesus let it all slip away.

Some think that Judas betrayed Jesus in order to force Him to play the power game and establish His rule. Those who hold this theory suggest that Judas felt that if Jesus were left with no alternative, He would be forced away from His reluctance to seize the throne. If that was the plan of Judas, it all backfired. Perhaps it was when he realized that his attempt to manipulate Jesus into using power only resulted in the death of one who had loved him infinitely that Judas hanged himself.

ANTHONY CAMPOLO

HIS PASSION

ONE *of* YOU

MARK 14:18 NKJV

*Now as they sat and ate, Jesus said, "Assuredly, I say
to you, one of you who eats with Me will betray Me."*

Jesus began to speak again now in low, solemn tones. His
words were weighty—heavy with foreboding:

"One of you will betray Me!"

It seemed like a thunderclap of condemnation.

How could it be? He had just washed each of them.
How could any of them be so cruel, so ungrateful?

In turn each, including Judas, asked, "Is it I?"

At that very moment Judas had the blood money
wrapped tightly, silently, in a secret money belt strapped to
his body. It must have branded him like a burning iron. It
took colossal gall to have this ghastly sum on his very person
while innocently pretending he was not guilty. The audacity
of it all is shocking. It seems impossible that a man could sink
to such depths of cunning bestiality. But he did.

The problem with Judas was that the central citadel of
his will had never come under Christ's control. He had never
fully capitulated to his Lord. The Saviour, by His Spirit, had
never been received as royalty nor recognized as sovereign by
this man. It was really that basic. And it explains why he or
any of us can descend to behave as brute beasts.

W. PHILLIP KELLER

SATAN ENTERED

LUKE 22:3 NRSV
Then Satan entered into Judas.

Even by extending our imaginations to their extremity it is difficult to understand Judas' dreadful deed. Obviously it was perpetrated first in a mind boiling with belligerence. It was spawned in a soul seething with resentment. . . .

Jesus and Judas had been intimate friends for nearly three years. They had shared the same life, tramped the same trails, eaten from the same bowls, drunk from the same wells, slept under the same trees, seen the same sunrises, shared in the same tragedies and triumphs, talked about the same truths, lived the same rugged way.

But Judas had been hurt. His pride had been pricked. His self-pity had been indulged. His hostility had been inflamed. Now he was at dagger points with his best friend. He was determined to destroy Him. Loved had turned to hate. . . .

The reason for all of this still lies somewhat shrouded in mystery. It still escapes us even though we endeavor to unravel its entangled strands.

One thing is sure: This man's dark, black soul was a suitable beachhead from which Satan attempted a major assault against the Saviour of the world.

The record given of those horrendous hours is couched in awesome language: "Satan entered into Judas."

W. PHILLIP KELLER

JESUS WASHES *the* DISCIPLES' FEET

It was just before the Passover Feast.
Jesus knew that the time had come for him to
leave this world and go to the Father. Having
loved his own who were in the world, he now
showed them the full extent of his love.

JOHN 13:1 NIV

JESUS WASHES *the* DISCIPLES' FEET

J esus did a lot to prepare His followers for the
trauma of His death. He told them why and
showed them how. He gave them inoculating
shocks that conditioned them for the greatest one.
He indicated how far He would go to serve by
touching the untouchables, loving the unlovables,
and stooping to wash dirty feet before His last meal
with the disciples. He mixed love with towel and
basin to give them a hint of what it means to serve.

Jesus' example of loving service that cli-
maxed at the cross included countless startling
earlier moments. Few capture our imagination
and emotions like the picture of Jesus kneeling
before Peter and the others to wash their feet.
Allow His example to touch your life as you consider the following reflections.

CAN YOU LOVE *as* HE LOVED?

JOHN 13:3–5 NLT

*Jesus knew that the Father had given him authority
over everything and that he had come from God and would
return to God. So he got up from the table, took off his robe,
wrapped a towel around his waist, and poured water into a
basin. Then he began to wash the disciples' feet and to wipe
them with the towel he had around him.*

Jesus knew that one of his disciples had already decided to
betray him. Another would deny him by the next morning.
Even this night, they would all desert him. In the next hours
they would repeatedly display ignorance, laziness, and lack of
trust. It was indeed a sorry lot that gathered in the upper
room. Even with good reasons to reject the entire group, Jesus
deliberately showed to them the full extent of his love. The
actions, words, and feelings that he shared with his disciples
conveyed the highest form of love because his disciples did
not deserve nor immediately appreciate this love.

Jesus knows us as fully as he knew those disciples. He
knows intimately of every time and every way that we have
denied or deserted him. Yet knowing us, he willingly died for
us. Jesus continually displays his love toward us and reaches
out to us. He continues to serve us in the Lord's Supper, and
he guides and encourages us by his Spirit. He serves us as we
serve one another. Are we prepared to love one another with
the same kind of love Jesus demonstrated for us?

LIFE APPLICATION COMMENTARY—JOHN

HE CAME *to* BE *a* SERVANT
JOHN 13:3−5 NKJV

Jesus, knowing that the Father had given all things into His hands, and that He had come from God and was going to God, rose from supper and laid aside His garments, took a towel and girded Himself. After that, He poured water into a basin and began to wash the disciples' feet, and to wipe them with the towel with which He was girded.

We must learn to worship as an everyday lifestyle. Even if we took part in wonderful, powerful worship once a week from a church pew, it wouldn't be enough. The Spirit of God accompanies us everywhere we go, and we can worship Him in the very midst of daily life. . . .

It's a question of whether you have eternal perspective. Wherever you go, whatever you do, the Lord Jesus longs to be your constant companion. You have the opportunity to praise and worship Him all through the day. He once washed the dirty feet of His disciples, so the details of your job make no difference.

If you will only practice His presence, you will find an eternal perspective taking root in your soul. You will begin to see this world through heavenly eyes. The trials will seem more trivial, and the blessings will be more obvious to you. You'll see every person as Christ sees him or her, and don't be surprised if you find yourself washing a foot or two, in time.

Wherever you go will be a fine place to be. And whatever you do will be filled with an irrepressible joy, because you're in the company of the King.

DAVID JEREMIAH

DAILY CLEANSING

JOHN 13:5 NIV

*After that, he poured water into a basin and began
to wash his disciples' feet, drying them with
the towel that was wrapped around him.*

The Lord Jesus loves his people so much, that every day he
is still doing for them much that is analogous to washing
their soiled feet. Their poorest actions he accepts; their deepest sorrow he feels; their slenderest wish he hears, and their
every transgression he forgives. He is still their servant as well
as their Friend and Master. . . . Humbly, patiently, he yet goes
about among his people with the basin and the towel. He
does this when he puts away from us day by day our constant
infirmities and sins. . . . It is a great act of eternal love when
Christ once for all absolves the sinner, and puts him into the
family of God; but what condescending patience there is
when the Saviour with much long-suffering bears the oft
recurring follies of his wayward disciple; day by day, and hour
by hour, washing away the multiplied transgressions of his
erring but yet beloved child! . . . While we find comfort and
peace in our Lord's daily cleansing, its legitimate influence
upon us will be to increase our watchfulness, and quicken our
desire for holiness. *Is it so?*

CHARLES HADDON SPURGEON

PROOF *of* LOVE

JOHN 13:6 NRSV
He came to Simon Peter, who said to him,
"Lord, are you going to wash my feet?"

Christ manifested his love to them by washing their feet, as that good woman (Luke 7:38) showed her love to Christ by washing his feet and wiping them. Thus he would show that as his love to them was constant so it was condescending—that in prosecution of the designs of it he was willing to humble himself—and that the glories of his exalted state, which he was now entering upon, should be no obstruction at all to the favour he bore to his chosen; and thus he would confirm the promise he had made to all the saints that he would *make them sit down to meat, and would come forth and serve them* (Luke 12:37), would put honour upon them as great and surprising as for a lord to serve his servants. The disciples had just now betrayed the weakness of their love to him, in grudging the ointment that was poured upon his head (Matthew 26:8), yet he presently gives this proof of his love to them. Our infirmities are foils to Christ's kindnesses, and set them off.

MATTHEW HENRY

THE FEET *of the* BETRAYER

JOHN 13:10–11 NIV

Jesus answered, "A person who has had a bath needs only to wash his feet; his whole body is clean. And you are clean, though not every one of you." For he knew who was going to betray him, and that was why he said not every one was clean.

How great is the example You showed of enduring evil! How great, too, is Your model of humility! How is it that the Lord gave us this example to show us that we shouldn't give up counseling our neighbors even if they aren't affected by our words? For incurable wounds are wounds that can't be healed by harsh medications or by more pleasant ones. Similarly, the soul, when it has been taken captive, gives itself up to wickedness, refuses to consider what is profitable for it, and won't accept goodness despite great counsel. As if it is deaf, it won't benefit from any advice. Not that it can't, but it won't. This happened in Judas's case. Nevertheless, Christ, although He knew this beforehand, didn't ever stop doing everything to counsel him. Since we know that Jesus practiced this, we also should never stop striving to set the careless right even if it seems no good comes from our counsel.

DIONYSIUS OF ALEXANDRIA

OUR CALLING

JOHN 13:14 NIV
*"Now that I, your Lord and Teacher, have washed
your feet, you also should wash one another's feet."*

Pride sucks the vitality out of our character. Bernard of
Clairvaux wisely taught that there are four Christian vir-
tues. The first is humility. The second is humility. The third is
humility. And the fourth is humility. Bernard also taught that
most of us would like to gain humility without humiliation.
Alas, it is not possible. Our arrogance is the least lovely of all
our personal qualities. Ego is the barrier that stands between
God and his dreams for our lives.

As servants we are to be priests. A priest is soil—inter-
mediary soil, a small patch of ground on which both God
and the needy stand to meet. Our work is priestly and it is
glorious. Like Jesus, our great High Priest, we too wear the
vestments of our mediation of grace. We make his incarnation possible once more. We are the willing amen of Walt
Whitman. We must likewise cry to our needy world, "If you
want us, look beneath the soles of your boots." Our humility may be easily seen in our love of helping others. Our
service is our office. If the King of heaven can wash feet, our
calling is clear.

CALVIN MILLER

OUR EXAMPLE

JOHN 13:14-15 KJV

If I then, your Lord and Master, have washed your feet; ye also ought to wash one another's feet. For I have given you an example, that ye should do as I have done to you.

In washing the feet of disciples who were already washed and clean, the Lord instituted a sign, to the end that, . . . we might know that we are not exempt from sin; which He thereafter washes away by interceding for us. . . . What connection, then, can such an understanding of the passage have with that which He afterwards gave Himself, when He explained the reason of His act in the words, "If I then, your Lord and Master, have washed your feet, ye also ought to wash one another's feet. For I have given you an example, that ye should do as I have done to you"? . . . Let us listen to the Apostle James, who states this precept with the greatest clearness when he says, "Confess your faults one to another, and pray one for another." For of this also the Lord gave us the example. For if He who neither has, nor had, nor will have any sin, prays for our sins, how much more ought we to pray for one another's in turn! And if He forgives us, whom we have nothing to forgive; how much more ought we, who are unable to live here without sin, to forgive one another!

AUGUSTINE

PEOPLE *of* CHARACTER

JOHN 13:15 NKJV
*"For I have given you an example,
that you should do as I have done to you."*

Character comes gradually in the process of allowing God to make us servants. But oh, the pain that lies in the pathway! Hurt is the unwelcome forge on which God hammers out our Christlikeness. We beg God to cover the hammer with felt. But the iron blows fall and the anvil tears. Some have actually had to die to serve Christ. And sometimes it is the very people we are called to serve who hold in their ungrateful lives the pain that breaks our spirits and crushes us beneath alienation and aloneness.

Unfortunately, serving people is the only way by which we can serve God. And serving people means that we are going to get hurt in the process. . . .

Jesus, according to Philippians 2, humbled himself and became a man. Now we must humble ourselves to become servants and people of character. The crucifixion can be a very nasty end to anyone who wants to be a servant. Why? Consider the methodology of servanthood: We must turn our cheek and walk two miles for everyone who forces us to walk one! Serving our antagonists and blessing our persecutors can be the terrible tedium that fashions us in his image.

CALVIN MILLER

HUMBLE SERVING

JOHN 13:16 NIV

"I tell you the truth, no servant is greater than his master,
nor is a messenger greater than the one who sent him."

Jesus humbled himself and served them like their servant. Though he was the Son of God, he did not claim his right. Rather he gave up his right and humbled himself to serve smelly and proud disciples. He could have claimed his right at least for this last meal, but he not only gave up his right, but also he determined to serve them humbly. He did not rebuke them, saying, "What did you learn for three years? Did I not deserve one last meal time to be served properly?" He rather took the form of a servant and began to wash their feet one by one. In this world, higher position means more money and higher authority; higher authority means more respect from others. As the master and teacher by washing their feet, Jesus showed them that humble serving is true loving.

UNIVERSITY BIBLE FELLOWSHIP

NOT *to* BE SERVED, BUT *to* SERVE

MATTHEW 20:28 NRSV

"The Son of Man came not to be served but to serve, and to give his life a ransom for many."

So great and wonderful was the work that Jesus had to do for the sinner, that nothing less was necessary than that He should give Himself to do that work. So great and wonderful was the love of Jesus towards us, that He actually gave Himself for us and to us. So great and wonderful is the surrender of Jesus, that all that same thing for which He gave Himself can actually and completely come to pass in us. For Jesus, the Holy, the Almighty, has taken it upon Himself to do it: He gave *Himself* for us. . . . And now the one thing that is necessary is that we should rightly understand and firmly believe this His surrender for us. . . .

When I receive Him, when I believe that He gave Himself to do this for me, I shall certainly experience it. I shall be purified through Him, shall be held fast as His possession, and be filled with zeal and joy to work for Him.

ANDREW MURRAY

JESUS SHARES *the* LAST SUPPER

—

"For this is My blood of the new covenant, which is shed for many for the remission of sins."

MATTHEW 26:28 NKJV

JESUS SHARES *the* LAST SUPPER

The Passover meal recalls the slavery in Egypt, the visit by the angel of death, and a long Exodus. The lamb consumed not only provides the main course; its blood also stains the doorposts, turning away the final plague. Jesus gathered His disciples for the Passover to end all Passovers.

During that last meal with His disciples, Jesus, the Lamb of God, offered His body and blood for sharing, always to be taken with a solemn reflection on His sacrifice and His future return. He offered it in spite of the unworthiness of His followers—one who had betrayed Him, another who would deny Him, and all who would abandon Him. He offered it because they needed a Savior, and He was that Savior.

As you revisit that supper, find your place at the table among the other unworthy ones, and share in the meal worthily. Feast on the banquet of Jesus' words.

SATAN'S PART

JOHN 13:27 NIV
As soon as Judas took the bread, Satan entered into him.
"What you are about to do, do quickly," Jesus told him.

Now the most powerful mediation needs a spirit of counsel because "if the prince of this world had known it, he would not have crucified the Lord of glory" (1 Corinthians 2:8). But the Son of God hid His glory of divinity, revealing only the weakness of the flesh without sin. Thereby He took away the envy of the hostile wickedness by the holiness of His life. Through His weakness the enemy hoped to be victorious over Him.

Christ also aroused Satan's envy by His accompanying miracles which He used to strengthen man's faith in Him as reconciler. Satan, the deceiver, having been deceived, inflicted on Christ, who was unworthy of punishment for sin, the penalty of sin; that is, a very cruel death. Yet the righteous—so struck unjustly for righteousness' sake—obtained a new righteousness from the enemy of death which was unjustly inflicted upon Him.

Since this death was not incumbent upon Him—for He was without sin—by sharing this victory with sinful man, He absolved the accused through the punishment of His innocence.

BERNARD OF CLAIRVAUX

I, THE SON *of* MAN, MUST DIE

MARK 14:21 NLT
"For I, the Son of Man, must die,
as the Scriptures declared long ago."

The life of Jesus went as swift and straight as a thunder-bolt. It was above all things dramatic; it did above all things consist in doing something that had to be done. It emphatically would not have been done, if Jesus had walked about the world forever doing nothing except tell the truth. And even the external movement of it must not be described as a wandering in the sense of forgetting that it was a journey. This is where it was a fulfillment of the myths rather than of the philosophies; it is a journey with a goal and an object, like Jason going to find the Golden Fleece, or Hercules the golden apples of the Hesperides. The gold that he was seeking was death. The primary thing that he was going to do was to die. He was going to do other things equally definite and objective; we might almost say equally external and material. But from first to last the most definite fact is that he is going to die.

G. K. CHESTERTON

PARTICIPATION *with* HIM

MARK 14:22–23 NKJV

And as they were eating, Jesus took bread, blessed and broke it, and gave it to them and said, "Take, eat; this is My body." Then He took the cup, and when He had given thanks He gave it to them, and they all drank from it.

This feeding with the body of Christ takes place, on the side of the Lord by the Spirit, on our side by faith. On the side of the Lord by the Spirit: for the Spirit communicates to us the power of the glorified body, whereby even our bodies, according to Scripture, become members of His body. . . . The Spirit gives us to drink of the life-power of His blood, so that that blood becomes the life and the joy of our soul. The bread is a participation in the body: the cup is a participation in the blood.

And this takes place on our side by faith: a faith that, above what can be seen or understood, reckons on the wonder-working power of the Holy Spirit to unite us really, alike in soul and body, with our Lord, by communicating Him inwardly to us.

ANDREW MURRAY

MY BODY, BROKEN

LUKE 22:19 NIV
*And he took bread, gave thanks and broke it, and gave
it to them, saying, "This is my body given for you;
do this in remembrance of me."*

All life has need of food: it is sustained by nourishment which it takes in from without. The heavenly life must have heavenly food; nothing less than Jesus Himself is the bread of life. . . . This heavenly food, Jesus, is brought near to us in two of the means of grace, the word and the Lord's Supper. The word comes to present Jesus to us from the side of the intellectual life, by our thoughts. The Lord's Supper comes in like manner to present Jesus to us from the side of the emotional life, by the physical senses. . . . The Supper is the pledge that the Lord will also change our body of humiliation and make it like His own glorified body by the working whereby He subdues all things to Himself. . . . In the Supper, Christ would take possession of the whole man, body and soul, to renew and sanctify it by the power of His holy body and blood. Even His body shares in His glory: even His body is communicated by the Holy Spirit. Even our body is fed with His holy body, and renewed by the working of the Holy Spirit.

ANDREW MURRAY

ONENESS *with* JESUS

LUKE 22:19 NIV
"Do this in remembrance of me."

This deeply inward union with Jesus, even with His body and blood, is the great aim of the Lord's Supper. All that it teaches and gives us of the forgiveness of sins, of the remembrance of Jesus, of the confirmation of the divine covenant, of union with one another, of the announcement of the Lord's death till He comes, must lead to this: complete oneness with Jesus through the Spirit. . . .

It is readily understood that the blessing of the Supper depends very much on preparation within the inner chamber, on the hunger and thirst with which one longs for the living God. . . . Do not imagine, however, that the Supper is nothing but an emblematic token of what we already have by faith in the word. No: it is a spiritual actual communication from the exalted Lord in heaven of the powers of His life: yet this, only according to the measure of desire and faith. Prepare for the Lord's Supper, therefore, with very earnest separation and prayer. And then expect that the Lord will, with His heavenly power, in a way to you incomprehensible, yet sure, renew your life.

ANDREW MURRAY

EXTRAVAGANT FORGIVING

LUKE 22:20 NIV
*In the same way, after the supper he took the cup,
saying, "This cup is the new covenant in my blood,
which is poured out for you."*

What has gratitude to do with calling? It is surely easier and more correct to see gratitude as a response to the cross of Christ. Around 1546 Michelangelo did a pencil drawing of the Pietà for Vittoria Colonna, his saintly aristocratic friend. With the dead body of Jesus supported by angels at her feet, Mary does not cradle her son as in his other renderings of the Pietà but raises her eyes and her hands to heaven in speechless wonder. On the upright beam of the cross Michelangelo inscribed a line from Dante's *Paradise*, which is the focus of the drawing's meditation: "No one thinks of how much blood it costs."

Certainly anyone thinking of how much blood it cost, and whose and why, can only stop and adore. So the adulterous woman, forgiven, bathes Jesus' feet with her kisses, her perfume, and her tears—her extravagant giving is the response to his even more extravagant forgiving. As Simone Weil expressed it eloquently, "our country is the Cross."

OS GUINNESS

CONTEMPLATE *with* AWE

LUKE 22:20 NIV
*In the same way, after the supper he took the cup,
saying, "This cup is the new covenant in my blood,
which is poured out for you."*

The Savior teaches nothing in a merely human way, but teaches His own with Divine and mystic wisdom. Therefore, we must not listen to His words with worldly ears. We must search out and learn the meaning hidden in them. For what the Lord seems to have simplified for the disciples requires even more attention than puzzling statements because of its overabundance of wisdom. In addition, the things He explained to His children require even more consideration than the things which seem to have been simply stated. Those who heard such explanations didn't ask questions, because the Lord's words pertaining to the entire design of salvation were meant to be contemplated with awe and a deep spiritual mind. We must not receive these words superficially with our ears, but must apply our minds to understanding the Spirit of the Savior and the unspoken meaning of His words.

CLEMENT OF ALEXANDRIA

A NEW COMMANDMENT

JOHN 13:34 KJV

A new commandment I give unto you, That ye love one another; as I have loved you, that ye also love one another.

The Scriptures also plainly and abundantly teach that all true saints have a loving, compassionate, and kind spirit. Without this, says the Apostle, we may speak with the tongues of men and angels yet we are only a sounding brass or a tinkling cymbal. Although we have the gift of prophecy, and understand all mysteries, and all knowledge, without this spirit we are nothing. No other virtue or disposition of mind is more often and expressly insisted upon as a mark of a true Christian. Love is often given as the evidence of who are Christ's disciples, and how they may be known.

Indeed, Christ calls the law of love His commandment. "A new commandment give I unto you, that you love one another; as I have loved you, that you also love one another" (John 13:34). "This is My commandment, that you love one another as I have loved you" (John 15:12). And verse 17, "These things I command you, that you love one another." He says in chapter 13:35, "By this shall all men know that you are My disciples, if you have love one to another." Again in chapter 14:21, "He that has My commandments, and keeps them, he it is that loves Me."

JONATHAN EDWARDS

TO LOVE *as* HE LOVED

JOHN 13:34 NASB

*"A new commandment I give to you, that you
love one another, even as I have loved you,
that you also love one another."*

Even as I have loved you: those words give us the *measure* of the love wherewith we must love each other. True love knows no measure: it gives itself entirely. . . .

Our love may recognize no measure other than His, because His love is the strength of ours. The love of Christ is no mere idea or sentiment; it is a real divine life power. So long as the Christian does not understand this, it cannot exert its full power in him. But when his faith rises to realize that Christ's love is nothing less than the imparting of Himself and His love to the beloved, and he becomes rooted in this love as the source whence his life derives its sustenance, then he sees that his Lord simply asks that he should allow His love to flow through him. He must live in a Christ-given strength: the love of Christ constrains him, and enables him to love as He did.

ANDREW MURRAY

LOVE ONE *to* ANOTHER

JOHN 13:35 KJV
By this shall all men know that ye are my disciples,
if ye have love one to another.

Before Christ promised the Holy Spirit, He gave a new commandment, and about that new commandment He said wonderful things. One thing was: "Even as I have loved you, so love ye one another." To them His dying love was to be the only law of their conduct and intercourse with each other. What a message to those fishermen, to those men full of pride and selfishness! "Learn to love each other," said Christ, "as I have loved you." And by the grace of God they did it. When Pentecost came, they were of one heart and one soul. Christ did it for them.

And now He calls us to dwell and to walk in love. He demands that though a man hate you, still you love him. True love cannot be conquered by anything in Heaven or upon the earth. The more hatred there is, the more love triumphs through it all and shows its true nature. This is the love that Christ commanded His disciples to exercise.

What more did He say? "By this shall all men know that ye are my disciples, if ye have love one to another."

ANDREW MURRAY

TRUST ME

JOHN 14:1 NIV
"Do not let your hearts be troubled.
Trust in God; trust also in me."

All of his words can be reduced to two: *Trust me.* . . .
Don't be troubled by the return of Christ. Don't be anxious about things you cannot comprehend. Issues like the
millennium and the Antichrist are intended to challenge and
stretch us, but not overwhelm and certainly not divide us. For
the Christian, the return of Christ is not a riddle to be solved
or a code to be broken, but rather a day to be anticipated.

Jesus wants us to trust him. He doesn't want us to be
troubled, so he reassures us with these truths. . . .

We don't know when he will come for us. We don't
know how he will come for us. And, we really don't even
know why he would come for us. Oh, we have our ideas and
opinions. But most of what we have is faith—faith that he
has ample space and a prepared place and, at the right time,
he will come so that we can be where he is.

He will do the taking. It's up to us to do the trusting.

MAX LUCADO

A PLACE *for* YOU

JOHN 14:2 NLT
"There are many rooms in my Father's home,
and I am going to prepare a place for you.
If this were not so, I would tell you plainly."

Soon Jesus would die on the cross, rise from the dead, and ascend into heaven, leaving his disciples on earth. To help prepare them for life without him, Jesus explained that he would be going to his Father in heaven and would be preparing a place for them there. He also promised to return.

The disciples were confused, not really believing that Jesus would have to die, not realizing that he would come back to life, and thus not understanding at all what he meant by going to the Father and "preparing a place" for them.

But we have the perspective of history. We know that Jesus died on the cross. And we know that he rose from the grave and later ascended into heaven. Thus, we can be confident that he is there now preparing for us.

What a great promise! If you have trusted in Christ as your Savior, your future is secure—he has a place for you in the "Father's house." No one can stop you; nothing can deter you; no one can steal your hope. . . because Jesus has promised.

And he's coming back to take you there.

DAVE VEERMAN

HIS PASSION

AWAITING HIS RETURN

JOHN 14:2 NIV
"In my Father's house are many rooms;
if it were not so, I would have told you.
I am going there to prepare a place for you."

Jesus is with His Twelve the night before He is taken under arrest and goes to the cross. While there, He abruptly unveils the truth of His impending death. It catches the disciples off guard. They became visibly shaken, and understandably so. Had we been among His disciples, we, too, would have expected Him to live forever, establish His kingdom, and take us with Him as He became the King of kings and Lord of lords, ruling over the whole earth.

But suddenly He introduces a change in the game plan—the Cross. Full of turmoil, doubt, and fear, the disciples stared in stunned amazement as He spoke of His imminent death. . . . To those anxious disciples He gave an unconditional promise. He doesn't say, "If you're expecting Me, I'll come back." He doesn't even say, "If you're walking with Me, I'll come back." No, His promise is absolutely unconditional. "I am going to prepare a place . . . I will return . . . I will receive you . . . you will be with Me." His return was no guesswork . . . it would occur! . . .

Clearly, Christ is going to return. Our question is this: How can we best "stay ready 'til quittin' time"?

CHARLES R. SWINDOLL

NO OTHER WAY

JOHN 14:6 NKJV
*Jesus said to him, "I am the way, the truth, and the life.
No one comes to the Father except through Me."*

What does it mean to come to the Father? It means nothing else but to come from death to life, from sin and condemnation to innocence and godliness, from distress and sorrow to eternal joy and blessedness. Christ is saying, "No one should try to come to the Father through a different way than through me. I alone am the way, the truth, and the life." Christ clearly rules out and powerfully disproves all teaching that salvation can be obtained by works. He completely denies that we can get to heaven by any other way. For Jesus says, "No one comes to the Father except through me." There is no other way. . . .

Though everyone else may abandon me and leave me lying in ruins, I will still have an eternal treasure that can never fail me. This treasure isn't the result of my own works or efforts. The treasure is Christ—the way, the truth, and the life. Only through Christ do I come to the Father. I will hold to this, live by this, die by it.

MARTIN LUTHER

CHRIST IS OUR WAY

JOHN 14:6 NKJV

Jesus said to him, "I am the way, the truth, and the life.
No one comes to the Father except through Me."

We can say the ways of the Lord are the courses of a
good life, guided by Christ. He says, "I am the Way,
and the Truth, and the Life." The way, then, is the immense
power of God. For Christ is our way—and a good way, too.
He is the way that has opened the kingdom of heaven to
believers. In addition, the Lord's ways are straight. It is writ
ten: "Make Thy ways known unto me, O Lord." . . . Christ,
then, is the beginning of our righteousness. He is the beginning of purity. . . . Christ is the beginning of frugality, for He
became poor even though He was rich. Christ is the beginning of patience, for when He was abused verbally, He didn't
lash back. When He was struck, He did not strike back. Christ
is the beginning of humility, for He took the form of a servant even though He was equal with God the Father in the
majesty of His power. Every virtue has its origin in Christ.

AMBROSE

POWERFUL NAMES

JOHN 14:6 KJV

*Jesus saith unto him, I am the way, the truth, and the life:
no man cometh unto the Father, but by me.*

He who is the Way doesn't sidetrack us or lead us into spacious wastelands. He who is the Truth doesn't mock us with lies. He who is the Life doesn't betray us with deathly delusions. Christ chose these winsome names for Himself to indicate His methods for our salvation. As the Way, He will guide us to the Truth. And the Truth will root us in the Life. Therefore, it is vital that we know the mysterious way (which He reveals) of attaining this life. "No man cometh to the Father but through Me." The way to the Father is through the Son. Now we must ask whether the way is by obedience to His teaching or by faith in His Godhead. For it is conceivable that our way to the Father could be by obeying the Son's teaching, rather than by believing that the Father dwells in the Son. Therefore, we must next seek out the true meaning of this instruction. For it isn't by cleaving to a preconceived opinion, but by studying the force of the words, that we can possess this faith.

HILARY OF POITIERS

WIDE ENOUGH *for* ALL WHO BELIEVE

JOHN 14:6 NLT

*Jesus told him, "I am the way, the truth, and the life.
No one can come to the Father except through me."*

When the disciples asked how they would get to the Father and his "house," Jesus answered that he was the *only* way.

This fact that Jesus is the only way to heaven isn't popular in our age of "it doesn't matter what you believe as long as you're sincere" and "all faiths lead to the same destination" ways of thinking. People argue that having just one way is too narrow and limiting. In reality, it is wide enough for all who believe. Instead of arguing and worrying about how limited it sounds, they should be grateful that there actually is one way to God. When standing at a precipice and wishing to get to the other side of the great divide, we don't pout and demand that a bridge be where we are. Instead, we travel to the bridge, the only bridge, a few miles away, grateful that there is a way across.

Jesus is the way—follow him. Jesus is truth—believe him. Jesus is life—live in him. There is no other bridge to the Father and his house.

DAVE VEERMAN

Overcoming Fear

JOHN 14:6 NLT

Jesus told him, "I am the way, the truth, and the life.
No one can come to the Father except through me."

Fear moistens our palms, buckles our knees, and chokes our breath. Debilitating fear makes cowards of even the strongest and most powerful warriors. Some try to fight their fears by ignoring them. Others mask their fears through anesthesia (alcohol and drugs) or false bravado (pretending that all is well). Some respond by rushing recklessly into danger. But the answer, the effective antidote to fear, comes from knowing the truth and knowing what lies ahead, down the path.

Jesus told his disciples that he was the Truth (John 14:6) and that heaven awaited all who trusted in him (John 14:1-4). Thus they need not fear, regardless of their circumstances, pressures, and troubles. Certainly these young men didn't know the future, but they knew the one who did—and he promised them peace.

What fears steal your hope and keep you awake at night? Trust the Savior, and sleep like a baby.

DAVE VEERMAN

GOD *in* HIM

JOHN 14:8 NIV
*Philip said, "Lord, show us the Father
and that will be enough for us."*

In the Gospels God spoke through His Son—Jesus. . . .
The disciples would have been foolish to say, "It's wonderful knowing You, Jesus; but we really would like to know the Father."

Philip even said, "Lord, show us the Father and that will be enough for us" (John 14:8).

Jesus responded, "Don't you know me, Philip, even after I have been among you such a long time? Anyone who has seen me has seen the Father. How can you say, 'Show us the Father'? Don't you believe that I am in the Father, and that the Father is in me? The words I say to you are not just my own. Rather, it is the Father, living in me, who is doing his work" (John 14:9–10). When Jesus spoke, the Father was speaking through Him. When Jesus did a miracle, the Father was doing His work through Jesus.

Just as surely as Moses was face-to-face with God at the burning bush, the disciples were face-to-face with God in a personal relationship with Jesus. Their encounter with Jesus was an encounter with God. To hear from Jesus *was* to hear from God.

HENRY BLACKABY AND CLAUDE KING

TO SEE ME IS *to* SEE GOD

JOHN 14:9 NKJV

Jesus said to him, "Have I been with you so long, and yet you have not known Me, Philip? He who has seen Me has seen the Father; so how can you say, 'Show us the Father'?"

We should carefully guard against separating Christ and God. This is what Philip was doing here. He ignored Christ and looked for God in heaven. . . . What else is this than unbelief and a secret denial of God? Christ had to correct Philip in order to tear him away from such a misconception. He said, "Philip, why are you trying to separate the Father from me? With your thoughts, you're climbing up into the clouds and leaving me here on earth talking uselessly. Don't you hear what I am saying? Whoever sees me, sees the Father too. Don't you believe that I am in the Father and the Father is in me?"

Those are loving yet serious words from the Lord, for he can't tolerate us fluttering around in uncertainty. Christ wants us firmly tied to him and his Word so that we don't search for God anywhere else except in him.

MARTIN LUTHER

PRAY *as* HE PRAYED

JOHN 14:13–14 NKJV
"And whatever you ask in My name,
that I will do, that the Father may be glorified in the Son.
If you ask anything in My name, I will do it."

Christ's life and work, His suffering and death—it was all prayer, all dependence on God, trust in God, receiving from God, surrender to God. Thy redemption, O believer, is a redemption wrought out by prayer and intercession: thy Christ is a praying Christ; the life He lived for thee, the life He lives in thee, is a praying life that delights to wait on God and receive all from Him. To pray in His Name is to pray as He prayed. Christ is our only example because He is our Head, our Saviour, and our Life. In virtue of His Deity and of His Spirit He can live in us: we can pray in His Name, because we abide in Him and He in us.

ANDREW MURRAY

FROM *the* HEART

JOHN 14:14 NIV
*"You may ask me for anything in my name,
and I will do it."*

True prayer is only another name for the love of God. Its excellence does not consist in the multitude of our words; for our Father knoweth what things we have need of before we ask Him. The true prayer is that of the heart, and the heart prays only for what it desires. *To pray,* then is *to desire*—but to desire what God would have us desire. He who asks what he does not from the bottom of his heart desire, is mistaken in thinking that he prays. Let him spend days in reciting prayers, in meditation or in inciting himself to pious exercises, he prays not once truly, if he really desires not the things he pretends to ask.

FRANÇOIS FENELON

THEY SANG *a* HYMN

MARK 14:26 NKJV
*And when they had sung a hymn,
they went out to the Mount of Olives.*

How fitting that on this very night Christ, the coming King, would give voice to songs penned centuries earlier just for Him. . . . Imagine the Son of God singing these words as the seconds ticked toward the cross. . . . "The LORD is with me; I will not be afraid. What can man do to me? . . . The stone the builders rejected has become the capstone; The LORD has done this and it is marvelous in our eyes."

Whatever Christ sang as the Passover meal concluded that night, the words had significance for Him that the others could never have comprehended. I wonder if His voice quivered with emotion. Or did He sing with exultation? Perhaps He did both, just as you and I have done at terribly bittersweet moments when our faith exults while our sight weeps. One thing we know: Christ, above all others, knew that He was singing more than words. That night He sang the score of His destiny.

BETH MOORE

THE HOUR *of* TEMPTATION

MATTHEW 26:34 NKJV

*Jesus said to him, "Assuredly, I say to you that this night,
before the rooster crows, you will deny Me three times."*

[P eter] imagined that in the hour of temptation he should come off better than any of them, and Christ tells him that he should come off worse—"take my word for it, who know thee better than thou knowest thyself." He tells him that he should deny him. Peter promised that he would not be so much as offended in him, not desert him; but Christ tells him that he will go further, he will disown him. He said, "Though all men, yet not I," and he did it sooner than any. He thought that he should never once do such a thing; but Christ tells him that he would do it again and again; for, when once our feet begin to slip, it is hard to recover our standing again.

MATTHEW HENRY

JESUS PROMISES
the HOLY SPIRIT

———

"But I tell you the truth: It is for your good that I am going away. Unless I go away, the Counselor will not come to you; but if I go, I will send him to you."

JOHN 16:7 NIV

JESUS PROMISES *the* HOLY SPIRIT

The disciples couldn't help themselves—their hearts *were* troubled. Jesus' repeated predictions about His impending death and departure troubled them. But, now that the meal was over and the table cleared, Jesus' tone changed. He began to speak urgently about life without His physical presence. He promised that the Father would send another Comforter and Counselor, someone who would be with them in ways that Jesus, limited by His humanity, could not be. That new, indwelling presence would be the Holy Spirit.

John chapters 13 to 17 include the lengthiest record of teaching by Jesus in the Gospels. The details of the Spirit's role, guidelines for prayer in a believer's life, and Jesus' own prayer for His followers, both present and future, will occupy our meditations in this section.

HE WILL BE *in* YOU

JOHN 14:17 NRSV

"This is the Spirit of truth, whom the world cannot receive, because it neither sees him nor knows him. You know him, because he abides with you, and he will be in you."

Be constant in prayer as well as in reading. Speak with God, and let God speak with you. Let Him instruct you in His commands; let Him direct you. No one can make poor those He makes rich, for those who have been supplied with heavenly food can't be poor. When you know that it is you who will be perfected, golden ceilings and houses with costly marble mosaics will seem dull to you in comparison to the dwelling in which God has lived and in which the Holy Spirit has begun to make His home. Let us then decorate this house with the colors of innocence. Let us illuminate it with the light of justice. Then it will never decay with the wear of age, nor will its wall colors or its gold become tarnished. Those things made artificially beautiful are perishing. Things that can't really be owned can't provide abiding assurance for their possessors. But remain in a beauty that is continually vivid, in perfect honor, in permanent splendor. It can neither decay nor be destroyed. It can only be fashioned into greater perfection.

CYPRIAN

GOD'S HOME

JOHN 14:17 (Amp.)
*The Spirit of Truth, Whom the world cannot receive
(welcome, take to its heart), because it does not see Him or
know and recognize Him. But you know and recognize Him,
for He lives with you [constantly] and will be in you.*

Just think about it—if you and I are believers in Jesus
Christ, we are the home of the Holy Spirit of God! We
should meditate on this truth over and over until it becomes
a reality in our lives. If we do, we will never be helpless,
hopeless, or powerless, for He promises to be with us to
strengthen us and empower us. We will never be without a
friend or without direction, for He promises to lead us and
to go with us.

I am so excited about being able to share these things
with you, and I sincerely pray that the things I am sharing
are opening up your heart to the wonder of it all. . . .

This truth I have been sharing is so precious I encourage you to guard it, to keep it in your heart. Don't allow it
to slip away from you. Since you are a believer in Jesus
Christ, the Holy Spirit is in you to help you not only to
maintain this revelation, but to give you many others besides.
Appreciate Him, honor Him, love and adore Him. He is so
good, so kind, so awesome. He is wonderful!

JOYCE MEYER

ALWAYS *with* YOU

JOHN 14:18 KJV
I will not leave you comfortless: I will come to you.

Jesus, seeing their anxious faces, noting Peter's fearful question, "Lord, I don't understand. Where are you going?" hastened to reassure them. "I will not leave you orphans," He promised the little group. "I will *not* leave you comfortless. I *will* manifest Myself to you."

So Jesus was telling His followers, "Look, having broken into the time space capsule of Planet Earth and lived for a time among you, you don't think I'm going to leave you there do you? For in that case, what would those have who come after you? Only the written record of Me as an historical figure. No contemporary expression of God, the Father, or of Me—Jesus—for themselves. No, I won't leave it that way. I *will* come to you in the form of One who loves you as I do and is able to care for you even as I do now." . . .

Jesus' promise to you and me is that the Helper will be with us always, day and night, standing by for any protection we need and for every emergency. Our only part is to recognize His presence and to call upon Him in joyous faith.

CATHERINE MARSHALL

WE WILL LIVE *in* YOU

JOHN 14:23 KJV

Jesus answered and said unto him, If a man love me,
he will keep my words: and my Father will love him, and
we will come unto him, and make our abode with him.

T*he kingdom of God is within you,* saith the Lord. Turn thee
with all thine heart to the Lord and forsake this miser-
able world, and thou shalt find rest unto thy soul. Learn to
despise outward things and to give thyself to things inward,
and thou shalt see the kingdom of God come within thee.
For the kingdom of God is peace and joy in the Holy Ghost,
and it is not given to the wicked. Christ will come to thee,
and show thee His consolation. . . .

Go to, faithful soul, prepare thy heart for this bridegroom that he may vouchsafe to come to thee and dwell,
within thee, for so He saith, *if any man loveth me he will keep*
my words: and my Father will love him, and we will come unto him
and make our abode with him. Give, therefore, place to Christ
and refuse entrance to all others. When thou hast Christ, thou
art rich, and hast sufficient. He shall be thy provider and faithful watchman in all things, so that thou hast no need to trust
in men, for men soon change and swiftly pass away, but Christ
remaineth for ever and standeth by us firmly even to the end.

THOMAS À KEMPIS

The House *of the* Lord

John 14:23 NIV

Jesus replied, "If anyone loves me, he will obey my teaching.
My Father will love him, and we will come to him
and make our home with him."

Our Head, which is Christ, has willed us to be His members. As a result, by the bond of love and faith He makes us one body in Himself. It is fitting for us to adhere our hearts to Him, since without Him we can't be anything. But through Him we can be what we are called to be. Don't let anything divide us from our well-established Head, lest by refusing to be His members, we be left separated from Him and wither like branches fallen from the vine. Therefore, in order to be considered the worthy dwelling place of our Redeemer, we must abide in His love with completely resolved minds. For He Himself says, "He that loveth Me will keep My word, and My Father will love him, and We will come unto him, and make Our abode with him." But we can't stay close to the Author of good unless we cut covetousness—for it is the root of all evil. . . . Therefore, we eliminate greed from the temple of faith. It only serves idols. Then we won't face anything hurtful or disorderly while in the house of the Lord.

Gregory I

HOLY CHARACTER

JOHN 14:26 NIV
"But the Counselor, the Holy Spirit, whom the Father will send in my name, will teach you all things and will remind you of everything I have said to you."

Under the Old Testament you know the Holy Spirit often came upon men as a divine Spirit of revelation to reveal the mysteries of God, or for power to do the work of God. But He did not then dwell in them. Now, many just want the Old Testament gift of power for work, but know very little of the New Testament gift of the indwelling Spirit, animating and renewing the whole life. When God gives the Holy Spirit, His great object is the formation of a holy character. It is a gift of a holy mind and spiritual disposition, and what we need above everything else, is to say: "I must have the Holy Spirit sanctifying my whole inner life if I am really to live for God's glory."

ANDREW MURRAY

NO POWER

JOHN 14:30 NIV
*"I will not speak with you much longer, for the prince
of this world is coming. He has no hold on me."*

Did the devil "serve" Jesus? Yes, unwittingly. He whispered to people: "Put Jesus on the cross. That will settle everything." They did just that. So when Jesus was safely nailed to the cross, the devil stood off with folded arms and said to himself, "That settles everything—it is finished." And then his eyes opened wide with astonishment: "Why, he is in charge, even on the cross." For he was dispensing forgiveness to his enemies, opening the gates of paradise to a dying thief, crying "It is finished!" "It is finished," not "I am finished," but the purpose for which I came, the redemption of a race, is finished. The devil gnawed his tongue in anguish: "What a man! He made me 'serve' his purpose!" When you can make the devil serve you, then you are victorious. You're safe, for everything furthers those who follow Christ. If you know what to do with it—use it.

E. STANLEY JONES

MY FATHER IS *the* HUSBANDMAN

JOHN 15:1 KJV

I am the true vine, and my Father is the husbandman.

Now, if there is no doubt that the Son of God is called the Vine in respect of His Incarnation, you can see our Lord's hidden truth in saying "The Father is greater than I." For after establishing this premise, He immediately continued: "I am the true Vine, and My Father is the Husbandman." As a result, you can know that the Father is greater because He prepares and cares for our Lord's flesh, as farmers prepare and care for their vines. Furthermore, our Lord's flesh was able to grow with age and be wounded through suffering. Therefore, the whole human race could rest under the shadow of the cross's outstretched limbs, guarded from the pestilent heat of the world's pleasures.

AMBROSE

PRODUCE MUCH FRUIT

JOHN 15:5 NLT

*"Yes, I am the vine; you are the branches. Those who
remain in me, and I in them, will produce much fruit.
For apart from me you can do nothing."*

The purpose of an apple tree is to bear apples. The purpose of a cherry tree is to bear cherries. The purpose of a grapevine is to bear grapes. Christians are also expected to bear fruit: love, joy, peace, patience, kindness, goodness, faithfulness, gentleness, and self control (Galatians 5:22–23), and to win souls (John 15:16). Here, Jesus says he is the vine and believers are the branches. Thus, the secret to our bearing fruit is staying attached to the vine. Jesus' point is that we are totally dependent upon him. Just as we could not become God's children through our own efforts but only through faith in Christ, so, too, we cannot bear fruit by wishing and hoping for it or by working hard at it on our own. Instead, we must allow Christ to produce his fruit through us. The secret is in "remaining."

We remain in Christ by communicating with him, doing what he says, living by faith, and relating in love to the community of believers.

So stay close, be nourished, and bear fruit.

DAVE VEERMAN

THE FRUIT *of the* FAITH

JOHN 15:5 NKJV
"I am the vine, you are the branches.
He who abides in Me, and I in him, bears much fruit;
for without Me you can do nothing."

By saying that believers live in him and he lives in them, Jesus is making it clear that Christianity is not something we put on externally. We don't put it on like clothes. We don't adopt it as new lifestyle that focuses on our own efforts, as do those who practice a holy lifestyle they have invented themselves. Rather, Christian faith is a new birth brought about by God's Word and Spirit. A Christian must be a person from the depths of his heart. Once the heart is born anew in Christ, these fruits will follow: confession of the gospel, love, obedience, patience, purity, and so on. . . .

The works we make up require us to strive harder, but they never do as well as natural growth. In contrast, natural growth stands, moves, lives, and does what it should naturally. So Christ says, "All other human teaching cannot succeed because it instructs people to make up works. But if you live in me, as natural branches live on the vine, you will certainly produce good fruit."

MARTIN LUTHER

NOTHING WITHOUT HIM

JOHN 15:5 KJV

*I am the vine, ye are the branches: He that abideth in me,
and I in him, the same bringeth forth much fruit:
for without me ye can do nothing.*

We are renewed day by day by making progress in our
righteousness and true holiness through the knowledge of God. For those who do so transfer their love from
temporal things to eternal things, from visible things to invis-
ible things, from fleshly things to spiritual things . . . They do
this in proportion to their help from God. For God said,
"Without me ye can do nothing." When the last day of life
finds them holding on tightly to their faith in the Mediator
through such progress and growth, they will be welcomed by
the holy angels. They will be led to God, whom they have
worshiped, and will be perfected by Him. As a result, they
will receive an immortal body at the end of the world. They
won't be led to punishment, but to glow. For our likeness of
God will be perfected into His image when our sight of God
is perfected.

AUGUSTINE

HE GIVES HIMSELF

JOHN 15:7 NIV
*"If you remain in me and my words remain in you,
ask whatever you wish, and it will be given you."*

We want fatherly assurance that there is an order to our painful reality that somehow transcends our problems. . . . This is our cry when we ask "why?" The problem of suffering is not about something; it's about someone. And so it follows that the answer is not something, but someone. And God, like any good daddy, doesn't give answers as much as He gives Himself. . . .

I learned early on in this wheelchair that God owed me no explanations. He did enough explaining on the cross. He didn't provide me with the words I was looking for at the beginning of my paralysis. Instead, He is the Word. The Word made flesh, hands nearly ripped off, nailed to a cross, vomit, spit, smeared, dried blood, hammering hatred, flies buzzing. . . . For one who suffers, I'm so glad Jesus endured a messy death on the cross. I'm so grateful that our God isn't a medicating mystic of a guru who sits on some mountaintop twiddling his thumbs, but is our Savior who suffered a messy, bloody death that was excruciatingly painful at the hands of vindictive and mean-spirited men.

God allows suffering so that nothing stands between Him and me. You see, when we suffer, we're much more apt to fall to our knees, and when we do, our hearts are open to the Lord.

JONI EARECKSON TADA

ASK WHAT YOU WISH

JOHN 15:7 NRSV

"If you abide in me, and my words abide in you, ask for whatever you wish, and it will be done for you."

So how do we pray in Jesus' name, that is, in conformity to his nature? Jesus himself says, "If you abide in me, and my words abide in you, ask for whatever you wish, and it will be done for you" (John 15:7). This "abide in me" is the all-inclusive condition for effective intercession. It is the key for prayer in the name of Jesus. We learn to become like the branch, which receives its life from the vine: "Abide in me as I abide in you. Just as the branch cannot bear fruit by itself unless it abides in the vine, neither can you unless you abide in me" (John 15:4). Nothing is more important to a life of prayer than learning how to become a branch.

As we live this way, we develop what Thomas à Kempis calls "a familiar friendship with Jesus." We become accustomed to his face. We distinguish the voice of the true Shepherd from that of religious hucksters in the same way professional jewelers distinguish a diamond from glass imitations—by acquaintanceship. When we have been around the genuine article long enough, the cheap and the shoddy become obvious. . . . We know even as we are known. This is how we pray in Jesus' name.

RICHARD J. FOSTER

That Your Joy Might Be Full

John 15:11 kjv

These things have I spoken unto you, that my joy might remain in you, and that your joy might be full.

In His dying discourse with His eleven disciples, Jesus Christ in the fourteenth, fifteenth, and sixteenth chapters of John, frequently declares His special and everlasting love to them in the plainest and most positive terms. In the most absolute manner, He promises them a future participation with Him in His glory. He tells them at the same time that He does this so that their joy might be full (John 15:11). Christ was not afraid of speaking too plainly and positively to them. He does not desire to hold them in suspense. He concludes His last discourse with a prayer in their presence in which He speaks positively to His Father of those eleven disciples as all knowing Him savingly, believing in Him, and having re-ceived and kept His Word.

Jonathan Edwards

NO GREATER LOVE

JOHN 15:13 NKJV
"Greater love has no one than this,
than to lay down one's life for his friends."

In the greatest showing of love imaginable, Christ came into human life, into the story that love had made, as Jesus of Nazareth. Christ, the Second Person of the Trinity, left the place of Creation and power and became mortal, open to temptation, to weakness and fatigue, to sorrow and joy, and laughter and tears. Who was this Jesus? God? Mortal? Both? Yes, both! How could such a thing be?

It is impossible, but Jesus reiterated that although many things are impossible for us, nothing is impossible for God.

Even human love is beyond explanation. I am grateful for my life with my husband; grateful for my children (who are miracles in themselves), and for their children; grateful for the friends who accept me as I am, with all my faults and flaws, doubts, and mistakes.

I struggle to write about God and God's love, knowing that I am totally inadequate, and yet feeling called to proclaim a love so marvelous that it can only be wondered at and rejoiced in with delight. . . .

Christ, the Second Person of the Trinity, is not limited by the mortal body of Jesus of Nazareth. Christ is the Word who shouted all things into being and who continually calls each one of us into fuller being, every day, every minute, right now.

MADELEINE L'ENGLE

PURE LOVE ALONE

JOHN 15:13 KJV
*Greater love hath no man than this,
that a man lay down his life for his friends.*

Jesus, Thy boundless love to me
No thought can reach, no tongue declare;
Unite my thankful heart with Thee
And reign without a rival there.
To Thee alone, dear Lord, I live;
Myself to Thee, dear Lord, I give.

O, grant that nothing in my soul
May dwell but Thy pure love alone!
Oh, may Thy love possess me whole,
My joy, my treasure, and my crown!
All coldness from my heart remove;
My every act, word, thought, be love.

O love, how cheering is thy ray!
All pain before thy presence flies;
Care, anguish, sorrow, melt away
Wherever thy healing beams arise.
O Jesus, nothing may I see,
Nothing desire or seek, but Thee!

PAUL GERHARDT

LAYING DOWN YOUR LIFE

JOHN 15:13 KJV
Greater love hath no man than this,
that a man lay down his life for his friends.

We aren't discouraged by punishment for our sins. It is meant to train us in self-discipline, so that as we press on in holiness, we can overcome our fear of death. If those who aren't afraid ("because of the faith which worketh by love") are hardly noticed, then there wouldn't be much glory in martyrdom. And the Lord couldn't say, "Greater love hath no man than this, that he lay down his life for his friends." John, in his epistle, expresses it in these words: "As He laid down His life for us, so ought we to lay down our lives for the brethren." Therefore, it would be useless to praise those who face death for righteousness' sake if death wasn't really a severe trial. But those who overcome the fear of death by their faith, will receive great glory and fair compensation for their faith. No one should be surprised, therefore, that death is a punishment for previous sins. Neither should it surprise us that the faithful die after their sins are forgiven to exercise the fearlessness of righteousness by conquering their fear of death.

AUGUSTINE

CHANGED *for the* BETTER

JOHN 15:15 NKJV

"No longer do I call you servants, for a servant does not know what his master is doing; but I have called you friends, for all things that I heard from My Father I have made known to you."

The Divine Word doesn't want us to be slaves of anything; our nature has been changed for the better. He has taken everything that was ours with the agreement that He will give what is His to us in return. Just as He took disease, death, condemnation, and sin, He also took our slavery. He doesn't keep what He took, but purged our nature of such evil. Our defects are being swallowed up and done away with in His stainless nature. Therefore, there won't be disease condemnation, sin, or death, in the life that we hope for. And slavery will also vanish. The Truth Himself testifies of this. He says to His disciples, "I call you no more servants, but friends." . . . If "the servant knoweth not what his lord doeth," and if Christ owns all the Father's things, then let those who are reeling with alcohol become sober at last. Let them now, as never before, look up at the truth and see that He who owns all the Father's things is Lord of all and isn't a slave.

GREGORY OF NYSSA

YOU ARE MY FRIENDS

JOHN 15:15 NLT

*"I no longer call you servants, because a master doesn't
confide in his servants. Now you are my friends, since
I have told you everything the Father told me."*

In the middle of his last instructions to his disciples before
he was betrayed, tried, and crucified, Jesus explained that
they should see themselves as his friends, not as his servants.
It was an important distinction. Good servants work hard for
the master and are loyal and faithful. But they don't ask why.
They aren't privileged to know the master's plans, reasons,
and motives. They simply obey.

Friends, however, enjoy a close relationship. They share
experiences and information. They know each other well,
and they move together in the same direction. Jesus had
revealed to these men all that he had learned from his Father.
They truly were his friends.

Twenty centuries later, we who name Christ as Savior
also stand as his friends. He has given us the Bible, his written Word, to study and apply and the Holy Spirit to teach us
(John 14:26). We can know the Master's business.

When you don't know which way to turn, ask God. He
will answer because Jesus is your friend. When you feel all
alone, turn your thoughts heavenward, remembering that
Jesus is your friend. He's there when you need him.

DAVE VEERMAN

I CHOSE YOU

JOHN 15:16 NRSV

*"You did not choose me but I chose you. And I appointed
you to go and bear fruit, fruit that will last, so that the Father
will give you whatever you ask him in my name."*

The disciples were ordinary Galileans, with no special claims on the interest of Jesus. But Jesus, the rabbi who spoke with authority, the prophet who was more than a prophet, the master who evoked in them increasing awe and devotion till they could not but acknowledge him as their God, found them, called them to Himself, took them into His confidence, and enrolled them as His agents to declare to the world the kingdom of God. "He appointed twelve, to be with him, and to be sent out to preach ..." (Mark 3:14, RSV). They recognized the one who had chosen them and called them friends as "the Christ, the Son of the living God" (Matthew 16:16), the man born to be king, the bearer of "the words of eternal life" (John 6:68), and the sense of allegiance and privilege which this knowledge brought transformed their whole lives.

J. I. PACKER

YOU DO NOT BELONG *to the* WORLD

JOHN 15:18–19 NRSV

"If the world hates you, be aware that it hated me before it hated you. If you belonged to the world, the world would love you as its own. Because you do not belong to the world, but I have chosen you out of the world—therefore the world hates you."

No one is free from the risk of persecution. . . . But how serious it is for Christians who are unwilling to suffer for their own sins when He who had no sin suffered for us! The Son of God suffered in order to make us children of God, but people won't suffer to continue being children of God! If we suffer from the world's hatred, Christ first endured the world's hatred. If we suffer rebukes in this world, if exile or torture, the Maker and Lord of the world experienced harder things than these. He also warns us, "If the world hates you, remember that it hated Me before you. If ye were of the world, the world would love their own: but because ye are not of the world, but I have chosen you out of the world, therefore the world hateth you. Remember the word that I said unto you, 'The servant is not greater than his lord.' If they have persecuted Me, they will also persecute you." Whatever our Lord God taught, He did so that disciples who learn have no excuse not to do what they learn.

CYPRIAN

THE COST *of* FOLLOWING

JOHN 15:20 NLT

"Do you remember what I told you? 'A servant is not greater than the master.' Since they persecuted me, naturally they will persecute you."

B ut make no mistake. No fancy words must ever disguise the fact that choosing suffering is not normal. Human beings avoid suffering and prefer not to think about death. Given a choice, we prefer better weather. We take aspirin. We appreciate a cushion. We come in out of the cold. We don't go down dark alleys. We don't drive cars without brakes. Anyone who chooses pain is odd, if not a masochist, in the eyes of most of us.

The Gospels, however, are unambiguously clear about the cost of discipleship and also that Jesus' call to discipleship is the echo of his father's call to him. Called to be the Messiah, Jesus knew he must suffer and be what appeared a contradiction in terms—a rejected Messiah. But he lays this necessity on the disciples too. Just as Jesus is the Messiah, the Christ, only insofar as he suffers and is rejected, so the disciples of Jesus are obedient to the call of Jesus only insofar as they are prepared to pay the cost.

OS GUINNESS

YOU'RE NOT ALONE

JOHN 15:26 NLT

"But I will send you the Counselor—the Spirit of truth. He will come to you from the Father and will tell you all about me."

Jesus is teaching the disciples about the Holy Spirit, the "Spirit of truth." Translated as "Counselor" or "Comforter," the Greek word literally means "one who comes alongside." So this title pictures one person coming close to another, alongside, to guide (as on a path in the woods), to advise (as a lawyer in a court of law), to counsel (as a psychiatrist or simply a trusted friend), to speak words of concern (as in a hospital room), or to comfort (as at a graveside).

Clearly, God sends his Spirit to help all believers. And he counsels and comforts by telling the truth about Jesus, assuring believers of Christ's true identity, forgiveness of sins, love, and salvation.

Do you feel lost, wondering which way to turn? You are not alone. The Holy Spirit stands beside you and will guide you God's way.

Do you feel accosted and accused? You're not alone. God's Spirit comes to your defense.

Do you feel confused, frustrated, anxious, or fearful? You're not alone. The Counselor is with you to give you hope and to tell you how to live.

Do you feel devastated by loss and overcome with grief? You're not alone. The Comforter is close, wrapping his arms around you and whispering words of love.

DAVE VEERMAN

WHAT FILLS YOUR THOUGHTS?

JOHN 16:7 (Amp.)

"However, I am telling you nothing but the truth when I say it is profitable (good, expedient, advantageous) for you that I go away. Because if I do not go away, the Comforter (Counselor, Helper, Advocate, Intercessor, Strengthener, Standby) will not come to you [into close fellowship with you]; but if I go away, I will send Him to you [to be in close fellowship with you]."

These words were spoken by Jesus just before He departed into heaven where He is seated at the right hand of the Father in glory. It is obvious from this Scripture that it is God's will that we be in close fellowship with Him.

Nothing is closer to us than our own thoughts. Therefore, if we will fill our mind with the Lord, it will bring Him into our consciousness and we will begin to enjoy a fellowship with Him that will bring joy, peace and victory to our everyday life.

He is always with us just as He promised He would be (Matthew 28:20; Hebrews 13:5). But we will not be conscious of His Presence unless we think about Him. I can be in a room with someone and if I have my mind on lots of other things, I can leave and never even know that person was there. This is the way it is with our fellowship privileges with the Lord. He is always with us, but we need to think on Him and be aware of His presence.

JOYCE MEYER

BECAUSE *of* HIM

JOHN 16:7 NIV

*"But I tell you the truth: It is for your good that
I am going away. Unless I go away, the Counselor will
not come to you; but if I go, I will send him to you."*

As for forgiveness, so equally for the coming upon us of
the Holy Spirit, the whole question is one of faith. As
soon as we see the Lord Jesus on the Cross, we know our sins
are forgiven; and as soon as we see the Lord Jesus on the
Throne, we know the Holy Spirit has been poured out upon
us. The basis upon which we receive the enduement of the
Holy Spirit is not our praying and fasting and waiting, but the
exaltation of Christ. Those who emphasize tarrying and hold
"tarrying meetings" only mislead us, for the gift is not for the
"favoured few" but for all, because it is not given on the
ground of what we are at all, but of what Christ is. The Spirit
has been poured out to prove *His* goodness and greatness, not
ours. Christ has been crucified, therefore we have been forgiven: Christ has been glorified, therefore we have been
endued with power from on high. It is all because of Him.

WATCHMAN NEE

FACE *the* TRUTH

JOHN 16:12 (Amp.)

*"I have still many things to say to you, but you are not able
to bear them or to take them upon you or to grasp them now."*

Jesus could have showed His disciples all the truth, but He
knew they were not ready for it. He told them that they
would have to wait until the Holy Spirit came down from
heaven to abide with them and to dwell in them.

After Jesus had ascended into heaven, He sent the Holy
Spirit to work with us, preparing us continually for God's
glory to be manifested through us in varying degrees.

How can we have the Holy Spirit working in our lives
if we will not face truth? He is called "The Spirit of Truth."
A major facet of His ministry to you and me is to help us
face truth—to bring us to a place of truth, because only the
truth will set us free.

Something in your past—a person, event or circum-
stance that hurt you—may be the source of your wrong attitude and behavior, but don't allow it to become an excuse to
stay that way. . . .

Ask God to start showing you the truth about yourself.
When He does, hang on! It won't be easy, but remember,
He has promised, "I will never leave you nor forsake you."
(Hebrews 13:5.)

JOYCE MEYER

GUIDED *by the* HOLY SPIRIT

JOHN 16:13 NLT
*"When the Spirit of truth comes,
he will guide you into all truth."*

Y ou all know what shunting is on a railway. A locomotive
with its train may be run in a certain direction, and the
points at some place may not be properly opened or closed,
and unobservingly it is shunted off to the right or to the left.
And if that takes place, for instance, on a dark night, the train
goes in the wrong direction, and the people might never
know it until they have gone some distance.

And just so God gives Christians the Holy Spirit with
this intention, that every day all their life should be lived in
the power of the Spirit. A man cannot live one hour a godly
life unless by the power of the Holy Ghost. He may live a
proper, consistent life, as people call it, an irreproachable life,
a life of virtue and diligent service; but to live a life acceptable to God, in the enjoyment of God's salvation and God's
love, to live and walk in the power of the new life—he cannot do it unless he be guided by the Holy Spirit every day
and every hour.

ANDREW MURRAY

JOY THAT STAYS

JOHN 16:22 NKJV
*"Therefore you now have sorrow; but I will see you again and
your heart will rejoice, and your joy no one will take from you."*

The joy of Christ doesn't go away. Have you noticed how
easily earthly joy can leave? Have you discovered how
simple it is for your gladness of today to become your sad-
ness of tomorrow, for your sweetness of the morning to turn
into the bitterness of the night? Have you discovered how
the people you thought were your friends today can become
your enemies tomorrow, the wisdom you thought was so
great yesterday is foolishness today?

Nothing seems to be too stable in the world. You can't
really count on too much anymore. But the joy of Christ is
a continual, never-ending, absolutely constant joy when we
follow the principles of the Word of God. This joy survives
all the difficult times in life. This joy is not hinged on hap-
penings, but it is hinged on a Person.

In John 16:22, Jesus says, "Therefore you now have sorrow; but I will see you again and your heart will rejoice, and
your joy no one will take from you." Isn't that something?
Jesus says the joy He wants to give every one of His children
is the kind of joy you don't have to lose. Nobody can take it
away from you!

DAVID JEREMIAH

THE FIRST LINE *of* DEFENSE

JOHN 16:23–24 NKJV

"And in that day you will ask Me nothing. Most assuredly,
I say to you, whatever you ask the Father in My name
He will give you. Until now you have asked nothing in My
name. Ask, and you will receive, that your joy may be full."

Study what Christ commands in this passage and put it into practice. Don't consider prayer as something that you do voluntarily, as if it wouldn't be a sin if you neglected to pray. Don't act as if it's enough for others to pray. But now you know that Christ earnestly commands prayer. If you don't pray, you risk the greatest disgrace and the highest penalty. Christ's command here is similar to the commandment that prohibits worshiping any other gods and blaspheming God's name. Those who never pray should know that they aren't Christians and don't belong in God's kingdom. Now don't you think that God has good reason to be angry with idolaters, murderers, thieves, blasphemers, and others who despise his Word? Don't you think he's right to punish these sins? Why, then, aren't you afraid of God's anger when you disrespect his command and confidently act as if you aren't obligated to pray?

So this passage should serve as a strong encouragement to pray diligently. Prayer is our comfort, strength, and salvation. It's our first line of defense against all of our enemies.

MARTIN LUTHER

TWO OBSTACLES *to* PRAYER

JOHN 16:24 NKJV
*"Until now you have asked nothing in My name.
Ask, and you will receive, that your joy may be full."*

There are two major obstacles to prayer. The first obstacle arises when the devil prompts you to think, "I am not yet prepared to pray. I should wait for another half-hour or another day until I have become more prepared or until I have finished taking care of this or that." Meanwhile, the devil distracts you for half an hour, so that you no longer think about prayer for the rest of the day. From one day to the next, you are hindered and rushed with other business. This common obstacle shows us how maliciously the devil tries to trick us. . . .

The second obstacle arises when we ask ourselves, "How can you pray to God and say the Lord's Prayer? You are too unworthy and sin every day. Wait until you are more devout. You might be in the mood to pray now, but wait until you have confessed your sin taken the Lord's Supper so that you can pray more fervently and approach God with confidence. Only then can you really pray the Lord's Prayer from your heart." This serious obstacle crushes us like a heavy stone. Despite our feelings of unworthiness, our hearts must struggle to remove this obstacle so that we can freely approach God and call upon him.

MARTIN LUTHER

CHRIST HAS OVERCOME

JOHN 16:33 NKJV

*"These things I have spoken to you, that in Me you
may have peace. In the world you will have tribulation;
but be of good cheer, I have overcome the world."*

We should learn to remind ourselves of Christ's victory. In Christ, we already have everything that we need. We only live to spread this message of victory to other people. With our word and example, we tell them about the victory that Christ secured for us and gave to us. Christ, our victor, accomplished everything. We don't need to add anything to it. We don't need to wipe away our own sins, or try to conquer death and the devil. Everything has already been done for us. We're not fighting the real battle. We're only suffering now in order to share in Christ's victory. It's not accomplished by what we do. . . .

We know from the past when believers were severely tested, the Holy Spirit reminded them of Christ's victory and strengthened them so that they could endure everything. They could even face martyrdom, relying on Christ's victory. May God help us also to hold on to Christ's victory during our troubles and when we're dying. Even though we don't understand these words of Christ completely, we can still believe in them in times of trouble and reassure ourselves.

MARTIN LUTHER

BE *an* OVERCOMER

JOHN 16:33 NLT

*"I have told you all this so that you may have peace in me.
Here on earth you will have many trials and sorrows.
But take heart, because I have overcome the world."*

Jesus was about to be arrested, tried, convicted, and crucified. Soon his disciples would be left to carry his message
throughout the world. Jesus knew that they would be tested,
tempted, and persecuted. So in these final instructions, he
warned them and gave them a promise.

Note that Jesus didn't say the disciples "might" or "could"
have trouble; he said they "will"—it was a certainty. Yet in their
troubles they could have peace and be encouraged.

Until Christ returns, Christians will always conflict
with the world. We stand out with a different allegiance, different values, and a different lifestyle. We threaten the status
quo by refusing to compromise our faith, living for Christ,
and calling people to turn from their sins and to give their
lives to the Savior.

That doesn't make us popular. We will have trouble.

With all this trouble, however, we can have peace.
Knowing that our Lord has defeated sin, death, and all of the
temptations and attacks of Satan gives us courage to face
adversity with calmness of spirit during any trial.

Whatever "trouble" you face, take heart! You can be an
overcomer because he has "overcome the world."

DAVE VEERMAN

IT'S JUST PART *of* LIFE

JOHN 16:33 (Amp.)

"I have told you these things, so that in Me you may have [perfect] peace and confidence. In the world you have tribulation and trials and distress and frustration; but be of good cheer [take courage; be confident, certain, undaunted]! For I have overcome the world. [I have deprived it of power to harm you and have conquered it for you.]"

If we get the idea in our heads that everything concerning us and our circumstances and relationships should always be perfect—no inconveniences, no hindrances, no unlovely people to deal with—then we are setting ourselves up for a fall. Or, actually, I should say that Satan is setting us up for a fall through wrong thinking.

I am not suggesting that we be negative; I am a firm believer in positive attitudes and thoughts. But I am suggesting that we be realistic enough to realize ahead of time that very few things in real life are ever perfect. . . .

I don't plan for failure, but I do remember that Jesus said that in this world we will have to deal with tribulation and trials and distress and frustration. These things are part of life on this earth—for the believer as well as the unbeliever. But all the mishaps in the world cannot harm us if we will remain in the love of God, displaying the fruit of the Spirit.

JOYCE MEYER

ARMED *with the* CROSS

JOHN 16:33 NKJV

"These things I have spoken to you, that in Me you may have peace. In the world you will have tribulation; but be of good cheer, I have overcome the world."

We must not pursue foolish and vain things or yield to fear in the midst of trouble. We are, no doubt, flattered by deception and weighed down by troubles, but because "the earth is full of the mercy of the Lord," Christ's victory is ours. He fulfills what He said: "Fear not, for I have overcome the world." So then, whether we fight against the world's ambition, the lusts of the flesh, or against the darts of heresy, we must always arm ourselves with the Lord's cross. . . . We should remember the Apostle Paul's instruction, "Let this mind be in you which was also in Christ Jesus: who being in the form of God counted it not robbery to be equal with God, but emptied Himself, taking the form of a bond-servant, being made in the likeness of men and found in fashion as a man. Wherefore God also exalted Him, and gave Him a name which is above every name, that in the name of Jesus every knee should bow, of things in heaven, of things on earth, and of things below, and that every tongue should confess that the Lord Jesus Christ is in the glory of God the Father."

LEO I

TRIBULATION *and* TEMPTATION

JOHN 16:33 KJV
*These things I have spoken unto you, that in me ye
might have peace. In the world ye shall have tribulation:
but be of good cheer; I have overcome the world.*

After saying, "In the world ye shall have tribulation," Christ added, "But be of good cheer, I have overcome the world." He taught the disciples to pray that they wouldn't fall into temptation. He said, "And lead us not into temptation," which means, "Do not let us fall into temptation." To show that this implied not that they wouldn't be tempted but that they would be saved from evil, He added, "But deliver us from evil." Perhaps you will say, "What difference is there between being tempted, and falling or entering into temptation?" Well, if a person is overcome by evil (and he will be overcome unless he struggles against it, and unless God protects him with His shield), that person has entered into temptation and has been taken captive to it. But if one resists and endures, one is tempted but hasn't entered into temptation or fallen under it. Therefore, the wicked one draws us into evil temptations when he tempts us. But God tests us as one untempted by evil. For God, it is said, "cannot be tempted of evil." The devil, therefore, drives us on by violence, drawing us to destruction. But God leads us by the hand, training us for our salvation.

DIONYSIUS OF ALEXANDRIA

ETERNAL LIFE

JOHN 17:3 NRSV
"And this is eternal life, that they may know you, the only true God, and Jesus Christ whom you have sent."

God loves us by giving us *eternal life* at the cost of his Son, Jesus Christ. But what is eternal life? Is it eternal self-esteem? Is it a heaven full of mirrors? Or snowboards, or golf links, or black-eyed virgins?

No. Jesus tells us exactly what he meant: "And this is eternal life, that they know you the only true God, and Jesus Christ whom you have sent" (John 17:3). What is eternal life? It is to know God and his Son, Jesus Christ. No thing can satisfy the soul. The soul was made to stand in awe of a Person—the only person worthy of awe. All heroes are shadows of Christ. We love to admire their excellence. How much more will we be satisfied by the one Person who conceived all excellence and embodies all skill, all talent, all strength and brilliance and savvy and goodness. This is what I have been trying to say. God loves us by liberating us from the bondage of self so that we can enjoy knowing and admiring him forever.

JOHN PIPER

THE WORK GOD GIVES

JOHN 17:4 KJV
*I have glorified thee on the earth: I have finished
the work which thou gavest me to do.*

The Lord Jesus Himself was given only a few short years
on earth to accomplish the entire plan of redemption.
Talk about a long "to do" list! Yet, at the end of His life, Jesus
was able to lift His eyes to His Father and say, "I have glorified thee on the earth: I have *finished the work* which thou
gavest me to do" (John 17:4 KJV, italics added).

I find that truly amazing. Rarely can I say at the end of
the day that I have completed the work I set out to do that
day. . . . How was it possible for Jesus to finish His life's
work—especially in such a short period of time?

In Jesus' words, we find a clue—a powerful Truth that sets
us free from the bondage of hurry and frustration about all we
have to do. Notice what work Jesus completed in the thirty-
three years He was here on the earth: "I have finished the
work *which thou gavest me to do."* That is the secret. Jesus didn't
finish everything His disciples wanted Him to do. (Some of
them were hoping He would overthrow the Roman govern-
ment!) He didn't finish everything the multitudes wanted
Him to do. (There were still people who were sick and lonely and dying.) But He did finish the work that *God* gave Him
to do.

NANCY LEIGH DEMOSS

LAST WORDS

JOHN 17:20 NIV
"My prayer is not for them alone. I pray also for those who will believe in me through their message."

To put Christ's words in their proper emotional context, we need to know only one thing: In less than twenty-four hours, he would be dead. He knew that. So this was a time of last things. It was not only his last supper, it was his last time with the disciples before he died. It was a time of last looks, last embraces, last words.

At the end of the evening, Jesus prays a last prayer for them. He prays not only on behalf of his disciples but for everyone who would believe in him through their words. . . .

Do you hear what he is asking? . . .

It is not just for that first privileged gathering of disciples. It is for each and every disciple that has followed after them.

That means it's for me.

And for you.

KEN GIRE

JESUS AGONIZES
in the GARDEN

———

Then Jesus went with them to a place called
Gethsemane; and he said to his disciples,
"Sit here while I go over there and pray."
MATTHEW 26:36 NRSV

JESUS AGONIZES *in the* GARDEN

The late hour, large meal, and emotional overload overwhelmed the disciples. Eyelids fought gravity, but lost. Those men may have been willing, but their bodies wanted sleep. Jesus sensed their helpless withdrawal as one more painful part of His own trials. No, they couldn't watch with Him for even one hour. The Garden of Gethsemane provided a deceptively quiet retreat from the long day.

He struggled alone in prayer. A few steps away, the bleary-eyed disciples faintly overheard His agony, noticed in the moonlight that His sweat glistened like blood, wondered why He was so troubled, but slowly succumbed to slumber. Their grogginess made them easy prey for fear when the mob came to arrest Jesus.

What did Jesus' prayer mean? How did Jesus' reluctance to face the cross fit with His determination to secure salvation for humanity? Monitor your own alertness as you think with others about the significance of those moments in Gethsemane and the importance Jesus placed on prayer.

THE HABIT of PRAYER

LUKE 22:41 NIV
*He withdrew about a stone's throw
beyond them, knelt down and prayed.*

O my brother, if thou and I would be like Jesus we must especially contemplate Jesus praying alone in the wilderness. *There is the secret of His wonderful life.* What He did and spoke to man *was first spoken and lived through with the Father.* In communion with Him, the anointing with the Holy Spirit was each day renewed. He who would be like Him in his walk and conversation must simply begin here, that he follow Jesus into solitude. . . . Besides the ordinary hour of prayer, he will feel at times irresistibly drawn to enter into the holy place, and not to come thence until it has been revealed anew to him that God is his portion. In his secret chamber, with closed door, or in the solitude of the wilderness, God must be found every day, and our fellowship with Him renewed. If Christ needed it, how much more we! What it was to Him it will be for us.

ANDREW MURRAY

GOD WAS THERE

MATTHEW 26:38 NASB

Then He said to them, "My soul is deeply grieved, to the point of death; remain here and keep watch with Me."

And if you come and say: "Lord, I yield myself in absolute surrender to my God," even though it be with a trembling heart and with the consciousness: "I do not feel the power, I do not feel the determination, I do not feel the assurance," it will succeed. Be not afraid, but come just as you are, and even in the midst of your trembling the power of the Holy Ghost will work.

Have you never yet learned the lesson that the Holy Ghost works with mighty power, while on the human side everything appears feeble? Look at the Lord Jesus Christ in Gethsemane. We read that He, "through the eternal Spirit," offered Himself a sacrifice unto God. The Almighty Spirit of God was enabling Him to do it. And yet what agony and fear and exceeding sorrow came over Him, and how He prayed! Externally, you can see no sign of the mighty power of the Spirit, but the Spirit of God was there. And even so, while you are feeble and fighting and trembling, in faith in the hidden work of God's Spirit do not fear, but yield yourself.

ANDREW MURRAY

AWESOME

MATTHEW 26:39 NIV
*Going a little farther, he fell with his face to the ground
and prayed, "My Father, if it is possible, may this cup be
taken from me. Yet not as I will, but as you will."*

A student at a university said to me, "I often wonder
about Jesus struggling at Gethsemane over the impending crucifixion. What was happening there? Jesus asking to
be spared the cup? It sounds crazy to me," he said.

I answered, "Ponder with me for a moment. The cup of
human sin was to be drunk to the last dregs by the purest
one of all. The most painful physical torture was that of being
crucified. Yet the Lord Jesus did not fear the physical pain.
The only indivisible entity in the world is the very Holy
Trinity. The possibility of His Father turning away from Him
when He was subjected to the accursedness of sin was para-
mount in His mind. But He knew that if that was the only
way to accomplish salvation, He would do it. . . .

"Look at the Cross, now Evil is seen for what it is—all
the vileness in the human heart is there in the face of the
perfectly pure. Evil is not covered up. See again the marvel
of God's love that offers forgiveness of such evil. . . ."

There was silence and then the student said one word:
"Awesome." He muttered again, "Just awesome."

RAVI ZACHARIAS

THE BITTER CUP

MATTHEW 26:39 KJV

*And he went a little farther, and fell on his face, and prayed,
saying, O my Father, if it be possible, let this cup pass
from me: nevertheless not as I will, but as thou wilt.*

His entire submission to, and acquiescence in, the will of God; "Nevertheless, not as I will, but as thou wilt." Our Lord Jesus, though he had a quick sense of the extreme bitterness of the sufferings he was to undergo, yet was freely willing to submit to them for our redemption and salvation, and offered himself, and gave himself, for us. The reason of Christ's submission to his sufferings, was his Father's will; "as thou wilt," (v. 39). He grounds his own willingness upon the Father's will, and resolves the matter wholly into that; therefore he did what he did, and did it with delight, because it was the will of God. In conformity to this example of Christ, we must drink of the bitter cup which God puts into our hands, be it ever so bitter; though nature struggle, grace must submit. We then are disposed as Christ was, when our wills are in every thing melted into the will of God, though ever so displeasing to flesh and blood; The will of the Lord be done.

MATTHEW HENRY

A Life Yielded *to* God

MATTHEW 26:39 NKJV

He went a little farther and fell on His face, and prayed,
saying, "O My Father, if it is possible, let this cup pass from
Me; nevertheless, not as I will, but as You will."

He never for a moment thought of seeking His own honor, or asserting His own power to vindicate Himself. His whole spirit was that of a life yielded to God to work in. It is not until Christians study the humility of Jesus as the very essence of His redemption, as the very blessedness of the life of the Son of God, as the only true relation to the Father, and therefore as that which Jesus must give us if we are to have any part with Him, that the terrible lack of actual, heavenly, manifest humility will become a burden and a sorrow, and our ordinary religion be set aside to secure this, the first and the chief of the marks of the Christ within us.

Are you clothed with humility? Ask your daily life. Ask Jesus. Ask your friends. Ask the world. And begin to praise God that there is opened up to you in Jesus a heavenly humility of which you have hardly known, and through which a heavenly blessedness you possibly have never yet tasted can come in to you.

ANDREW MURRAY

ABBA, FATHER

MARK 14:36 NKJV

And He said, "Abba, Father, all things are possible for You. Take this cup away from Me; nevertheless, not what I will, but what You will."

Calling God "Abba" is rooted in Jesus' agony in the Garden of Gethsemane:

"And He said, 'Abba, Father, all things are possible for You. Take this cup away from Me; nevertheless, not what I will, but what You will'" (Mark 14:36).

Abba was an ordinary family word of Jesus' day. It conveyed intimacy, tenderness, dependence, and complete lack of fear or anxiety. Modern English equivalents would be Daddy or Papa.

No Jew would have dreamed of using this very intimate term to address God. However, Jesus always used this word in His prayers (Aramaic *abba* or its Greek equivalent *pater)*, with the exception of His cry from the cross.

And Jesus instructed His disciples to use this word in their prayers as well. We are empowered to speak to God just as a small child speaks to His father.

DAVID JEREMIAH

YOUR WILL BE DONE

LUKE 22:42 NKJV
*"Father, if it is Your will, take this cup away from Me;
nevertheless not My will, but Yours, be done."*

Gaze in adoring wonder at the scene. The solitary figure
etched against gnarled olive trees. The bloodlike sweat
falling to the ground. The human longing: "Let this cup
pass." The final relinquishment: "Not my will but yours be
done" (Luke 22:39–46). We do well to meditate often on this
unparalleled expression of relinquishment.

Here we have the incarnate Son praying through his
tears and not receiving what he asks. Jesus knew the burden of
unanswered prayer. He really did want the cup to pass, and he
asked that it would pass. "If you are willing" was his questioning, his wondering. The Father's will was not yet absolutely
clear to him. "Is there any other way?" "Can people be
redeemed by some different means?" The answer—no!
Andrew Murray writes, "For our sins, He suffered beneath the
burden of that unanswered prayer."

Here we have the complete laying down of human will.
The battle cry for us is, "My will be done!" rather than, "Thy
will be done."

RICHARD J. FOSTER

ABSOLUTE SURRENDER

LUKE 22:42 NIV
"Not my will, but yours be done."

And when you do yield yourself in absolute surrender, let it be in the faith that God does now accept of it. That is the great point, and that is what we so often miss—that believers should be thus occupied with God in this matter of surrender. I pray you, be occupied with God. We want to get help, every one of us, so that in our daily life God shall be clearer to us, God shall have the right place, and be "all in all." And if we are to have that through life, let us begin now and look away from ourselves, and look up to God. Let each believe—while I, a poor worm on earth and a trembling child of God, full of failure and sin and fear, bow here, and no one knows what passes through my heart, and while I in simplicity say, O God, I accept Thy terms; I have pleaded for blessing on myself and others, I have accepted Thy terms of absolute surrender—while your heart says that in deep silence, remember there is a God present that takes note of it, and writes it down in His book, and there is a God present who at that very moment takes possession of you. You may not feel it, you may not realize it, but God takes possession if you will trust Him.

ANDREW MURRAY

TO DO *the* FATHER'S WILL

LUKE 22:42 NIV
"Father, if you are willing, take this cup from me;
yet not my will, but yours be done."

Now, if the Son was obedient to do His Father's will, the servant should be much more obedient to his Master's will! . . . This is the will of God which Christ both did and taught: humility in conversation; steadfastness in faith; modesty in words, justice in deeds; mercy in works; discipline in morals, inability to do a wrong, and ability to bear a wrong done; to keep peace with the brethren; to love God with all our hearts; to love Him as a Father; to fear Him as God; to prefer nothing above Christ (because He did not prefer anything above us); to adhere inseparably to His love; and to stand by His cross bravely and faithfully. When there is any battle against His name and honor, it is His will that we exhibit the consistency of confession; in torture, the confidence with which we do battle; in death, the patience with which we are crowned. This is to do the commandment of God. This is to fulfill the will of the Father.

CYPRIAN

ANGELS *to* STRENGTHEN US

LUKE 22:43 KJV
*And there appeared an angel unto him
from heaven, strengthening him.*

Just a little while before that He had said, "I have overcome the world," and yet there was need for special strength, and His Father sent an angel to strengthen Him.

This has been a word of peace to me to-day. We accept our Father's will, and know that He has given us the victory over all the power of the enemy. Nevertheless there are times when we do need special strength if we are not to break down before the end. Our Father knows this; He does not say, You accepted all at the beginning; this that tries your spirit now was included in that.

His love understands and He sends an angel to strengthen us.

AMY CARMICHAEL

WATCH *and* PRAY

MATTHEW 26:41 KJV
Watch and pray, that ye enter not into temptation:
the spirit indeed is willing, but the flesh is weak.

"Watch, therefore, and pray that you enter not into temptation." Such prayers warn you that you need the Lord's help. You shouldn't rely on yourself to live well. Don't pray for the riches and honors of this world, or for any worthless possession. But pray that you won't enter into temptation. You wouldn't ask for this in prayer if you could accomplish it for yourself. . . . In fact, when you begin to exercise this wisdom, you will have a reason to give thanks. "For what have you which you have not received? But if you have received it, beware that you boast not as if you had not received it," that is, as if you could have had it by your own power. When you have received the gift, ask the One who began giving it to you that it may be perfected.

AUGUSTINE

GOING AWAY AGAIN *to* PRAY

MATTHEW 26:44 NRSV
*So leaving them again, he went away and
prayed for the third time, saying the same words.*

It isn't wrong or unprofitable to spend much time in prayer
as long as it doesn't hinder us from doing other good and
necessary works duty calls us to . . . For to spend a long time
in prayer isn't, as some think, the same thing as praying "with
much speaking." Multiplied words are one thing, but the sustained warmth of desire is another. It is written that the Lord
continued all night in prayers and that His prayer was pro
longed when He was in agony. Isn't this an example for us
from our Intercessor who, along with the Father, eternally
hears our prayers? . . . If we are paying attention to our souls,
far be it from us to use "much speaking" in prayer, or to
refrain from prolonged prayer. To talk a lot in prayer is to
cheapen and overuse our words while asking for something
necessary. But to prolong prayer is to have our hearts throb
with continual pious emotions toward the One we pray to.
In most cases, prayer consists more of groaning than of
speaking, of tears rather than words. He sees our tears. Our
groaning isn't hidden from Him. For He made everything by
a word and doesn't need human words.

AUGUSTINE

LET US BE GOING

MARK 14:42 NKJV
"Rise, let us be going. See, My betrayer is at hand."

There in the garden the Son of God bore His private cross. Very soon He would bear it publicly, but when He rose from knees bruised with anguish, His face, dusted with earth, was set like flint. . . . Christ knew what He was going to have to do when He came to planet Earth. Remember? He is the Lamb slain from the foundation of the world. He was as good as dead from the beginning. Jesus lived for one purpose alone: to do the will of His Father. . . .

Sometimes obeying God in a matter will be the hardest thing we've ever done in our lives. We are not wrong to feel. We are wrong to disobey. Hash it out with God. Ask for the cup to be removed, but resolve to do His will no matter what. Glory is at stake. That's why He drew the three close enough to see—to teach them to pray, not sleep, in their anguish. This time they slept. They had little power to do otherwise. But a time would come when each would rise from his own Gethsemane and bear his own cross.

BETH MOORE

THE GREATEST THING WE CAN DO

1 THESSALONIANS 5:17 KJV
Pray without ceasing.

More time and early hours for prayer would act like magic to revive and invigorate many a decayed spiritual life. More time and early hours for prayer would be manifest in holy living. A holy life would not be so rare or so difficult a thing if our devotions were not so short and hurried. A Christly temper in its sweet and passionless fragrance would not be so alien and hopeless a heritage if our closet stay were lengthened and intensified. We live shabbily because we pray meanly. . . .

To pray is the greatest thing we can do: and to do it well there must be calmness, time, and deliberation; otherwise it is degraded into the littlest and meanest of things. True praying has the largest results for good; and poor praying, the least. We cannot do too much of real praying; we cannot do too little of the sham. We must learn anew the worth of prayer, enter anew the school of prayer. There is nothing which it takes more time to learn. . . . We must demand and hold with iron grasp the best hours of the day for God and prayer, or there will be no praying worth the name.

EDWARD M. BOUNDS

PERSEVERING PRAYER

——

EPHESIANS 6:18 NLT
*Pray at all times and on every occasion in the power
of the Holy Spirit. Stay alert and be persistent
in your prayers for all Christians everywhere.*

Of all the mysteries of the prayer world the need of per-severing prayer is one of the greatest. That the Lord, who is so loving and longing to bless, should have to be supplicated time after time, sometimes year after year, before the answer comes, we cannot easily understand. It is also one of the greatest practical difficulties in the exercise of believing prayer. When, after persevering supplication, our prayer remains unanswered, it is often easiest for our slothful flesh, and it has all the appearance of pious submission, to think that we must now cease praying, because God may have His secret reason for withholding His answer to our request.

It is by faith alone that the difficulty is overcome. When once faith has taken its stand on God's word and the Name of Jesus, and has yielded itself to the leading of the Spirit to seek God's will and honor alone in its prayer, it need not be discouraged by delay. It knows from Scripture that the power of believing prayer is simply irresistible; real faith can never be disappointed.

ANDREW MURRAY

HE IS OUR EXAMPLE

MARK 1:35 NIV
Very early in the morning, while it was still dark,
Jesus got up, left the house and went off
to a solitary place, where he prayed.

Prayer alone prevails over God. But Christ has willed that it doesn't operate for evil. He gave it all its virtue when used for good. And so it knows only . . . how to transform the weak, restore the sick, purge the possessed, open prison bars, and loosen the bonds of the innocent. Likewise, it washes away faults, repels temptations, extinguishes persecutions, consoles the faint-spirited, cheers the down-trodden, escorts travelers, calms waves, frightens robbers, nourishes the poor, governs the rich, raises the fallen, rescues the falling, confirms the standing. Prayer is the wall of faith. It arms us and hurls missiles against the enemy who watches us on all sides. So we never walk unarmed. By day, we are aware of our post—by night, of our vigil. Under the armor of prayer, we guard the banner of our General. We wait in prayer for the angel's trumpet. . . . What more do we need then, but the duty of prayer? Even the Lord Himself prayed, to whom be honor and virtue for ages and ages!

TERTULLIAN

EARLY *on* THEIR KNEES

MARK 1:35 KJV
And in the morning, rising up a great while before day, he went out, and departed into a solitary place, and there prayed.

The men who have done the most for God in this world have been early on their knees. He who fritters away the early morning, its opportunity and freshness, in other pursuits than seeking God will make poor headway seeking him the rest of the day. If God is not first in our thoughts and efforts in the morning, he will be in the last place the remainder of the day.

Behind this early rising and early praying is the ardent desire which presses us into this pursuit after God. Morning listlessness is the index to a listless heart.... Christ longed for communion with God; and so, rising a great while before day, he would go out into the mountain to pray. The disciples, when fully awake and ashamed of their indulgence, would know where to find him. We might go through the list of men who have mightily impressed the world for God, and we would find them early after God.

A desire for God which cannot break the chains of sleep is a weak thing and will do but little good for God after it has indulged itself fully. The desire for God that keeps so far behind the devil and the world at the beginning of the day will never catch up.

FRANÇOIS FENELON

SLEEPY *in* PRAYER

LUKE 6:12 NKJV
*Now it came to pass in those days that He went out to the
mountain to pray, and continued all night in prayer to God.*

Let us pray urgently and groan with continual requests.
For not long ago, I was scolded in a vision because we
were sleepy in our prayers and didn't pray with watchfulness.
Undoubtedly, God, who "rebukes whom He loves," rebukes
in order to correct and corrects to preserve. Therefore, let us
break away from the bonds of sleep and pray with urgency
and watchfulness. As the Apostle Paul commands us,
"Continue in prayer, and watch in the same." For the apostles continually prayed day and night. Also, the Lord Jesus
Himself, our teacher and example, frequently and watchful-
ly prayed. We read in the Gospel of Luke, "He went out into
a mountain to pray, and continued all night in prayer to
God." Certainly, what He prayed for He prayed on our behalf since He wasn't a sinner but bore the sins of others. In
another place we read, "And the Lord said to Peter, 'Behold,
Satan has desired to sift you as wheat: but I have prayed for
thee, that thy faith fail not.'" If He labored, watched, and
prayed for us and our sins, we should all the more be continually in prayer. First of all, pray and plead with the Lord.
Then, through Him, be restored to God the Father!

CYPRIAN

URGED *to* PRAY

LUKE 18:1 KJV

And he spake a parable unto them to this end,
that men ought always to pray, and not to faint.

He who knows what we need before we ask Him has urged us to pray by saying: "Men ought always to pray and not to faint." The Lord told the story of a widow who wanted justice done to her enemy. By her unceasing requests, she persuaded an evil judge to listen to her. The judge wasn't moved because of justice or mercy but because he was overcome by her wearisome pleas. The story encourages us that the Lord God, who is merciful and just, pays attention to our continual prayers more than when this widow won over the indifferent, unjust, and wicked judge by her unceasing requests . . . The Lord gives a similar lesson in the parable of the man who had nothing to give to a traveling friend. . . . By his very urgent and insistent requests, he succeeded in waking the friend, who gave him as many loaves as he needed. But this friend was motivated by his wish to avoid further annoyances, not by generosity. Through this story the Lord taught that those who are asleep are compelled to give to the person who disturbs them, but those who never sleep will give with much more kindness. In fact, He even rouses us from sleep so that we can ask from Him.

AUGUSTINE

PRAY DILIGENTLY

MATTHEW 6:6 NLT

"But when you pray, go away by yourself, shut the door behind you, and pray to your Father secretly. Then your Father, who knows all secrets, will reward you."

Prayer is a mighty weapon if it is done in the right mind-set. Prayer is so strong that continual pleas have overcome shamelessness, injustice, and savage cruelty. . . . Let us pray diligently. Prayer is a mighty weapon if used with earnestness and sincerity, without drawing attention to ourselves. It has turned back wars and benefited an entire undeserving nation . . . So then, if we pray with humility, beating our chests like the tax gatherer and saying what he did, "Be merciful to me a sinner," we will obtain everything we ask for . . . We need much repentance, beloved, much prayer, much endurance, and much perseverance to gain the good things that have been promised to us.

CHRYSOSTOM

JESUS IS
ARRESTED

—

*"Don't you realize that I could ask my
Father for thousands of angels to protect us,
and he would send them instantly? But if I
did, how would the Scriptures be fulfilled
that describe what must happen now?"*

MATTHEW 26:53–54 NLT

JESUS IS ARRESTED

Whispered voices and soft wind in the olive trees gave way to the rumble of mob feet. Torches flared in the darkness, casting shadows on angry and determined faces. Sleep gave way to terror as disciples realized they were the objective of the armed hunt. A confusing confrontation followed. Judas, backed by clubs and swords, approached and kissed Jesus, picking Him out of the dim lineup. Others stepped up to take custody. In the chaos, Peter lashed out with a sword, hewing someone's ear in a stunning display of characteristic impulsiveness and poor swordsmanship. Jesus' apparent unwillingness to resist arrest further flustered the disciples and they saw no other recourse but to run. Those who had vowed to stand to the end dashed into the night.

The cowardice of the disciples seems culpable until we begin to think about the ways we stand with Jesus in the darkness of the world. Thinking about their responses under pressure gives us opportunities to consider how often we run for cover at the first sign of danger. And perhaps even more significantly, we can gain a deeper understanding of the way God responds when we prove unfaithful under fire.

A CARELESS FOLLOWER?

LUKE 22:48 NKJV

*But Jesus said to him, "Judas, are you
betraying the Son of Man with a kiss?"*

What if I should be guilty of the same accursed sin as Judas, that son of perdition? Do I live in the world as carelessly as others do, and yet make a profession of being a follower of Jesus? Surely if I act thus inconsistently I am a Judas, and it were better for me that I had never been born. Dare I hope that I am clear in this matter? Then, O Lord, keep me so. O Lord, make me sincere and true. Preserve me from every false way. Never let me betray my Saviour. I do love Thee, Jesus, and though I often grieve Thee, yet I would desire to abide faithful even unto death. O God, forbid that I should be a high-soaring professor, and then fall at last into the lake of fire, because I betrayed my Master with a kiss.

CHARLES HADDON SPURGEON

HIS PERMISSION

JOHN 18:4–6 NKJV

Jesus therefore, knowing all things that would come upon Him, went forward and said to them, "Whom are you seeking?" They answered Him, "Jesus of Nazareth." Jesus said to them, "I am He." And Judas, who betrayed Him, also stood with them. Now when He said to them, "I am He," they drew back and fell to the ground.

Judas then, having received a band of men and officers from the Chief Priests and Pharisees, cometh thither with lanterns, and torches, and weapons. And these men had often at other times sent to seize Him, but had not been able; whence it is plain, that at this time He voluntarily surrendered Himself. . . . Seest thou His invincible power, how being in the midst of them He disabled their eyes? For that the darkness was not the cause of their not knowing Him, that they had torches also. And even had there been no torches, they ought at least to have known Him by His voice; or if they did not know it, how could Judas be ignorant? For he too stood with them, and knew Him no more than they, but with them fell backward. And Jesus did this to show, that not only they could not seize Him, but could not even see Him when in the midst, unless He gave permission. Showing, that what was done proceeded not from their power, but from His consent, and declaring that He was not one opposed to God but obedient to the Father even unto death.

CHRYSOSTOM

THEY SHOULD HAVE KNOWN

JOHN 18:6 KJV
As soon then as he had said unto them,
I am he, they went backward, and fell to the ground.

As soon as he said, "I am he," they went backward and fell to the ground. How amazing is it, that they should renew the assault, after so sensible an experience both of his power and mercy! But probably the priests among them might persuade themselves and their attendants, that this also was done by Beelzebub; and that it was through the providence of God, not the indulgence of Jesus, that they received no farther damage.

JOHN WESLEY

CARNAL WEAPONS

MATTHEW 26:51–52 KJV

And, behold, one of them which were with Jesus stretched out his hand, and drew his sword, and struck a servant of the high priest's, and smote off his ear. Then said Jesus unto him, Put up again thy sword into his place: for all they that take the sword shall perish with the sword.

We have seen that the apostles were but scantily armed, there being only two swords in their possession. Peter evidently carried one of these, and stood ready to make good his boast that he would suffer, and, if need be, die in his Lord's service. He evidently struck a downward blow at Malchus' head, and Malchus would have been killed had he not dodged. Jesus spoke these words, "Suffer ye thus far," to those who held him, asking them to loose him sufficiently to enable him to touch the ear of Malchus. By the healing of Malchus' ear and the words spoken to Peter, Jesus shows that the sword is not to be used either to defend the truth or to advance his kingdom. Had he not thus spoken and acted, Pilate might have doubted his words when he testified that his kingdom was not of this world (John 18:36). While we know better than to rely upon the aid of the sword for the advance of truth, we are often tempted to put undue trust in other "carnal weapons" which are equally futile. Wealth and eloquence and elaborate church buildings have but little saving grace in them. It is the truth which wins.

J. W. MCGARVEY AND PHILIP Y. PENDLETON

ZEAL IS NOT ENOUGH

JOHN 18:10 NIV

Then Simon Peter, who had a sword, drew it and
struck the high priest's servant, cutting off his right ear.
(The servant's name was Malchus.)

Peter was willing to die for Christ. He was not lying. He sincerely meant those words. They came from the depths of his heart.

Now Peter was awakened to participate in a nightmare. Before him stood a large crowd armed with swords and clubs. Suddenly, they seized Jesus.

Peter was not prepared. Oh, he had been warned, "Keep watching and praying." Instead, he had slept. Peter knew his spirit, but he had not reckoned with his flesh. And so he found himself weeping bitter tears of defeat and condemnation.

Are you aware of the weakness of your flesh? Oh, the zeal is there, and so is the dedication and the commitment . . . but there is also the flesh!

May you, may I, remember to watch ourselves carefully . . . and may we pray much. Only constant vigilance and close communion keep us from the bitter weeping.

So many who were once standing in zeal are today falling into temptation. Zeal alone cannot keep you from falling. It takes vigilance and prayer.

KAY ARTHUR

THE ANGELS WERE SILENT

MATTHEW 26:53 NLT
"Don't you realize that I could ask my Father for thousands of angels to protect us, and he would send them instantly?"

When we comprehend the great price God was willing to pay for the redemption of man, we only then begin to see that something is horribly wrong with the human race. It must have a Savior, or it is doomed! Sin cost God His very best. Is it any wonder that the angels veiled their faces, that they were silent in the consternation as they witnessed the outworking of God's plan? How inconceivable it must have seemed to them, when they considered the fearful depravity of sin, that Jesus should shoulder it all. But they were soon to unveil their faces and offer their praises again. A light was kindled that day at Calvary. The cross blazed with the glory of God as the most terrible darkness was shattered by the light of salvation. Satan's depraved legions were defeated and they could no longer keep all men in darkness and defeat.

BILLY GRAHAM

ONE LAST HEALING

LUKE 22:51 NASB
But Jesus answered and said, "Stop! No more of this."
And He touched his ear and healed him.

The last thing the Lord Jesus did before His hands were bound was to heal.

Have you ever asked yourself, If I knew this was the last thing I should do, what would I do? I have never found the answer to that question. There are so very, very many things that we would want to do for those whom we love, that I do not think we are likely to be able to find the chief one of all these. So the best thing is just to go on simply, doing each thing as it comes as well as we can.

Our Lord Jesus spent much time in healing sick people, and in the natural course of events it happened that the last thing He did with His kind hands was to heal a bad cut. (I wonder how they could have the heart to bind His hands after that.) In this, as in everything, He left us an example that we should follow in His steps. Do the thing that this next minute this next hour, brings you, faithfully and lovingly and patiently; and then the last thing you do, before power to do is taken from you (if that should be), will be only the continuation of all that went before.

AMY CARMICHAEL

This Is *the* Hour *of* Darkness

Luke 22:53 NKJV
*"When I was with you daily in the temple,
you did not try to seize Me. But this is
your hour, and the power of darkness."*

When the chief priests, Temple officers, and elders came to the Garden of Gethsemane to arrest Jesus, they succeeded only because a sovereign God permitted them to succeed. Jesus pointed out that He was teaching daily in the Temple, yet they never laid a finger on Him. Now they were after Him with swords and staves. "But this is your hour, and the power of darkness is yours" (Luke 22:53 JBP). Who gave them that hour? Who allowed them the power to capture Him? It was God, without whose leave not even a sparrow can fall to the ground. God is omnipotent, never slumbering, just, righteous, and forever in control. He was not taken by surprise. All was working then, as it is always working, into a pattern for good.

Our own difficulties often appear to be random. Our tragedies look wildly uncontrolled. They are not. They are *subject*. Limits are set. God is quietly at work, standing in the shadows, ceaselessly watching over His children.

"The light shines on in the dark, and the darkness has never mastered it" (John 1:5 NEB).

Elisabeth Elliot

THEY FLED

MATTHEW 26:56 KJV
Then all the disciples forsook him, and fled.

He never deserted them, but they in cowardly fear of their lives, fled from Him in the very beginning of His sufferings. This is but one instructive instance of the frailty of all believers if left to themselves; they are but sheep at the best, and they flee when the wolf cometh. They had all been warned of the danger, and had promised to die rather than leave their Master; and yet they were seized with sudden panic, and took to their heels. It is one thing to promise, and quite another to perform. It would have been to their eternal honour to have stood at Jesus' side right manfully; they fled from honour; may I be kept from imitating them! Where else could they have been so safe as near their Master, who could presently call for twelve legions of angels? They fled from their true safety. These very apostles who were timid as hares, grew to be bold as lions after the Spirit had descended upon them. What anguish must have filled the Saviour as He saw His friends so faithless!

CHARLES HADDON SPURGEON

A Man *of* Sorrows

ISAIAH 53:3 NKJV

He is despised and rejected by men, a Man of sorrows and acquainted with grief. And we hid, as it were, our faces from Him; He was despised, and we did not esteem Him.

Christ also, when He was in the world, was despised and rejected of men, and in His greatest necessity was left by His acquaintance and friends to bear these reproaches. Christ was willing to suffer and be despised, and darest thou complain of any? Christ had adversaries and gainsayers, and dost thou wish to have all men thy friends and benefactors? Whence shall thy patience attain her crown if no adversity befall thee? If thou art unwilling to suffer any adversity, how shalt thou be the friend of Christ? Sustain thyself with Christ and for Christ if thou wilt reign with Christ.

If thou hadst once entered into the mind of Jesus, and hadst tasted yea even a little of his tender love, then wouldst thou care nought for thine own convenience or inconvenience, but wouldst rather rejoice at trouble brought upon thee, because the love of Jesus maketh a man to despise himself.

THOMAS À KEMPIS

JESUS STANDS TRIAL

—

*Then they all said, "Are You then
the Son of God?" So He said to them,
"You rightly say that I am."*
LUKE 22:70 NKJV

JESUS STANDS TRIAL

Never has the term "kangaroo court" had a more apt application than the trial of Jesus. He was hopped from judge to judge in what appeared to be a life-sized sleight-of-hand trick. The proceedings had all the superficial trappings of legitimacy and all the details of a deadly and unjust conspiracy. No maneuver went untried in the perversion of justice. The verdict was never in doubt, but the effort demanded maximum participation by all concerned.

In the end, each of us had at least two representatives in the events that transpired during that sham trial: Jesus, who took our place as the accused, and a host of other candidates who took our place as the accusers. Each of our substitutes performed their role. Our stand-ins succeeded in condemning Jesus to die, and He succeeded in dying on our behalf. Each of our substitutes accomplished their immediate objective, although their ultimate purposes could not have been in greater disagreement. We review these events to acknowledge once again our participation and gratefully own the ultimate benefits we gained.

A FOREGONE CONCLUSION

MARK 14:55 NKJV
Now the chief priests and all the council sought testimony against Jesus to put Him to death, but found none.

This trial is clearly a farce. The outcome was determined long before the trial was convened, for Mark records that the chief priests sought for testimony because they were determined to put him to death. This reminds me of those accounts of the early western vigilantes who announced to their victims that they would be nice to give them a fair trial and then hang them. The trial was illegal right from the very beginning: First, it was held at night, and Jewish law insisted that all trials of criminals before the priests be held in the daytime. Second, it met in the wrong place. The Sanhedrin was to meet only in the hall set aside for its purposes, and only meetings held there were valid. But this meeting was held in the residence of the high priest. Third, the Sanhedrin was prohibited by law from reaching a verdict on the same day that the trial was held, and here the verdict is passed immediately at the end of this farcical trial.

RAY C. STEDMAN

FALSE EVIDENCE

The chief priests and the whole Sanhedrin were looking for false evidence against Jesus so that they could put him to death.

This was not a trial but a farce. There was no intention of giving Jesus the opportunity to declare His innocence of their trumped-up notions. Motivated by envy, they had already decided that Jesus must die. . . .

This was not a trial but an orchestrated plot. The religious leaders devised it. They ordered officers to carry out the arrest. They found false witnesses. They delivered Christ to Pilate and stirred up the people to cheer for the release of the real criminal, Barabbas. They intimidated Pilate. They mocked Christ. And they walked brazenly toward Calvary, having decided against Christ without having first humbled themselves to listen to His words and genuinely consider His powerful claims. . . .

As we read the Gospels, it is clear that Jesus died not as the helpless victim of evil forces, nor as a result of some inflexible decree, but because He freely submitted to the Father's plan. He had come to do the will of the Father. . . .

Here, in the everyday events of Roman jurisprudence, the pivotal event of human history was taking place. As men and women wandered through their empty way of life, God was intervening in the act of redemption.

ALISTAIR BEGG

I Am

MATTHEW 26:63 NRSV
*But Jesus was silent. Then the high priest said to him,
"I put you under oath before the living God, tell us
if you are the Messiah, the Son of God."*

Isaiah had prophesied: "As a sheep before her shearers is dumb, so he opened not his mouth" (Isaiah 53:7). Evidently our Lord understood that the testimony against him was so fragmentary, so weak, that it required no answer. He made no effort to defend himself or to answer the lies of the witnesses, but remained silent. The high priest was stunned by Jesus' silence, and so he did something absolutely illegal. He put Jesus under oath to testify against himself. Matthew said that the high priest put Jesus under oath. He said to him, "I adjure you by the living God" (Matthew 26:63b RSV). This was a very solemn oath. In response to that, Jesus breaks his silence and answers the high priest's question, "Are you the Messiah, the Son of the Blessed One?" What the priest is really asking is, "Are you the one who the Old Testament predicts will come, the Messiah, the Promised One? Are you the Son of God?" This is a clear-cut question directly placed and the high priest puts Jesus under oath to answer. Jesus responds very simply, "I am."

RAY C. STEDMAN

UNMISTAKABLE CLAIMS

MARK 14:61–62 NIV

*Again the high priest asked him, "Are you the Christ, the
Son of the Blessed One?" "I am," said Jesus. "And you
will see the Son of Man sitting at the right hand of the
Mighty One and coming on the clouds of heaven."*

At first, Jesus wouldn't answer, so the high priest put him
under oath. Being under oath Jesus had to answer (and
I'm so glad he did). He responded to the question, "Are You
the Christ, the son of the Blessed One?" by saying "I am."

An analysis of Christ's testimony shows that he claimed
to be (1) the Son of the Blessed One (God); (2) the One who
would sit at the right hand of power, and (3) the Son of Man
who would come on the clouds of heaven. Each of the affir-
mations is distinctively messianic. The cumulative effect of all
three is significant. The Sanhedrin, the Jewish court, caught all
three points, and the high priest responded by tearing his garments and saying, "What further need do we have of witnesses?" They had finally heard it from him themselves. He
was convicted by the words of his own mouth. . . .

It is clear, then, that this is the testimony Jesus wanted
to bear about himself. We also see that the Jews understand
his reply as a claim to his being God.

JOSH MCDOWELL

SEATED *at the* RIGHT HAND *of* POWER

MARK 14:61–62 NRSV

*Again the high priest asked him, "Are you the Messiah, the
Son of the Blessed One?" Jesus said, "I am; and 'you will see
the Son of Man seated at the right hand of the Power,'
and 'coming with the clouds of heaven.'"*

How can someone doubt God's presence and help who
has experienced various dangers and has been saved
from them by His simple nod, who has passed through the sea
that the Savior calmed and that supplied a solid road for the
people? I believe that finding miracles like these performed
and perfected at God's command is the foundation of faith
and the basis for confidence. Therefore, even in the midst of
trials there is no reason to turn from our faith. But we have
an unshaken hope in God. When this habit of confidence
is firmly rooted in the soul, God Himself will dwell in our
deepest thoughts. His power can't be overcome. Therefore the
soul in which He dwells won't be overcome by dangers surrounding it. We see this truth demonstrated in Gods own victory. While He intended to bless humanity. He was severely
insulted by malicious, ungodly people. However, He suffered
through His passion unharmed and gained a mighty victory
over sin and an everlasting crown of triumph. Therefore He
accomplished His providential purpose, loved the righteous,
and destroyed the cruelty of the unrighteous.

EUSEBIUS

STRONG SILENCE

MARK 14:61–62 NLT
"Are you the Messiah . . .?" . . . "I am."

Throughout the crowded closing hours of His life, Jesus did and said nothing that could in any way be construed as a withdrawal or watering-down of the astounding claims to kingship and deity He had made. Although He did not disallow the claim that He was King, He hastened to make clear that His kingdom was not of this world, but a spiritual one (John 18:36). Nor did He deny that He was "the Christ, the Son of the Blessed" (Mark 14:61), but quietly accepted the ascription. In the face of such a statement, it is difficult to understand how hostile critics can suggest as they do, that He never claimed deity for Himself. He always spoke and acted in a manner entirely consistent with such a claim.

J. OSWALD SANDERS

UNANIMOUS VERDICT

MARK 14:63–65 NIV
The high priest tore his clothes. "Why do we need any more witnesses?" he asked. "You have heard the blasphemy. What do you think?" They all condemned him as worthy of death. Then some began to spit at him; they blindfolded him, struck him with their fists, and said, "Prophesy!"

It is a bit beyond us to grasp how God, very God, on the basis of His own admission and forthright declaration should stand incriminated by coarse, crass men. On this horrendous day the earth was to grow dark and the heavens withhold their light from men who were absolute murderers.

The verdict of the Sanhedrin was unanimous.

He was guilty of death.

He was condemned to die.

They had won the day.

The case was closed.

To celebrate they decided to indulge in a ghastly game of terrible torture. Here were men who were supposed to protect the interests of their people subjecting an innocent person to appalling abuse. . . .

The roughnecks blindfolded the Master. . . . They pummeled His weary body. They spat in His face until their foul-smelling saliva ran down over His flushed cheeks. They jeered at him, challenging Him to prophesy who had last struck Him a stinging blow. They slashed and smashed His face until it was purple and swollen with great welts.

W. PHILLIP KELLER

BETRAYAL *of an* INNOCENT

MATTHEW 27:4 NIV
"I have sinned," he said, "for I have betrayed innocent
blood." "What is that to us?" they replied.
"That's your responsibility."

The presence of Judas is mentioned by each of the
Gospels. His treachery made a deep impression upon
them. The arresting party which accompanied Judas consist-
ed of the band of officers and men from the temple guard or
Levitical police, Pharisees, scribes, servants, chief priests, captains of the temple and elders. They were well supplied with
lights, for while the Passover is always held when the moon
is full, the moon at this time of night would be near setting,
and the valley of the Kidron, in which Gethsemane lay,
would be darkened by the shadow of the adjoining mountain. He who has changed his mind about the past is in the
way to change everything; he who has an after care may have
little or nothing more than a selfish dread of the consequences of what he has done. Considering the prophecy
which had been uttered with regard to Judas' act (Matthew
26:24), he had good reason to fear the consequences. While
he testifies as to the innocence of Jesus, he expresses no affection for him. The Pharisees did not share with Judas the wish
to undo what had been done.

J. W. McGARVEY AND PHILIP Y. PENDLETON

TAKEN *to* PILATE

Very early in the morning the leading priests, other leaders,
and teachers of religious law—the entire high council—
met to discuss their next step. They bound Jesus
and took him to Pilate, the Roman governor.

One principal point in the Gospel narrative is Christ's
condemnation before Pontius Pilate, the governor of
Judea, to teach us that the punishment to which we were
liable was inflicted on that Just One. We could not escape the
fearful judgment of God; and Christ, that he might rescue us
from it, submitted to be condemned by a mortal, nay, by a
wicked and profane man. For the name of Governor is mentioned not only to support the credibility of the narrative,
but to remind us of what Isaiah says: 'The chastisement of
our peace was upon him" and "with his stripes we are
healed" (Isaiah 53:5). For, in order to remove our condemnation, it was not sufficient to endure any kind of death. To
satisfy our ransom, it was necessary to select a mode of death
in which he might deliver us, both by giving himself up to
condemnations and undertaking our expiation. Had he been
cut off by assassins, or slain in a seditious tumult, there could
have been no kind of satisfaction in such a death. But when
he is placed as a criminal at the bar, where witnesses are
brought to give evidence against him, and the mouth of the
judge condemns him to die, we see him sustaining the character of an offender and evil-doer.

JOHN CALVIN

SHAMEFULLY TREATED

MARK 15:3 KJV
*And the chief priests accused him of many things:
but he answered nothing.*

Christ gave Pilate a direct answer, but would not answer the witnesses, because the things they alleged were known to be false, even Pilate himself was convinced they were so. Pilate thought that he might appeal from the priests to the people, and that they would deliver Jesus out of the priests' hands. But they were more and more urged by the priests, and cried, Crucify him! Crucify him! Let us judge of persons and things by their merits, and the standard of God's word, and not by common report. The thought that no one ever was so shamefully treated, as the only perfectly wise, holy, and excellent Person that ever appeared on earth, leads the serious mind to strong views of man's wickedness and enmity to God. Let us more and more abhor the evil dispositions which marked the conduct of these persecutors.

MATTHEW HENRY

PILATE'S CONCERN

JOHN 18:37 NIV

"You are a king, then!" said Pilate. Jesus answered, "You are right in saying I am a king. In fact, for this reason I was born, and for this I came into the world, to testify to the truth. Everyone on the side of truth listens to me."

The Jewish leaders accused Jesus of three crimes. They claimed that He was guilty of misleading the nation, forbidding the paying of taxes, and claiming to be a king (Luke 23:2). These were definitely political charges, the kind that a Roman governor could handle. Pilate focused on the third charge—that Jesus claimed to be a king—because this was a definite threat to Rome. If he could deal with this "revolutionary" properly, Pilate could please the Jews and impress the Emperor at the same time.

"Are You the king of the Jews?" Pilate asked. Jesus gave him a clear reply: "It is as you say." However, Jesus then asked Pilate a question about his question (John 18:34–37). Was Pilate thinking "kingship" in the Roman sense? If so, then Jesus is not that kind of a king. Jesus explained to the governor that His kingdom was not of this world, that He had no armies, that His followers did not fight. Rather, His kingdom was a reign of truth.

This conversation convinced Pilate that Jesus was not a dangerous revolutionary. "I find no fault in Him," was Pilate's decision.

WARREN W. WIERSBE

TRIAL BEFORE HEROD

LUKE 23:8–9 KJV

And when Herod saw Jesus, he was exceeding glad: for he was desirous to see him of a long season, because he had heard many things of him; and he hoped to have seen some miracle done by him. Then he questioned with him in many words; but he answered him nothing.

Before Herod, whom Jesus called "that fox" (Luke 13:32), Jesus maintained a similar lofty silence. The dissolute king welcomed the diversion created by the advent of Jesus. He had long desired to see this man of whom he had heard so much perform some miracle. Herod "questioned with him in many words; but *he answered him nothing*" (Luke 23:9). Herod's volubility, "many words," met only a calm and impressive silence that was very disconcerting for the king and the chief priests and scribes who vociferously accused Him.

Jesus had counseled His disciples not to waste their pearls of truth on those who would not appreciate them (Matthew 7:6), and He was practicing His own precept. Herod was merely seeking entertainment, and Jesus refused to gratify his vulgar desire. Such silence in the face of certain death was the hallmark of His inner fortitude.

J. OSWALD SANDERS

A KINGDOM NOT *of* THIS WORLD

JOHN 18:36 NIV
*Jesus said, "My kingdom is not of this world. If it were,
my servants would fight to prevent my arrest by the Jews.
But now my kingdom is from another place."*

Jesus' kingdom was of such a nature that it was not pro-
cured by military might or power. Its rule is neither terri-
torial nor political. If history has proven anything, it is that
the spread of the gospel by the sword or by coercion has
done nothing but misrepresent the message and bring disre-
pute to the gospel.

To be sure, Jesus was not talking here about pacifism or
warfare. He was making a definite difference between the
way His kingdom grows and the way earthly nations establish control. He was making a significant point to a prosecu-
tor with political motives. His kingship cannot and will not
be established by force or threat. This fact alone would have
given Pilate reason enough to go beyond the surface of what
was going on. It was really the nations of this world that were
on the witness stand, and God who was doing the judging.
Pilate ought to have known immediately that this was no
Caesar standing in front of him. This was someone with a
drastically different kind of authority.

RAVI ZACHARIAS

WHAT IS TRUTH?

JOHN 18:38 KJV

*Pilate saith unto him, What is truth? And when
he had said this, he went out again unto the Jews, and
saith unto them, I find in him no fault at all.*

"What is truth?" Among the sages of that time there were
many opinions concerning truth; and some had even
supposed that it was a thing utterly out of the reach of men.
Pilate perhaps might have asked the question in a mocking
way; and his not staying to get an answer indicated that he
either despaired of getting a satisfactory one, or that he was
indifferent about it. This is the case with thousands: they
appear desirous of knowing the truth, but have not patience to
wait in a proper way to receive an answer to their question.

Having asked the above question, and being convinced
of our Lord's innocence, he went out to the Jews to testify
of his convictions and to deliver him, if possible, out of their
hands.

ADAM CLARKE

ALL *or* NOTHING

MARK 14:61–62 NRSV
*But he was silent and did not answer. Again the high
priest asked him, "Are you the Messiah, the Son of the
Blessed One?" Jesus said, "I am; and 'you will see the
Son of Man seated at the right hand of the Power,'
and 'coming with the clouds of heaven.'"*

Once faced with the staggering proposition that He is
God, I was cornered, all avenues of retreat blocked, no
falling back to that comfortable middle ground about Jesus
being a great moral teacher. If He is not God, He is nothing,
least of all a great moral teacher. For what He taught includes
the assertion that He is indeed God. And if He is not, that
one statement alone would have to qualify as the most mon-
strous lie of all time—stripping Him at once of any possible
moral platform.

I could not, I saw, take Him on a slightly lower plateau
because it is easier to do so, less troublesome to my intellect,
less demanding of my faith, less challenging to my life. That
would be substituting my mind for His, using Christianity
where it helped to buttress my *own* notions, ignoring it
where it didn't. . . .

Jesus said take it, all or nothing. If I was to believe in
God at all, I had to take Him as He reveals Himself, not as I
might wish Him to be.

CHARLES W. COLSON

NOBLE SILENCE

MATTHEW 27:14 NIV

But Jesus made no reply, not even to a single charge—
to the great amazement of the governor.

It was a surprise, even to ordinary people, that someone who was accused and attacked by false testimony refused to protect Himself. He was able to defend Himself and to show that He wasn't guilty of any of the alleged charges. He could have listed the praiseworthy deeds of His own life and His miracles done by divine power in order to allow the judge to deliver a more honorable judgment concerning Him. But, by the nobleness of His nature, He condemned His accusers. Without hesitation, the judge would have set Him free if He had offered a defense. This is clear from his statement, "Which of the two do ye wish that I should release unto you, Barabbas or Jesus, who is called Christ?" and from what the Scripture adds, "For he knew that for envy they had delivered Him." Jesus, however, is continually attacked by false witnesses and, while wickedness remains in the world, is continually exposed to accusation. Yet, even now, He remains silent in the presence of these things and makes no audible answer. Instead, He places His defense in the lives of His genuine disciples. They are an outstanding testimony, one superior to all false witness, that refutes and overthrows all unfounded accusations and charges.

ORIGEN

NO NEED *for* DEFENSE

MATTHEW 27:14 NIV
*But Jesus made no reply, not even to a single charge—
to the great amazement of the governor.*

Pilate was irritated that Jesus did not speak in his own defense. He had already seen enough of our Lord's wisdom to assure him that it would be an easy matter for him to expose the malicious emptiness of these charges—charges which Pilate himself knew to be false, but about which he had to keep silent, for, being judge, he could not become our Lord's advocate. Our Lord's silence was a matter of prophecy (Isaiah 53:7). Jesus kept still because to have successfully defended himself would have been to frustrate the purpose for which he came into the world.

J. W. McGARVEY AND PHILIP Y. PENDLETON

CHARGES, MANY—DEFENSE, NONE

MARK 15:5 NIV
But Jesus still made no reply, and Pilate was amazed.

The whole council, which, on this extraordinary occasion, was convened; the result of which was, to bind Jesus, and deliver him up to the Roman governor, to be put to death by him, as a seditious person, and an enemy to Caesar, and accordingly they did so. The charges were many, and very heinous, and which Pilate thought called for self-defense. But Jesus yet answered nothing—He still continued silent, and made no defense for himself, which the governor was willing to give him an opportunity to make. What should be the meaning of his silence, when he was so capable of defending himself, and was so innocent? The things he was charged with were of the highest nature, and by persons of the greatest figure in the nation; so that his silence exposed him to a great deal of danger.

JOHN GILL

I Have Found No Fault

Luke 23:14 NKJV

*"You have brought this Man to me, as one who misleads
the people. And indeed, having examined Him in your
presence, I have found no fault in this Man concerning
those things of which you accuse Him."*

Pilate well understood the difference between armed forces
and our Lord's followers. But instead of being softened by
Pilate's declaration of his innocence, and considering whether
they were not bringing the guilt of innocent blood upon
themselves, the Jews were the more angry. The Lord brings his
designs to a glorious end, even by means of those who follow
the devices of their own hearts. The fear of man brings many
into this snare, that they will do an unjust thing, against their
consciences, rather than get into trouble. Pilate declares Jesus
innocent, and has a mind to release him; yet, to please the people, he would punish him as an evil-doer. If no fault be found
in him, why chastise him? Pilate yielded at length; he had not
courage to go against so strong a stream. He delivered Jesus to
their will, to be crucified.

MATTHEW HENRY

WASHING HIS HANDS *of* JESUS

MATTHEW 27:24 NIV

When Pilate saw that he was getting nowhere, but that instead an uproar was starting, he took water and washed his hands in front of the crowd. "I am innocent of this man's blood," he said. "It is your responsibility!"

In this story of Good Friday it is the best things in the world that are at their worst. That is what really shows us the world at its worst. . . . In the lightning flash of this incident, we see great Rome, the imperial republic, going downward under her Lucretian doom. Skepticism has eaten away even the confident sanity of the conquerors of the world. He who is enthroned to say what is justice can only ask, "What is truth?" So in that drama which decided the whole fate of antiquity, one of the central figures is fixed in what seems the reverse of his true role. Rome was almost another name for responsibility. Yet he stands forever as a sort of rocking statue of the irresponsible. Man could do no more. Even the practical had become the impracticable. Standing between the pillars of his own judgment-seat, a Roman had washed his hands of the world.

G. K. CHESTERTON

PILATE GAVE JESUS *to* THEM

JOHN 19:16 NLT
Then Pilate gave Jesus to them to be crucified.

Finally, Pilate handed Him over to be crucified.

In many ways Pilate is a most pitiable character, for he lived in fear on every side. He feared Caesar, if perchance he conveyed that he did not deal with someone who was a threat to Rome. He feared the implications of what he was doing, because his wife had warned him that she had had a dream about Jesus and that he should not have a share in punishing that innocent man. He feared Jesus Himself, not quite sure who he was dealing with.

Pilate may well be the quintessential example of what politics has come to mean. He knew what was right but succumbed to the seduction of his position. In life's most severe tests of motives, there is a politician in each and every one of us. While Pilate was ignorant of the role he was playing, the priests justified their heinous deed, quoting Scripture in support of their cause. Divine purpose, political maneuvering, and religious fervor met in the plan of redemption.

RAVI ZACHARIAS

CHRIST, OUR INTERCESSOR

ISAIAH 53:12 KJV
Therefore will I divide him a portion with the great,
and he shall divide the spoil with the strong; because he
hath poured out his soul unto death: and he was numbered
with the transgressors; and he bare the sin of many,
and made intercession for the transgressors.

When we read that Christ was led away from the judg-ment-seat to execution and was crucified between thieves, we have a fulfillment of the prophecy which is quot-ed by the Evangelist, "He was numbered with the transgres-sors" (Isaiah 53:12; Mark 15:28). When we read that he was acquitted by the same lips that condemned him (for Pilate was forced once and again to bear public testimony to his innocence), let us call to mind what is said by another prophet, "I restored that which I took not away" (Psalm 69:4). Thus we perceive Christ representing the character of a sinner and a criminal, while, at the same time, his inno-cence shines forth and it becomes manifest that he suffers for another's and not for his own crime.

JOHN CALVIN

JESUS IS DENIED
by PETER

---

*So they arrested him and led him to
the high priest's residence, and Peter
was following far behind.*

Luke 22:54 nlt

JESUS IS DENIED *by* PETER

First came the dash through the garden in the darkness, whipped and scratched by unseen branches, with fear in hot pursuit. Then came the breathless shadowing of the mob back into town and the shameful slinking around the high priest's residence until John's familiar face got him and Peter through the gate. As always, Peter had no plan. He was acting on pure impulse. But the gate that opened to let him in caught him in a trap.

Curious looks and unspoken questions threatened to destroy his anonymity. Then a girl unmasked the clumsy fisherman by recognizing him as a companion of Jesus. The shock of exposure activated his impetuous tendencies. Peter lied. He lied again. Then he lied with an attitude. As the cursed denial escaped his lips, a rooster contradicted his claims.

As you reflect on the following comments about Peter's denial, consider how often you begin a new day with the weight of poorly chosen words and actions from the previous day.

THE WILL *to* OBEY

MATTHEW 26:33 NLT
*Peter declared, "Even if everyone else
deserts you, I never will."*

Those who want to obey God, but can't, already possess a good will, although it is small and weak. But they are able to obey when they obtain a strong and robust will. When the martyrs obeyed the great commandments, they acted by a great will that is, with great love. The Lord speaks of this great love: "Greater love hath no man than this, that a man lay down his life for his friends." . . . The Apostle Peter didn't possess this love when he fearfully denied the Lord three times. . . . Even though Peter's love was small and imperfect, it was still present when he said to the Lord, "I will lay down my life for Thy sake." Peter believed he could carry out what he felt he was willing to do by himself. . . . However, God works in us so that we can have the will to obey. Once we have this will, God works with us to perfect us. The apostle Paul says, "I am confident of this very thing, that He which hath begun a good work in you will perform it until the day of Jesus Christ."

AUGUSTINE

KEEPING YOUR DISTANCE

LUKE 22:54 KJV
Peter followed afar off.

It began in sneaking. He followed Christ when he was had away prisoner; this was well, and showed a concern for his Master. But he followed afar off, that he might be out of danger. He thought to trim the matter, to follow Christ, and so to satisfy his conscience, but to follow afar off, and so to save his reputation, and sleep in a whole skin. It proceeded in keeping his distance still, and associating himself with the high priest's servants, when he should have been at his Master's elbow. His fall itself was disclaiming all acquaintance with Christ, and relation to him, disowning him because he was now in distress and danger.

MATTHEW HENRY

WILLING *to* BE KNOWN

MATTHEW 26:58 KJV
*But Peter followed him afar off unto the high priest's palace,
and went in, and sat with the servants, to see the end.*

B ut Peter followed afar off, comes in here, with an eye to
the following story of his denying him. He forsook him
as the rest did, when he was seized, and what is here said of
his following him is easily reconcilable with his forsaking
him; such following was no better than forsaking him, for, he
followed him, but it was afar off. Some sparks of love and
concern for his Master there were in his breast, and therefore
he followed him; but fear and concern for his own safety
prevailed, and therefore he followed afar off. It looks ill, and
bodes worse, when those that are willing to be Christ's disciples, are not willing to be known to be so. Here began
Peter's denying him; for to follow him afar off, is by little and
little to go back from him. There is danger in drawing back.

MATTHEW HENRY

207

UNCOMMITTED

JOHN 18:25–26 KJV

And Simon Peter stood and warmed himself. They said there-
fore unto him, Art not thou also one of his disciples?
He denied it, and said, I am not. One of the servants of the
high priest, being his kinsman whose ear Peter cut off, saith,
Did not I see thee in the garden with him?

Wonderful, by what a lethargy that hot and furious one
was possessed, when Jesus was being led away! After
such things as had taken place, he doth not move, but still
warms himself, that thou mayest learn how great is the
weakness of our nature if God abandoneth. And, being questioned, he denies again.

Neither did the garden bring him to remember what
had taken place, nor the great affection which Jesus there had
shown by those words, but all these from pressure of anxiety
he banished from his mind. But why have the Evangelists
with one accord written concerning him? Not as accusing
the disciple, but as desiring to teach us, how great an evil it
is not to commit all to God, but to trust to one's self. But do
thou admire the tender care of his Master, who, though a
prisoner and bound, took great forethought for His disciple,
raising Peter up, when he was down, by His look, and
launching him into a sea of tears.

CHRYSOSTOM

THREE TIMES

JOHN 18:27 NIV
Peter denied it.

First, it was the temple authorities themselves who did not care for His strong reminder that true religion was one of heart. They had torn the law on paper apart from the law imprinted on the heart, and they would use the law to kill Him, to crucify *Agape*.

A few days later the disciples were unable to stay awake and care for Him when He needed them most. They left Him alone—*storge* absent. Then it was Judas who dared to betray Jesus with a kiss. He used a symbol of friendship with which to betray his love, and *phileo* was made commonplace.

Finally, there was Peter, who when he was challenged, denied that he even knew Him. This was the same man who had bragged that others might betray Jesus but not he. His denial took place three times. All three of the loves demanded at the moment were conspicuously absent in the disciple into whom Jesus had poured so much. . . .

Of all the disciples who floundered and stumbled, Peter was at the forefront. Yet it was to him that Jesus issued that pastoral call: "Feed my sheep."

RAVI ZACHARIAS

BRAVERY *or* BRAVADO?

MARK 14:70 NIV

Again he denied it. After a little while, those
standing near said to Peter, "Surely you are
one of them, for you are a Galilean."

We are all familiar with how Peter's bravado had caused him to vow that he'd never deny the Lord. In the Garden of Gethsemane, it was Peter who drew his sword in an attempt to defend Jesus. But now his determination to show himself faithful to Christ has carried him right into the courtyard of the high priest where he is warming his hands around the fire with the very guards that had arrested Jesus and brought him there. That was a brave thing to do; he was in terrible danger. I think it was the pride of Peter's heart that brought him this far. He was so determined not to let the Lord down, so determined to show that Jesus was wrong when he said Peter would deny him. But now that he is there in the midst of the enemies of Jesus, fears begin to possess his heart, and the bravado melts away—his courage is gone.

RAY C. STEDMAN

ONE LOOK

LUKE 22:60–61 NRSV

At that moment, while he was still speaking, the cock crowed.
The Lord turned and looked at Peter.

C hrist looked upon Peter, not doubting but that Peter
would soon be aware of it; for he knew that, though he
had denied him with his lips, yet his eye would still be towards
him. Though Peter had now been guilty of a very great
offence, Christ would not call to him, lest he should shame
him or expose him; he only gave him a look which none but
Peter would understand the meaning of, and it had a great deal
in it. It was a significant look: it signified the conveying of
grace to Peter's heart, to enable him to repent; the crowing of
the cock would not have brought him to repentance without
this look, nor will the external means without special effica-
cious grace. Power went along with this look, to change the
heart of Peter, and to bring him to himself, to his right mind.

MATTHEW HENRY

MAY HE LOOK UPON US

LUKE 22:61 KJV
And the Lord turned, and looked upon Peter.

Whene'er my careless hands hang down,
O let me see thy gathering frown,
And feel thy warning eye;
And starting cry from ruin's brink
Save, Jesus, or I yield, I sink,
O save me, or I die!

If near the pit I rashly stray,
Before I wholly fall away,
The keen conviction dart!
Recall me by that pitying look,
That kind, upbraiding glance, which broke
Unfaithful Peter's heart.

In me thine utmost mercy show,
And make me like thyself below,
Unblamable in grace;
Ready prepared, and fitted here,
By perfect holiness, to appear
Before thy glorious face.

CHARLES WESLEY

BITTER TEARS

LUKE 22:61–62 NRSV

*The Lord turned and looked at Peter. Then Peter
remembered the word of the Lord, how he had said to him,
"Before the cock crows today, you will deny me three times."
And he went out and wept bitterly.*

That was the turning-point in the history of Peter. Christ
had said to him: "Thou canst not follow me now." Peter
was not in a fit state to follow Christ, because he had not
been brought to an end of himself; he did not know himself,
and he therefore could not follow Christ. But when he went
out and wept bitterly, then came the great change. Christ
previously said to him: "When thou art converted, strength-
en thy brethren." Here is the point where Peter was converted from self to Christ.

I thank God for the story of Peter. I do not know a man
in the Bible who gives us greater comfort. When we look at
his character, so full of failures, and at what Christ made him
by the power of the Holy Ghost, there is hope for every one
of us. But remember, before Christ could fill Peter with the
Holy Spirit and make a new man of him, he had to go out
and weep bitterly; he had to be humbled.

ANDREW MURRAY

WHEN WE EAT OUR WORDS

LUKE 22:61 NASB

And the Lord turned and looked at Peter.

We, like Peter, remember our boastful promise: "Though all men shall forsake Thee, yet will not I." We eat our own words with the bitter herbs of repentance. When we think of what we vowed we would be, and of what we have been, we may weep whole showers of grief. Can we, when we are reminded of our sins, and their exceeding sinfulness, remain stolid and stubborn? The Lord followed up the cock's warning voice with an admonitory look of sorrow, pity, and love. That glance was never out of Peter's mind so long as he lived. It was far more effectual than ten thousand sermons would have been. The penitent apostle would be sure to weep when he recollected the Saviour's full forgiveness, which restored him to his former place. To think that we have offended so kind and good a Lord is more than sufficient reason for being constant weepers. Lord, smite our rocky hearts, and make the waters flow.

CHARLES HADDON SPURGEON

WHAT HE KNOWS

And the Lord turned, and looked upon Peter. And Peter
remembered the word of the Lord, how he had said unto him,
Before the cock crow, thou shalt deny me thrice.

The Lord turned and looked upon him. Christ is here called the Lord, for there was much of divine knowledge, power, and grace, appearing in this. Though Christ had now his back upon Peter, and was upon his trial (when, one would think, he had something else to mind), yet he knew all that Peter said.

Christ takes more notice of what we say and do than we think he does. When Peter disowned Christ, yet Christ did not disown him, though he might justly have cast him off, and never looked upon him more, but have denied him before his Father. It is well for us that Christ does not deal with us as we deal with him.

MATTHEW HENRY

WITH WEEPING

———

LUKE 22:62 NLT
And Peter left the courtyard, crying bitterly.

Peter's denying Christ began by keeping at a distance from him. Those that are shy of godliness, are far in the way to deny Christ. Those who think it dangerous to be in company with Christ's disciples, because thence they may be drawn in to suffer for him, will find it much more dangerous to be in company with his enemies, because there they may be drawn in to sin against him. When Christ was admired and flocked after, Peter readily owned him; but will own no relation to him now he is deserted and despised. Yet observe, Peter's repentance was very speedy. Let him that thinketh he standeth take heed lest he fall; and let him that has fallen think of these things, and of his own offences, and return to the Lord with weeping and supplication, seeking forgiveness, and to be raised up by the Holy Spirit.

MATTHEW HENRY

JESUS IS TORTURED *and* MOCKED

The soldiers led Jesus away into the palace
(that is, the Praetorium) and called together
the whole company of soldiers. They put a
purple robe on him, then twisted together a
crown of thorns and set it on him.

MARK 15:16–17 NIV

JESUS IS TORTURED *and* MOCKED

The road that stretched out before Jesus between Pilate's court and the cross has been traditionally called the "painful way," the Via Dolorosa. That's an understatement. A gauntlet of suffering extracted a horrific price from Christ long before the agonies of the cross began. The soldiers whipped Him and mocked Him, crowning Him with thorns. They forced Jesus to carry the cross and then humiliated Him by requiring a stranger to bear it for Him. He heard women weeping for Him and realized sadly that they did not realize what awaited them. People experience pain in many ways, and Jesus was acquainted with all of them.

We find the sights and sounds of Jesus' final hours repulsive. Faced with the horrific acts humans commit against one another, we are sickened. The idea that God would submit to such mistreatment at the hands of creatures He created stuns us. But when we realize that God endured this suffering on our behalf, we come to a moment of crisis. Either we accept the fact that our sins required a painful solution, or we decide to take lightly the cross of Christ. In the pages that follow, you will glimpse the lengths God went out of love for you.

WHAT CROWN WILL YOU WEAR?

MATTHEW 27:28-29 NIV

They stripped him and put a scarlet robe on him, and then
twisted together a crown of thorns and set it on his head.
They put a staff in his right hand and knelt in front of him
and mocked him. "Hail, king of the Jews!" they said.

What sort of garland did Christ Jesus . . . submit to on behalf of humanity? One made of thorns and this-tles—a symbol of our sins, produced by the soil of the flesh. However, the power of the cross removed these thorns, blunt-ing death's every sting in the Lord's enduring head. Yes, even beyond this symbol, contempt, shame, disgrace, and fierce cruelty disfigured and lacerated the Lord's temples. This was so that now you might be crowned with laurel, myrtle, olive, and any famous branch—with roses too—and both kinds of lily, violets of all sorts, and perhaps with gems and gold—garlands that will rival even the crown Christ obtained after-wards. . . . The Father first made Him a little lower than the angels for a time and then crowned Him with glory and honor. If you owe your own head to Him for these things, repay it if you can; He presented His for yours. Otherwise, don't be crowned with flowers at all; if you can't be crowned with thorns, you may never be crowned with flowers.

TERTULLIAN

O SACRED HEAD, NOW WOUNDED

MARK 15:17 NKJV

And they clothed Him with purple; and they twisted a crown of thorns, put it on His head.

O sacred head, now wounded,
  with grief and shame weighed down,
Now scornfully surrounded
  with thorns, thine only crown:
O sacred head, what glory, what bliss till now was thine;
Yet, though despised and gory, I joy to call thee mine.

What thou, my Lord, has suffered
  was all for sinners' gain;
Mine, mine was the transgression,
  but thine the deadly pain.
Lo, here I fall, my Savior! 'Tis I deserve thy place;
Look on me with thy favor, and grant to me thy grace.

What language shall I borrow to thank thee,
  dearest friend,
For this thy dying sorrow, thy pity without end?
O make me thine forever; and should I fainting be,
Lord, let me never, never outlive my love to thee.

BERNARD OF CLAIRVAUX

WHOSE THORNS?

MARK 15:17 NASB

*And they dressed Him up in purple, and after
weaving a crown of thorns, they put it on Him.*

Every good deed we do to our neighbors is entered in the Gospel, which is written on heavenly tablets and read by all who are worthy of the knowledge of the whole of things. But on the other hand, there is a part of the Gospel which condemns those who do the same evil deeds done to Jesus. The Gospel includes the treachery of Judas and the shouts of the wicked crowd when it said, "Away with such a one from the earth," "Crucify Him, crucify Him," the mockings of those who crowned Him with thorns, and everything of that kind. There are those who still have thorns with which they crown and dishonor Jesus namely, those people who are choked by the cares, riches, and pleasures of life. Though they have received the Word of God, they don't carry it out. Therefore, we must beware, lest we crown Jesus with thorns of our own.

ORIGEN

ENDURING WHEN INSULTED

MARK 15:19 NIV
*Again and again they struck him on the head with
a staff and spit on him. Falling on their knees,
they paid homage to him.*

When a ship is in danger of sinking, the sailors don't know what they throw out of the boat—whether they lay hands on their own or other people's property. They throw overboard all the ship's contents without discriminating between what is precious and what is not. But when the storm has ended, they consider all they have thrown out and shed tears. They aren't aware of the calm due to their losing what they threw overboard. It is the same when passion blows hard and storms rise up. People fling out their words without knowing how to be orderly and appropriate. But when the passion has stopped, they remember what kind of words they spoke. . . . Let this console you when you suffer from insults. Are you insulted? God is also insulted. Are you verbally abused? God was also abused verbally. Are you treated with scorn? Why, so was our Master. He shares these things with us, but not the unfavorable things. For He never insulted someone else unjustly: God forbid! He never verbally abused anyone, never did a wrong. . . . For to endure insults is God's part. To be abusive is the part of the devil.

CHRYSOSTOM

HIS GENTLENESS

MATTHEW 27:30 NIV
*They spit on him, and took the staff
and struck him on the head again and again.*

My trials are merely a fraction of the spitting and blows Christ endured. We face these dangers for Him and with His help. Even taken altogether, these dangers don't deserve the crown of thorns which robbed our Conqueror of His crown. Yet for His sake I am crowned for a hard life. I don't consider these trials even worth the gall or vinegar alone. But by these we were cured of the bitter taste of life. My struggles aren't worthy of the gentleness He showed in His passion. Was He betrayed with a kiss? He corrects us with a kiss, but doesn't strike us. Was He arrested suddenly? He definitely reproves them, but follows willingly. And if through zeal you cut off the ear of Malchus with a sword, He will be angry and will heal it. And if one of us runs away in a linen sheet, He will defend that person. If you ask for the fire of Sodom to come down on His captors, He won't pour it out. And if He sees a thief hanging on the cross for his crime, He will bring him into Paradise through His goodness. Let all who love people be loving in their actions, as Christ was in His sufferings. Nothing could be worse than refusing to forgive our neighbor of even the smallest wrongs when God died for us.

GREGORY NAZIANZEN

WHO WAS *in* CONTROL?

LUKE 23:26 NLT
They led Jesus away.

Both character and holiness are best found where our need for Jesus is extreme. And our needs are most apparent where life dumps trials on us! To be tested in the extreme is to learn spiritual dependency. When our torn souls settle on the impaling stakes, we can define our need. It comes *in extremis*! We cringe when we think of letting other people gain control of our lives. Yet the time when we best develop character is when we are no longer in charge of our circumstances. To be under the heel of someone else's will or to suffer the indignity of crushing circumstances, these incarcerations of body give wings to the spirit.

We have to remember that Jesus was never more his own man than when he was bound, flogged, and crucified. He did not come across to any casual Roman observer as a man who was winning. When you are forced to die naked before your own mother, it can make you seem a loser with none on earth to vouch for your character. But Jesus was winning. And through his long ordeal of human abandonment, he remained in perfect union with his Father.

CALVIN MILLER

HOW *to* SUFFER

MARK 15:20 NLT
Then they led him away to be crucified.

If one day we will receive comfort from afflictions, rest from labor, health after sickness, and eternal life from death, it isn't right to agonize over temporal, human pain. . . . We should consider such matters to be the test and exercise of a righteous life. For how can we have patience if there isn't previous labor and sorrow? Or how can our strength be tested without attacks from the enemy? . . . Finally, how can we see righteousness unless the sin of very wicked people appears previously? As a result, our Lord and Savior Jesus Christ reminds us how to suffer. When He was beaten, He bore it patiently. Although verbally abused, He didn't lash out in return. When He suffered, He didn't speak threats but gave His back to the torturers and His cheeks to buffetings. He didn't turn His face away from the spitting but was willingly led to His death so that we could see the image of righteousness in Him. By following these examples, we can tread on serpents, scorpions, and all of the enemy's power.

ATHANASIUS

NO ORDINARY DAY

JOHN 19:16 NIV
So the soldiers took charge of Jesus.

It was the outskirts of Jerusalem, a city more memorable than either Rome, London, or New York; the residence of David, the royal city, the seat of Israel's kings. The city witnessed the magnificence of Solomon's reign, and here the temple stood. Here the Lord Jesus had taught and wrought miracles, and into this city He had ridden a few days earlier seated upon an ass as the multitudes cried, "Hosanna to the son of David: Blessed is he that cometh in the name of the Lord; Hosanna in the highest" (Matthew 21:9)—so fickle is human nature. Israel had rejected their King and therefore He was conducted beyond the bounds of the city, so that He "suffered without the gate" (Hebrews 13:12). The actual place of the crucifixion was Golgotha, signifying "the place of a skull." Nature had anticipated the awful deed, since the contour of the ground resembled a death's head. Luke gives the Gentile name "Calvary" (Luke 23:33), for the guilt of that death rested on both Jew and Gentile. . . .

To the soldiers it was an ordinary event, the execution of a criminal; and thus it is with most who hear the Gospel. It falls on their ears as a religious commonplace. To the Roman soldiers, at least for a while, Christ appeared only as a dying Jew; thus it is with the multitude today.

ARTHUR W. PINK

THE PATH *to the* CROSS

JOHN 19:17 NKJV
And He, bearing His cross, went out to a place called the
Place of a Skull, which is called in Hebrew, Golgotha.

The most notorious road in the world is the Via Dolorosa,
"the Way of Sorrows." According to tradition, it is the
route Jesus took from Pilate's hall to Calvary. . . . There are
fourteen stations in all, each one a reminder of the events of
Christ's final journey.

Is the route accurate? Probably not. When Jerusalem
was destroyed in A.D. 70 and again in A.D. 135, the streets of
the city were destroyed. As a result, no one knows the exact
route Christ followed that Friday.

But we do know where the path actually began.

The path began, not in the court of Pilate, but in the
halls of heaven. The Father began his journey when he left
his home in search of us. Armed with nothing more than a
passion to win your heart, he came looking. His desire was
singular—to bring his children home. The Bible has a word
for this quest: *reconciliation*. . . .

Reconciliation touches the shoulder of the wayward
and woos him homeward.

The path to the cross tells us exactly how far God will
go to call us back.

MAX LUCADO

THE OLD RUGGED CROSS

*Carrying the cross by himself, Jesus went to the place
called Skull Hill (in Hebrew, Golgotha).*

On a hill far away stood an old rugged cross,
The emblem of suffering and shame;
And I love that old cross where the dearest and best
For a world of lost sinners was slain.

O that old rugged cross, so despised by the world,
Has a wondrous attraction for me;
For the dear Lamb of God left His glory above
To bear it to dark Calvary.

In that old rugged cross, stained with blood so divine,
A wondrous beauty I see,
For 'twas on that old cross Jesus suffered and died,
To pardon and sanctify me. . . .

So I'll cherish the old rugged cross,
Till my trophies at last I lay down;
I will cling to the old rugged cross,
And exchange it some day for a crown.

GEORGE BENNARD

228   HIS PASSION

THAT WOODEN BEAM

MARK 15:21 NLT

A man named Simon, who was from Cyrene, was coming in from the country just then, and they forced him to carry Jesus' cross. (Simon is the father of Alexander and Rufus.)

For Simon it was just a hunk of wood. He was strong and the Romans had swords. He would carry it.

For us, it's a cross, a symbol rich in meaning, and the man Simon helped was the world's Savior. Who wouldn't do as much? If we were there, we would gladly have come forward to help Jesus.

We bear the cross, not because we love pain, but because Jesus loves us. It's the Christians' way of saying to everyone: I have died with Christ, this Savior has first place in my heart, and I will serve him as Lord.

Today the cross comes in different shapes. Christians must shoulder it when they suffer loss for Christ's sake—enduring a dread disease, losing a friend or a job, remaining chaste while unmarried, and a thousand more. Let us carry the cross courageously.

LIFE APPLICATION BIBLE COMMENTARY—MARK

THE CROSS YOU CARRY

LUKE 23:26 NRSV

As they led him away, they seized a man, Simon of Cyrene,
who was coming from the country, and they laid the cross
on him, and made him carry it behind Jesus.

We see in Simon's carrying the cross a picture of the work of the Church throughout all generations. Let us comfort ourselves with this thought, that in our case, as in Simon's, it is not our cross, but Christ's cross which we carry, and how delightful is it to carry the cross of our Lord Jesus!

You carry the cross after Him. You have blessed company; your path is marked with the footprints of your Lord. The mark of His blood-red shoulder is upon that heavy burden. 'Tis His cross, and He goes before you as a shepherd goes before his sheep. Take up your cross daily, and follow Him. And remember, though Simon had to bear the cross for a very little while, it gave him lasting honour. Even so the cross we carry is only for a little while at most, and then we shall receive the crown, the glory. Surely we should love the cross, and, instead of shrinking from it, count it very dear, when it works out for us "a far more exceeding and eternal weight of glory."

CHARLES HADDON SPURGEON

FOLLOW HIM

LUKE 23:27 NRSV
*A great number of the people followed him,
and among them were women who were beating
their breasts and wailing for him.*

See Him in raiment rent, with His blood dyed:
Women walk sorrowing by His side.

Heavy that cross to Him, weary the weight:
One who will help Him stands at the gate.

Multitudes hurrying, pass on the road:
Simon is sharing with Him the load.

Who is this traveling with the curst tree—
This weary prisoner—who is He?

Follow to Calvary, tread where He trod:
This is the Lord of life—Son of God.

EDWARD MONRO AND MRS. M. DEARMER

THE DIFFICULT TIMES

ROMANS 5:3–4 NIV
Not only so, but we also rejoice in our sufferings,
because we know that suffering produces perseverance;
perseverance, character; and character, hope.

Often in the most difficult of times, it seems as if our Heavenly Father is strangely silent. I have come to believe this is a gift. God wants His people to understand how much His world is in pain. He wants us to identify with the suffering that surrounds us.

This is an extremely difficult lesson to learn in a setting where we're used to having things more or less our own way. Our expectations and our sense of entitlement are high, and our tolerance for others and their problems is usually low.

But God doesn't need men and women working for His cause who have brilliant minds but hard and shriveled souls. He's not necessarily searching for beautiful people, not talented and educated people to be His servants. What He needs is believers who know what it is to be broken.

Pain and suffering can teach a proud person humility and compassion for others. On the other hand, hard times can make a man or woman bitter and resentful.

Paul writes to the Romans, "We know that suffering produces perseverance; perseverance, character; and character, hope" (Romans 5:3–4). Have you not found that to be true? That some of life's most valuable insights are discovered during difficult times?

DAVID MAINS

HE WENT BEFORE US

MARK 15:24 NKJV
They crucified Him.

The Lord desired that we rejoice and leap for joy in persecutions. When persecutions occur, then crowns of faith are given, then the soldiers of God are tested, then heaven is opened to martyrs. For we haven't enrolled for war in order to think only about peace and withdraw from battle. But in this very warfare of persecution, the Lord walked first. He is the Teacher of humility, endurance, and suffering. What He tells us to do, He did first. And what He urges us to suffer, He suffered first for us. Beloved, observe that He alone bore all the Father's judgment and will come Himself to judge. He has already declared His future judgment and recognition. He has foretold and testified that He will confess before His Father those who confess Him and will deny those who deny Him. If we could escape death, we might reasonably fear death. But since it is necessary for a mortal man to die, we should embrace the occasion as coming from God's promise to reward us in the end with eternal life. We shouldn't fear being slain, since we are sure that we will be crowned when we are slain.

CYPRIAN

ALAS! AND DID MY SAVIOR BLEED?

LUKE 23:33 KJV
*And when they were come to the place, which
is called Calvary, there they crucified him.*

Alas! And did my Savior bleed, and did my Sovereign die?
Would he devote that sacred head for sinners such as I?

Thy body slain, sweet Jesus, Thine—and bathed in its own blood—
While the firm mark of wrath divine, his soul in anguish stood.

Was it for crimes that I have done, he groaned upon the tree?
Amazing pity, grace unknown, and love beyond degree!

Well might the sun in darkness hide, and shut its glories in,
When Christ, and mighty Maker, died for his own creature's sin.

Thus might I hide my blushing face while his dear cross appears;
Dissolve my heart in thankfulness, and melt mine eyes to tears.

Bur drops of grief can ne'er repay the debt of love I owe;
Here, Lord, I give myself away; 'tis all that I can do.

ISAAC WATTS

JESUS IS
CRUCIFIED

---

*When they came to the place called
the Skull, there they crucified him, along
with the criminals—one on his right,
the other on his left.*

LUKE 23:33 NIV

JESUS IS CRUCIFIED

The cross represents the intersection of God's salvation plan and human history. It stands as a physical statement of God's love and commitment. Those timbers held the collision between a sinful race and a gracious God. Jesus, with His body and life, bridged the intersection. He became the living and dying ligament that established God's chosen means for settling the desperate human condition. Jesus made a way where otherwise there would have been no way. He is the way.

This section will offer glimpses of the cross. It remains an inexhaustible subject. Allow yourself to view the horror and wonder through other eyes, and you may well see what you have never seen before. You may discover anew the spiritual magnetism of the cross, described by Jesus Himself when He said, "And when I am lifted up on the cross, I will draw everyone to myself" (John 12:32 NLT).

WHAT WILL YOU DO *with* JESUS?

LUKE 23:33 NIV
*When they came to the place called the Skull, there
they crucified him, along with the criminals—
one on his right, the other on his left.*

God had reasons for decreeing that Jesus should gracelessly hang between two thugs. He wanted to demonstrate the depths of shame to which His Son was willing to descend. At His birth He was surrounded by beasts, and, now, in His death, with criminals. Let no one say that God has stayed aloof from the brokenness of our fallen world. He descended that we might ascend with Him to newness of life. . . .

These thieves represent the entire human race. Ultimately, the world is not divided geographically, racially, or economically. Nor can we draw a line separating the relatively good people from the relatively bad ones. All races, nations, and cultures are divided at the cross. On one side are those individuals who believe, and on the other are those who choose to justify themselves, determined to stand before God on their own record. Heaven and hell are not places far away, but near us. Everything depends on what we do with Jesus.

ERWIN LUTZER

A UNIQUE DEATH

LUKE 23:32 NIV
Two other men, both criminals,
were also led out with him to be executed.

Though we find it hard and even repulsive to imagine, Jesus was only one of many people tortured to death by crucifixion. He had two companions at the brow of Calvary. But his experience on the cross included several added sobering features. A unique death for a unique man:

First, it was shameful. He was stripped of his clothing and pinned naked between heaven and earth. There's no mention of the soldiers casting lots for the clothing of the other victims. He was ridiculed by the crowds and taunted by one of the criminals. Jesus suffered the humiliation of the sign posted over his head that attempted to mock his claim to be king.

Second, he was absolutely innocent—and he could prove it! He was there by choice. The nails didn't keep him on the cross. His decision to remain there was stronger than his desire to avoid the pain. Think for a moment how tempting it must have been to have a self-pity party.

Third, he bore the sins of the world—including yours and mine—on the cross.

Fourth, he sensed the forsaking action of God as his Father turned away from him, covered as he was in our sins.

NEIL WILSON

LOOKING FORWARD

MARK 15:25 NKJV
Now it was the third hour, and they crucified Him.

The fear of the Lord is our cross. Those who are crucified no longer have the power to move or turn their limbs in any direction they please. Similarly, we shouldn't fix our wishes and desires on what pleases and delights us now, but according to how the Law of the Lord constrains us. Those who are fastened to the wood of the cross no longer consider present things or think about their preferences. They aren't distracted by anxiety and care for tomorrow and aren't disturbed by the desire for any possession. They aren't inflamed by pride, strife, or rivalry. They don't grieve during present pain and don't remember past injuries. For while they are still breathing in the body, they consider themselves dead to every earthly thing. Instead, they send the thoughts of their heart ahead to where they know they will shortly follow. So when we are crucified by fear of the Lord, we should definitely be dead to all these things. That is, we shouldn't only die to wickedness, but also to every earthly thing. We should fix the eye of our minds onto the place we constantly hope to reach. For in this way we can destroy all our desires and fleshly affections.

JOHN CASSIAN

OUR HOPE

JOHN 19:18 NASB
There they crucified Him.

Wasn't God really crucified? And, having been crucified, didn't He really die? And, having died, didn't He really rise again? If not, Paul would have falsely "determined to know nothing among us but Jesus and Him crucified." He would have falsely imposed on us that Christ was buried and rose again. Then our faith is also false. And all that we hope for from Christ is a dream. You who acquit the murderers of God from guilt are a disgrace! For Christ didn't suffer from them if He really never suffered. . . .

The Son of God was crucified. I am not ashamed because mankind must be ashamed of it. And the Son of God died. It is, by all means, to be believed because it is absurd. And He was buried and rose again. The fact is certain, because it is impossible. But how will all this be true if He wasn't true Himself, if He hadn't had within Himself that which might be crucified, might die, might be buried, and might rise again?

TERTULLIAN

HE UNDERSTANDS YOUR SUFFERING

MATTHEW 27:34 NIV

There they offered Jesus wine to drink, mixed with gall;
but after tasting it, he refused to drink it.

Before the nail was pounded, a drink was offered. Mark says the wine was mixed with myrrh. Matthew described it as wine mixed with gall. Both myrrh and gall contain sedative properties that numb the senses. But Jesus refused them. He refused to be stupefied by the drugs, opting instead to feel the full force of his suffering.

Why? Why did he endure all these feelings? Because he knew you would feel them too.

He knew you would be weary, disturbed, and angry. He knew you'd be sleepy, grief-stricken, and hungry. He knew you'd face pain. If not the pain of the body, the pain of the soul . . . pain too sharp for any drug. He knew you'd face thirst. If not a thirst for water, at least a thirst for truth, and the truth we glean from the image of a thirsty Christ is—he understands.

MAX LUCADO

TAUNTED *for* OUR SAKES

MATTHEW 27:43 NRSV
*"He trusts in God; let God deliver him now, if he wants to;
for he said, 'I am God's Son.'"*

What a paradox it was! Christ came and manifested to Israel—to the world—His miraculous powers of healing, His complete authority over Satan and his kingdom; yet at the cross of Calvary, they taunted Jesus with statements like, "He believes in God, let God rescue Him" (see Matthew 27:43). They were statements that implied that Jesus was being smitten by God. What audacity! What sin lay in their darkened hearts! What blindness!

Then Isaiah goes on to explain the reason for, the purpose of, the cross. He was pierced through for our transgressions. He was crushed—killed—for our iniquities. Our deserved chastening fell on Him, that we might have peace, reconciliation with God. By His scourging or stripes we are healed.

Healed? Healed of what?

Peter tells us in his first epistle: "And He Himself bore our sins in His body on the cross, that we might die to sin and live to righteousness; for by His wounds you were healed. For you were continually straying like sheep, but now you have returned to the Shepherd and Guardian of your souls" (1 Peter 2:24–25).

By His stripes we were healed of our sins . . . of their power and their dominion over us (Romans 6).

What a healing! What a Savior!

KAY ARTHUR

RADICAL OBEDIENCE

LUKE 23:35 NLT
*The crowd watched, and the leaders laughed and scoffed.
"He saved others," they said, "let him save himself
if he is really God's Chosen One, the Messiah."*

The cross of Christ made those who abused their authority subject to their former subjects. The cross teaches us, first of all, to resist sin to the point of death and to die willingly for the sake of religion. It also sets an example of obedience for us, and in the same way it punishes the stubbornness of those who once ruled us. Listen to how the Apostle Paul taught us obedience by the cross of Christ: "Let this mind be in you, which was in Christ Jesus who, being in the form of God, thought it not robbery to be equal with God, but made Himself of no reputation, taking upon Him the form of a servant, being made in the likeness of men; and, being found in fashion as a man, He became obedient unto death, even the death of the cross." So, then, as a skilled master teaches both by example and command, so Christ taught us obedience, even to the point of death, by dying to Himself in obedience.

RUFINUS

THE SIGN

LUKE 23:38 NLT
*A signboard was nailed to the cross above him with
these words: "This is the King of the Jews."*

Please note that the sign bears immediate fruit. Remember the response of the criminal? Moments from his own death, in a maelstrom of pain, he turns and says, "Jesus, remember me when you come into your kingdom" (Luke 23:42). . . .

Luke seems to make the connection between the reading of the sign and the offering of the prayer. In one passage he writes: "At the top of the cross these words were written: THIS IS THE KING OF THE JEWS" (Luke 23:38). Four quick verses later we read the petition of the thief: "Jesus, remember me when you come into your kingdom."

The thief knows he is in a royal mess. He turns his head and reads a royal proclamation and asks for royal help. It might have been this simple. If so, the sign was the first tool used to proclaim the message of the cross. Countless others have followed, from the printing press to the radio to the stadium crusade to the book you are holding. But a crude wooden sign preceded them all. And because of the sign, a soul was saved. All because someone posted a sign on a cross.

MAX LUCADO

TO SAVE US

MATTHEW 27:42 NASB

"He saved others; He cannot save Himself. He is the King of Israel; let Him now come down from the cross, and we shall believe in Him."

Jesus was not executed in a quiet building, away from the city's noise and activity. He was executed on a public highway, on a day when perhaps hundreds of people were traveling. The fact that His indictment was written in three languages—Greek, Hebrew, and Latin—indicates that a cosmopolitan crowd passed by Golgotha, "the place of the skull." This in itself was humiliating, for the passersby could stare and shout bitter mockery at the victims. Again, this mockery from the crowd had been predicted (Psalm 22:6–8).

It was bad enough that the common rabble mocked Him, but even the Jewish leaders joined the attack. They reminded Him of His promise to rebuild the temple in three days (John 2:19; Matthew 26:61). "If You can do that, You can come down from the cross and prove to us that You are God's Son!" In reality, it was the fact that He *stayed* on the cross that proved His divine Sonship.

The Jewish rulers mocked His claim to be the Saviour. "He saved others; He cannot save Himself (Matthew 27:42, NASB). He *had* saved others. But if He saved Himself, then nobody else could be saved! He did not come to save His life, but to give it as a ransom for sinners.

WARREN W. WIERSBE

THE DARKNESS

MATTHEW 27:45 NLT
*At noon, darkness fell across the
whole land until three o'clock.*

Why night, at noon?

Darkness is always associated with the judgment of God for great sin. Here we see the judgment of God against the evil men who treated His Son with cruel contempt; and, in a profound sense, we stand condemned with them, for it was our sins that put Jesus on the cross. Should we ever love sin, we would love the very evil that caused nails to be driven through our Savior's hands and feet. . . .

But there is another reason for the darkness. It represents the judgment of the Father against His Son. In those hours of darkness, Jesus became legally guilty of our sin, and for that He was judged. Think of it: legally guilty of genocide, child abuse, alcoholism, murder, adultery, homosexual activity, greed, and the like. How appropriate that when the Sinless One was "made sin for us," the event was veiled from human eyes.

ERWIN LUTZER

INTO *the* DIVINE PRESENCE

MARK 15:37–38 NRSV
Then Jesus gave a loud cry and breathed his last. And the curtain of the temple was torn in two, from top to bottom.

The interior journey of the soul from the wilds of sin into the enjoyed Presence of God is beautifully illustrated in the Old Testament tabernacle. The returning sinner first entered the outer court where he offered a blood sacrifice on the brazen altar and washed himself in the laver that stood near it. Then through a veil he passed into the holy place where no natural light could come, but the golden candlestick which spoke of Jesus the Light of the World threw its soft glow over all. There also was the shewbread to tell of Jesus, the Bread of Life, and the altar of incense, a figure of unceasing prayer. . . . Another veil separated from the Holy of Holies where above the mercy seat dwelt the very God Himself in awful and glorious manifestation. While the tabernacle stood, only the high priest could enter there, and that but once a year, with blood which he offered for his sins and the sins of the people. It was this last veil which was rent when our Lord gave up the ghost on Calvary and . . . this rending of the veil opened the way for every worshipper in the world to come by the new and living way straight into the divine Presence.

A. W. TOZER

THE PRESENCE *of* GOD

MARK 15:37–38 NRSV

*Then Jesus gave a loud cry and breathed his last. And the
curtain of the temple was torn in two, from top to bottom.*

With the veil removed by the rending of Jesus' flesh,
with nothing on God's side to prevent us from entering, why do we tarry without? Why do we consent to abide
all our days just outside the Holy of Holies and never enter
at all to look upon God? We hear the Bridegroom say, "Let
me see thy countenance, let me hear thy voice; for sweet is
thy voice and thy countenance is comely." We sense that the
call is for us, but still we fail to draw near, and the years pass
and we grow old and tired in the outer courts of the tabernacle. What doth hinder us? . . . Insist that the work be done
in very truth and it will be done. The cross is rough, and it is
deadly, but it is effective. It does not keep its victim hanging
there forever. There comes a moment when its work is finished and the suffering victim dies. After that is resurrection
glory and power, and the pain is forgotten for joy that the
veil is taken away and we have entered in actual spiritual
experience the Presence of the living God.

A. W. TOZER

THE BARRIER IS GONE

MATTHEW 27:50–51 NIV

And when Jesus had cried out again in a loud voice,
he gave up his spirit. At that moment the curtain of the
temple was torn in two from top to bottom.

What appeared to be the cruelty of man was actually the sovereignty of God. Matthew tells us: "And when Jesus had cried out again in a loud voice, he gave up his spirit. *At that moment* the curtain of the temple was torn in two from top to bottom" (27:50–51 NIV, italics mine).

It's as if the hands of heaven had been gripping the veil, waiting for this moment. Keep in mind the size of the curtain—sixty feet tall and thirty feet wide. One instant it was whole; the next it was ripped in two from top to bottom. No delay. No hesitation.

What did the torn curtain mean? For the Jews it meant no more barrier between them and the Holy of Holies. No more priests to go between them and God. No more animal sacrifices to atone for their sins.

And for us? What did the torn curtain signify for us?

We are welcome to enter into God's presence—any day, any time. God has removed the barrier that separates us from him. The barrier of sin? Down. He has removed the curtain.

MAX LUCADO

THE EARTHQUAKE

MATTHEW 27:54 NIV
When the centurion and those with him who
were guarding Jesus saw the earthquake and all
that had happened, they were terrified.

Our Lord's victorious shout was followed immediately by a shattering earthquake. The rocks that rent were not detached boulders, but cliffs, masses of rock. Earthquake shocks are not uncommon in Jerusalem, but through divine overruling this particular quake synchronized with the tremendous event that had just transpired in the spiritual realm, as though to attest the might and majesty of Him whose lifeless body now hung limp on the cross. . . .

This was not an isolated phenomenon attributable to natural causes. The coincidences are too striking. It exactly coincided with two other miraculous manifestations, the mysterious darkness and the rending of the veil. It coincided with the loud cry and the death of the Son of God. It coincided with the opening of certain graves, apparently only the graves of saints.

Some have seen in this divine visitation an answer to the earthquake on Sinai that evidenced the awe-full presence of God. In the Old Testament, an earthquake often denoted God's presence and intervention among men.

J. OSWALD SANDERS

THE RAISING *of the* SAINTS

MATTHEW 27:52–53 NIV
The tombs broke open and the bodies of
many holy people who had died were raised to life.
They came out of the tombs, and after Jesus' resurrection
they went into the holy city and appeared to many people.

It must be noted that, while the tombs were opened at the moment of Christ's death, the bodies of the saints are recorded to have come "out of the graves *after* His resurrection." . . .

The opening of the graves was a vivid and eloquent symbolic demonstration that by His death Christ had for ever broken the bonds of death. "He death by dying slew," and for ever robbed the grave of its terror and victory.

The resurrection of these saints was a clear indication that the prison doors of Hades had been wrenched from their hinges. The words "they were raised" surely mean what they say. They rose, but not in order that they might live again on earth. They "appeared to many," but not to stay. . . . Their bodies were apparently revived for this purpose, but it was not their final resurrection.

In this momentous event we have a sign that Jesus had conquered death, and a foreshadowing of the glorious resurrection that awaits the believer.

J. OSWALD SANDERS

FINISHED

MARK 15:37 NIV
With a loud cry, Jesus breathed his last.

Jesus was crucified at nine o'clock in the morning; and from nine until noon, He hung in the light. But at noon, a miraculous darkness covered the land. This was not a sandstorm or an eclipse, as some liberal writers have suggested. It was a heaven-sent darkness that lasted for three hours. It was as though all of creation was sympathizing with the Creator. There were three days of darkness in Egypt before Passover (Exodus 10:21–23); and there were three hours of darkness before the Lamb of God died for the sins of the world. . . .

Though He was "crucified through weakness" (2 Corinthians 13:14), He exercised wonderful power when He died. Three miracles took place simultaneously: The veil of the temple was torn in two from top to bottom; an earthquake opened many graves; some of the saints arose from the dead. The rending of the veil symbolized the wonderful truth that the way was now open to God (Hebrews 10:14–26). There was no more need of temples, priests, altars, or sacrifices. Jesus had finished the work of salvation on the cross.

WARREN W. WIERSBE

SURELY

MARK 15:39 NIV

And when the centurion, who stood there in front of Jesus,
heard his cry and saw how he died, he said,
"Surely this man was the Son of God!"

A centurion (person of rank in the Roman guard) had accompanied the soldiers to the execution site. Undoubtedly, he had done this many times. Yet this crucifixion was completely different—the unexplained darkness, the earthquake, even the executed himself who had uttered the words, "Father, forgive them, for they do not know what they are doing" (Luke 22:34 NIV). The centurion observed Jesus' relatively quick and alert death. This Gentile Roman officer realized something that most of the Jewish nation had missed: *"Surely this man was the Son of God!"* Whether he understood what he was saying, we cannot know. He may simply have admired Jesus' courage and inner strength, perhaps thinking that Jesus was divine like one of Rome's many gods. He certainly recognized Jesus' innocence. While the Jewish religious leaders stood around celebrating Jesus' death, a lone Roman soldier was the first to acclaim Jesus as the Son of God after his death.

LIFE APPLICATION BIBLE COMMENTARY—MARK

FOR *the* GLORY *of* GOD

LUKE 23:47 NIV
*The centurion, seeing what had happened, praised God
and said, "Surely this was a righteous man."*

We cannot always or even often control events, but we can control how we respond to them. When things happen which dismay or appall, we ought to look to God for His meaning, remembering that He is not taken by surprise nor can His purposes be thwarted in the end. What God looks for is those who will *worship* Him. Our look of inquiring trust glorifies Him.

One of the witnesses to the crucifixion was a military officer to whom the scene was surely not a novelty. He had seen plenty of criminals nailed up. But the response of this Man who hung there was of such an utterly different nature than that of the others that the centurion knew at once that He was innocent. His own response then, rather than one of despair that such a terrible injustice should take place, or of anger at God who might have prevented it, was *praise* (Luke 23:47 NEB).

This is our first responsibility: to glorify God. In the face of life's worst reversals and tragedies, the response of a faithful Christian is praise—not *for* the wrong itself certainly, but for who God is and for the ultimate assurance that there is a pattern being worked out for those who love Him.

ELISABETH ELLIOT

HE CHOSE *to* SUFFER *for* US

PSALM 22:7–8 NKJV

*All those who see Me ridicule Me; they shoot out the lip,
they shake the head, saying, "He trusted in the LORD,
let Him rescue Him; let Him deliver Him,
since He delights in Him!"*

How could the Lord Jesus bring himself to suffer at the hands of men? After all, he is the Lord of all the earth, the one through whom men themselves were made in God's image. Even if he was willing to suffer as a mark of his love for us, how could it happen? Would this not detract from his power and dignity?

The answer, as one would expect, is to be found in the Scriptures. The prophets, inspired by the Lord himself, fore-told his coming as a man, since if he were to destroy death and bring in eternal life it was essential that he should take upon himself human flesh. And to take on human flesh in-volves suffering: the two are virtually indistinguishable. Has there ever been a human being who went through life with-out suffering?

But it was not just a matter of accepting the inevitable. The Lord *chose* to suffer, so that he could fulfill God's prom-ises to our ancestors by revealing the depth of his love for them, suffering and dying for us and then raising us as he was raised, drawing together a new people of God.

EPISTLE OF BARNABAS

DESPISED *and* REJECTED

ISAIAH 53:3 NKJV

He is despised and rejected by men, a Man of sorrows and
acquainted with grief. And we hid, as it were, our faces from
Him; He was despised, and we did not esteem Him.

Deity becoming incarnate is in itself a marvel of the ages.
That incarnate Deity should be so predominantly characterized by sorrow makes us aware that, as we think on this
title, we are entering into the holy of holies in the sanctuary
of Christ's life. We are standing before one of the most sub-
lime and sacred truths of eternity. It is too deep for us to
plumb its mystery and majesty.

The sorrow and anguish of Jesus defy description or
definition. His love was wounded in betrayal and denial by
those of His most intimate circle. He was burdened with the
awesome responsibility for the redemption of the world. . . .

The nails that tore through His sacred hands and feet
were our sins. The thorns that pierced His brow and marred
His visage were our sins. The scourge that lacerated the flesh
of His back to ribbons was our sins. The wagging heads that
mocked Him and the tongues that vilified Him were our sins.

"He was wounded for our transgressions." As the Man
of Sorrows He took on Himself our burden and penalty of
sin. He bore it for us. He carried our sorrow. He suffered our
condemnation. He endured our agony. He died our death.

HENRY GARIEPY

A CLOSER LOOK

ISAIAH 53:4 NKJV
*Surely He has borne our griefs and carried our sorrows;
yet we esteemed Him stricken, smitten by God, and afflicted.*

D oes it please you to go through all of My pain and to
experience grief with Me? Then consider the plots
against Me and the irreverent price of My innocent blood.
Consider the disciple's pretended kisses, the crowd's insults
and abuse, and, even more, the mocking blows and accusing
tongues. Imagine the false witnesses, Pilate's cursed judgment,
the immense cross pressed on My shoulders and tired back,
and My painful steps to a dreadful death. Study Me from head
to foot. I am deserted and lifted high up above My beloved
mother. See My hair clotted with blood, and My head encir-
cled by cruel thorns. For a stream of blood is pouring down
like rain on all sides of My Divine face. Observe My sunken,
sightless eyes and My beaten cheeks. See My parched tongue
that was poisoned with gall. My face is pale with death. Look
at My hands that have been pierced with nails and My
drawn-out arms. See the great wound in My side and the
blood streaming from it. Imagine My pierced feet and blood-
stained limbs. Then bow, and with weeping adore the wood
of the cross. With a humble face, stoop to the earth that is wet
with innocent blood. Sprinkle it with tears, and carry Me and
My encouragement in your devoted heart.

LACTANTIUS

SOMETHING HAD *to* BE DONE

ISAIAH 53:5 NRSV
Upon him was the punishment that made us whole.

Couldn't God simply pronounce forgiveness? Was it necessary for Christ to go through the painful process of dying? . . .

If God simply pronounced forgiveness, that would make forgiveness cheap. Our sin is too serious for such a response. We are too significant for our wrongdoing to be taken so lightly. People who have not been corrected during their childhood, whose wrongdoing has been regarded lightly, will invariably be insecure people. Subconsciously they reason that if they were significant individuals, their actions would be taken seriously. . . .

Because God regards us as significant people, He cannot simply pronounce forgiveness for our sins. They must be punished adequately. And Jesus took the punishment because God knew that if we were to take it on ourselves, there would be no hope for us.

Besides, to simply forgive would make a mockery of justice. A world without justice is an insecure and chaotic world. There is right, and there is wrong. And when wrong is done, it is serious. So something serious must be done about it.

AJITH FERNANDO

GOD'S PURPOSE *at the* CROSS

ISAIAH 53:6 KJV
*All we like sheep have gone astray; we have
turned every one to his own way; and the LORD
hath laid on him the iniquity of us all.*

"Suffered." This word carries not only the everyday meaning of bearing pain, but also the older and wider sense of being the object affected by someone else's action. The Latin is *passus,* whence the noun "passion." Both God and men were agents of Jesus' passion. "this Jesus, delivered up according to the plan and foreknowledge of God, you crucified and killed by the hands of lawless men" (Acts 2:23, from Peter's first sermon). God's purpose at the cross was as real as was the guilt of the crucifiers.

What was God's purpose? Judgment on sin, for the sake of mercy to sinners. The miscarrying of human justice was the doing of divine justice. Jesus knew on the cross all the pain, physical and mental, that man could inflict and also the divine wrath and rejection that my sins deserve; for he was there in my place, making atonement for me. "All we like sheep have gone astray . . . and the LORD has laid on him the iniquity of us all" (Isaiah 53:6).

J. I. PACKER

THE HIGHEST GLORY

ISAIAH 53:11 NLT

*When he sees all that is accomplished by his anguish,
he will be satisfied. And because of what he has experienced,
my righteous servant will make it possible for many to be
counted righteous, for he will bear all their sins.*

Truly the symbol of the cross is considered despicable according to the world and among people. But in heaven and among the faithful, it is the highest glory. . . .

But what is boasting in the cross? Boasting in the fact that Christ took on the form of a slave for my sake and suffered for me when I was the slave, the enemy, the unfeeling one. He loved me so much that He gave Himself over to a curse for me. What can compare to this? If servants only receive praise from their masters, who they are bound to kin by nature, and are elated by it, how much more must we boast when our Master, God Himself, isn't ashamed of the cross Christ endured for us. Therefore, we must not be ashamed of His unspeakable tenderness. He wasn't ashamed of being crucified for you—will you be ashamed to confess His infinite care for you?

CHRYSOSTOM

TAKING OUR SIN

ISAIAH 53:12 NKJV
He bore the sin of many.

Jesus did not come merely to disclose God's character. He came to make it possible to be remade in the likeness of that character. He came to redeem us from what we are and to remake us in the likeness of what he is. He is not merely a teacher, a doer—he is a redeemer.

He came not merely to give his word, his example. He came to give himself. He became like us that we might become like him. He was baptized into the world's toil for thirty years, baptized into our temptations for these years, and baptized into our sin at the end. He became sin for us at the cross. He died between two malefactors like one of them and cried the cry of derelicion that you and I cry when we *sin:* "My God, my God, why hast thou forsaken *me?"* If "life is sensitivity," then here was infinite life, for here was infinite sensitivity—every man's hunger his hunger; every man's bondage his bondage; and every man's sin his sin. "He bore in his own body our sins upon a tree." Don't ask me to explain it. I can't explain it; I bow in humility and repentance at the cross, at the wonder of it, that God should give himself for me. I bow and am redeemed!

E. STANLEY JONES

THE LAMB *of* GOD

JOHN 1:29 NKJV

The next day John saw Jesus coming toward him,
and said, "Behold! The Lamb of God who
takes away the sin of the world!

We're all familiar with the kind of story in which some terrible disaster or calamity is averted by a hero who sacrifices himself for the common good. It may be a plague or a famine or a monster—Greek mythology is full of stories like this: the evil power is somehow placated or frustrated by the power of self-sacrifice.

Now nobody pours scorn on this idea. It's accepted in fairy-tales. But some people seem to find the idea of God's Son overcoming evil in real life by the power of self-sacrifice very difficult to accept.

Of course, no story involves a sacrifice like Christ's. He accepted death on behalf of the whole world, so that the whole world could be cleansed—a world that was doomed to perish. Jesus alone, by his divine power, was able to take on himself the burden of the sins of the world. He carried it to the cross where he offered himself as a sacrifice for our sins. Like a sheep to the slaughter he humbled himself, and by his death delivered us from the peril into which our sins had put us.

ORIGEN

God So Loved

John 3:16 KJV
*For God so loved the world, that he gave
his only begotten Son, that whosoever believeth
in him should not perish, but have everlasting life.*

Who can describe the blessed bond of the love of God? What man is able to tell the excellence of its beauty as it ought to be told? The height to which love exalts is unspeakable. Love unites us to God. Love covers a multitude of sins. Love bears all things, is long-suffering in all things. There is nothing cruel, nothing arrogant in love. Love allows no divisions; love gives rise to no rebellions; love does all things in harmony. By love have all the elect of God been made perfect; without love nothing is well-pleasing to God. In love has the Lord taken us to Himself. On account of His love for us, Jesus Christ our Lord gave His blood for us by the will of God, His flesh for our flesh, and His soul for our souls.

You see, beloved, how great and wonderful a thing love is and that it is impossible to adequately declare its perfection. Who is fit to be found in it except those whom God has graciously privileged? Let us pray, therefore, and implore of His mercy, that we may live blameless in love, free from all human partialities for one above another.

CLEMENT OF ROME

TAKE UP THY CROSS

MATTHEW 10:38 NKJV
*And he who does not take his cross
and follow after Me is not worthy of Me.*

Why fearest thou then to take up the cross which lead-
eth to a kingdom? In the Cross is health, in the Cross
is life, in the Cross is protection from enemies, in the Cross
is heavenly sweetness, in the Cross strength of mind, in the
Cross joy of the spirit, in the Cross the height of virtue, in
the Cross perfection of holiness. There is no health of the
soul, no hope of eternal life, save in the Cross. Take up therefore, thy cross and follow Jesus and thou shalt go into eternal life. He went before thee bearing His Cross and died for
thee upon the Cross, that thou also mayest bear thy cross and
mayest love to be crucified upon it. For if thou be dead with
Him, thou shalt also live with Him, and if thou be a par-
taker of His sufferings, thou shalt be also of His glory.

THOMAS À KEMPIS

HE WILL HELP YOU BEAR IT

MARK 8:34 NLT

*Then he called his disciples and the crowds to come over and listen.
"If any of you wants to be my follower," he told them, "you must
put aside your selfish ambition, shoulder your cross, and follow me."*

It is not in the nature of man to bear the cross, to love the
cross, to keep under the body and to bring it into subjec-
tion, to fly from honours, to bear reproaches meekly, to
despise self and desire to be despised, to bear all adversities
and losses, and to desire no prosperity in this world. If thou
lookest to thyself, thou wilt of thyself be able to do none of
this; but if thou trustest in the Lord, endurance shall be given
thee from heaven, and the world and the flesh shall be made
subject to thy command. Yea, thou shalt not even fear thine
adversary the devil, if thou be armed with faith and signed
with the Cross of Christ.

Set thyself, therefore, like a good and faithful servant of
Christ, to the manful bearing of the Cross of thy Lord, who
out of love was crucified for thee. Prepare thyself for the bearing many adversities and manifold troubles in this wretched
life; because so it shall be with thee wheresoever thou art, and
so in very deed thou shalt find it, wherever thou hide thyself.
This it must be; and there is no means of escaping from tribulation and sorrow except to bear them patiently. Drink thou
lovingly thy Lord's cup if thou desirest to be His friend and
to have thy lot with Him. Leave consolations to God, let Him
do as seemeth best to Him concerning them.

THOMAS À KEMPIS

PUBLIC ACKNOWLEDGMENT

MATTHEW 10:32–33 NLT
*"If anyone acknowledges me publicly here on earth, I will
openly acknowledge that person before my Father in heaven.
But if anyone denies me here on earth, I will deny that
person before my Father in heaven."*

Why did Christ urge His disciples to take up the cross
and follow Him? . . . With respect to the suffering He
would experience and His disciples would endure, He sug-
gests, "For whosoever will save his life, shall lose it; and whosoever will lose his life, shall find it." And because His disciples
must suffer for His sake, Christ said to them, "Behold, I send
you prophets and wise men and scribes; and some of them ye
shall kill and crucify." . . . Therefore He knew both those who
would suffer persecution and those who would be whipped
and killed because of Him. He didn't speak about any other
cross but of the suffering He would experience . . . As a result,
He gave them this encouragement: "Fear not them which kill
the body, but are not able to kill the soul; but rather fear Him
who is able to send both soul and body into hell." He urged
them to hold tightly to their professions of faith in Him. For
He promised to confess before His Father those who confess
His name before men. But He announced that He would
deny those who deny Him and would be ashamed of those
who were ashamed to confess allegiance to Him.

IRENAEUS

THE WORLD CRUCIFIED *to* US

MATTHEW 16:26 NLT
*"And how do you benefit if you gain the whole
world but lose your own soul in the process?
Is anything worth more than your soul?"*

If, then, we wish to be saved, let us lose our lives to the
world as those who have been crucified with Christ. For
our glory is in the cross of our Lord Jesus Christ. The world
is to be crucified to us and we to the world, so that we may
gain the salvation of our lives. This salvation begins when we
lose our lives for the sake of the Word. But if we think that
the salvation of our life (or the salvation in God and joy of
being with Him) is a blessed thing, then any loss of life
should be a good thing. For the sake of Christ, death must
precede the blessed salvation. Therefore, it seems to me that
according to the analogy of self-denial, we should all lose our
own lives. Let us all lose our own sinful lives, so that having
lost what is sinful, we can receive that which is saved by
righteousness. In no way will we profit from gaining the
whole world. . . . But when we have the choice, it is much
better to forfeit the world, and to gain our life by losing it
for Christ, than to gain the world by forfeiting our life.

ORIGEN

WHILE WE WERE STILL SINNERS

ROMANS 5:8 NRSV

*But God proves his love for us in that while
we still were sinners Christ died for us.*

The cross is the greatest event in the history of salvation, greater even than the resurrection. The cross is the victory, the resurrection, the triumph; but the victory is more important than the triumph, although the latter necessarily follows from it. The resurrection is the public display of the victory, the triumph of the Crucified One. But the victory itself was complete. "It is finished" (John 19:30).

The cross is the supreme evidence of the love of God. For there the Lord of all life gave up unto death His most Beloved, His only begotten Son, the Mediator and Heir of creation (Colossians 1:16; Hebrews 1:2–3). Christ the Lord died on the cross, He for Whom the stars circle in the ether and for Whom every gnat dances in the sunshine (Hebrews 2:10). Truly "in this God proves his love toward us, in that Christ died for us while we were still sinners" (Romans 5:8).

ERICH SAUER

NO ORDINARY COURAGE

———

ROMANS 6:6 NIV
*For we know that our old self was crucified with him
so that the body of sin might be done away with,
that we should no longer be slaves to sin.*

Those who have not denied themselves cannot follow Jesus. For choosing to follow Jesus and to actually follow Him springs from no ordinary courage. Those who deny themselves wipe out their former, wicked lives. For example, those who once were immoral deny their immoral selves and become self-controlled forever. . . . Those who have become righteous don't confess themselves but Christ. Those who find wisdom, because they possess wisdom, also confess Christ. And those who, "with the heart believe unto righteousness, and with the mouth make confession unto salvation," and testify for Christ's works by confessing them to others, will be confessed by Christ before His Father in heaven. . . . As a result, let every thought, every purpose, every word, and every action become a denial of ourselves and a testimony about Christ and in Christ. I am persuaded that the perfect person's every action is a testimony to Christ Jesus and that abstinence from every sin is a denial of self, leading to Christ. Those people are crucified with Christ. They take up their own crosses to follow Him who, for our sake, bears His own cross.

ORIGEN

WE ARE WINNERS

ROMANS 6:6 NKJV

Knowing this, that our old man was crucified with Him,
that the body of sin might be done away with,
that we should no longer be slaves of sin.

Part of our passion comes from the daily realization that *we are winners*. To the victor go the spoils, and we enjoy every benefit of the victory that was won on Calvary, when Christ defeated death. Now we need only surrender fully to Him and serve under His command. When we realize that our future is secured, that there is no way Satan can snatch us from God's hand, we take on the positive and exuberant spirit of champions.

But how exactly do we surrender? As we share in Christ's victory, we share in His crucifixion. As we become Christians, we are crucified with Him (see Romans 6:6; Galatians 2:20). That means all the self-defeating parts of us —the rebelliousness, the strife, the resentment, the selfishness, the slavery to our lusts—all these things are nailed to the cross with Christ. It is the sum of those evils, what we call the *old self,* that is crucified. Then as surely as Christ rose in perfect form on the third day, we rise again to walk in newness of life, in passion, and in the spirit of champions.

If only we could remember! If only we could surround ourselves with monuments and memorials—the Statue of True Liberty; the Tomb of the Unknown Sinner—to keep ourselves from forgetting, even for an instant, that we need no longer struggle with a defeated enemy.

DAVID JEREMIAH

EMPTY ME

ROMANS 6:6 NKJV

Knowing this, that our old man was crucified with Him,
that the body of sin might be done away with,
that we should no longer be slaves of sin.

Heaven knows, these works of crucifixion that ultimately free us to true life are not sought. Left to my own devices, I will conduct Calvary in my own self-interest, for the sake of displaying to others that I have done so, and thereby winning their approval. Such false humility is a blight on Christendom and characterizes too many of its leaders. It is a horror that leers at me. . . .

No. No, this must be a work of God, contrived by him, in his own timing and in his own way. My role, as I am instructed by the many who have gone before me, is to bow, to accept that this painful agony will be made into a good thing, to surrender to the perfect working of the will of my Maker though I cannot see the outcome. My role is to surrender and not fight against the wooden stake being pounded into the arrogance, the pettiness, the narcissism, the concentration upon my own achievements and abilities. My role is to pray, "Empty me. Empty me even of life if that is the way you can work your work in your way. I choose to trust that your plan for me is good."

KAREN MAINS

BANKING *on the* TRUTH

ROMANS 6:7 NLT
For when we died with Christ
we were set free from the power of sin.

Why do you believe that the Lord Jesus died? What is your ground for that belief? Is it that you *feel* He has died? No, you have never felt it. You believe it because the Word of God tells you so. When the Lord was crucified, two thieves were crucified at the same time. You do not doubt that they were crucified with Him, either, because the Scripture says so quite plainly.

You believe in the death of the Lord Jesus and you believe in the death of the thieves with Him. Now what about your own death? Your crucifixion is more intimate than theirs. They were crucified at the same time as the Lord but on different crosses, whereas you were crucified on the self same cross as He, for you were in Him when He died. How can you know? You can know for the one sufficient reason that God has said so. It does not depend on your feelings. . . . Let me tell you, You have died! You are done with! You are ruled out! The self you loathe is on the Cross in Christ. . . . This is the Gospel for Christians.

WATCHMAN NEE

THE GIFT of GOD

ROMANS 6:23 NRSV

*For the wages of sin is death, but the free gift
of God is eternal life in Christ Jesus our Lord.*

God is the judge. Since He is perfectly just, all His actions must serve the universal law of justice. We are like the prisoner. We all deserve the death sentence, because we are all guilty of numerous sins: "All have sinned and fall short of the glory of God." In His fairness, God must judge our sin with the harshest punishment. "The wages of sin is death." He cannot allow us to inhabit His perfect heaven, that place without a spot of uncleanness, a thought of wrongdoing, or a charge of guilt.

In the supreme act of mercy God displayed divine favor and forbearance to us guilty offenders. He took our punishment upon Himself. That is what Jesus Christ did for us at Calvary: "The gift of God is eternal life in Christ Jesus our Lord." By His sacrifice, all who put their trust in Him are declared "not guilty" and freed! That was true mercy and grace.

BILL BRIGHT

HE DID NOT SPARE HIS SON

ROMANS 8:32 NKJV

He who did not spare His own Son, but delivered Him up for us all, how shall He not with Him also freely give us all things?

If God rejoices over the little one that is found, how do you despise those God earnestly cares for? We should give up even our lives for one of these little ones. But are the lost ones weak and contemptible? Then it is even more important that we do everything we can to preserve them. Even Christ left the ninety-nine sheep and went after the one. He took advantage of the safety of so many to prevent the loss of one. Luke says that He even brought the lost one home on His shoulders. And "There was greater joy over one sinner that repenteth, than over ninety and nine just persons." By His leaving the saved ones for it, and by His taking more pleasure in this one, He showed how greatly He valued it. So then, don't be careless about such souls. . . . . For our neighbor's sake, don't refuse to do any of the tasks that seem lowly and trouble some. Although we have to do the service for someone small and shabby, although the work is hard and we must pass over mountains and valleys, endure everything for your neighbor's salvation. For a soul is so important to God that "He spared not His own Son."

CHRYSOSTOM

REMEMBER *the* CROSS

1 CORINTHIANS 2:2 NIV
*For I resolved to know nothing while I was
with you except Jesus Christ and him crucified.*

Be mindful of the duties which thou hast undertaken, and set always before thee the remembrance of the Crucified. Truly oughtest thou to be ashamed as thou lookest upon the life of Jesus Christ, because thou hast not yet endeavoured to conform thyself more unto Him, though thou hast been a long time in the way of God. A religious man who exercises himself seriously and devoutly in the most holy life and passion of our Lord shall find there abundantly all things that are profitable and necessary for him, neither is there need that he shall seek anything better beyond Jesus. Oh! If Jesus crucified would come into our hearts, how quickly, and completely should we have learned all that we need to know!

THOMAS À KEMPIS

THE WONDROUS CROSS

1 CORINTHIANS 2:2 NLT
*For I decided to concentrate only on
Jesus Christ and his death on the cross.*

When I survey the wondrous cross
On which the Prince of glory died,
My richest gain I count but loss,
And pour contempt on all my pride.

Forbid it, Lord, that I should boast,
Save in the death of Christ my God!
All the vain things that charm me most,
I sacrifice them to His blood.

See from His head, His hands, His feet,
Sorrow and love flow mingled down!
Did e'er such love and sorrow meet,
Or thorns compose so rich a crown?

ISAAC WATTS

THE TRUE PICTURE

---

1 CORINTHIANS 2:2 NKJV
*For I determined not to know anything among
you except Jesus Christ and Him crucified.*

Jesus Christ evokes many images in the minds of people. Some picture Him as a baby in a manger—the Christ of Christmas. Others picture Him as a child, perhaps living in the home of a carpenter or confounding the religious leaders of Jerusalem. Many picture Him as a compassionate and powerful healer who restored the sick and raised the dead. Still others picture a bold and fiery preacher speaking the Word of God to great crowds. And there are those who see Him as the consummate man—a model of goodness, kindness, sympathy, concern, care, tenderness, forgiveness, wisdom, and understanding.

Yet the one image of Christ that surpasses all the rest is Jesus Christ on the cross. To know Christ crucified is to know Him as the author and finisher of your faith—the truest picture of His person and work.

Christ's suffering on the cross is the focal point of the Christian faith. That's where His deity, humanity, work, and suffering are most clearly seen

JOHN MACARTHUR

CRUCIFIXION MEANS . . .

GALATIANS 2:20 NIV

I have been crucified with Christ and I no longer live, but Christ lives in me. The life I live in the body, I live by faith in the Son of God, who loved me and gave himself for me.

Studying the Crucifixion accounts in the gospel has become a way for me to keep vigilance over my soul during times of fearful destruction. Exercising a blind sort of faith, I have chosen to trust that eventually something new and remarkable would be rebuilt by God. . . .

This is my litany of learning:

Crucifixion means being betrayed by people who are trusted, being abandoned by those most counted on and loved.

This was what it was like for you, Lord Christ. Help me, like you, to submit to the meaning of this pain.

Crucifixion means being pinioned to pain that lasts long enough to do the work of God only this kind of suffering is able to do.

This was what it was like for you, Lord Christ. Help me, like you, to submit to the meaning of this pain.

Crucifixion means feeling a silence on the part of God that makes it seem as though he is not present, as though, indeed, he has abandoned us.

This was what it was like for you, Lord Christ. Help me, like you, to submit to the meaning of this pain.

(continued)

KAREN MAINS

Crucifixion Means . . .

GALATIANS 2:20 NIV
*I have been crucified with Christ and I no longer live, but
Christ lives in me. The life I live in the body, I live by faith
in the Son of God, who loved me and gave himself for me.*

(continued from previous page)

Crucifixion means being stripped of all those things we hold dear and from which we gain our identity, being stripped to the point of nakedness.

This was what it was like for you, Lord Christ. Help me, like you, to submit to the meaning of this pain.

Crucifixion means enduring a period of bruising, beating, and battering, to which we bow with our own silence and acceptance.

This was what it was like for you, Lord Christ. Help me, like you, to submit to the meaning of this pain.

Crucifixion means entering into a profound aloneness; people can stand beside us, but they cannot truly experience our suffering.

This was what it was like for you, Lord Christ. Help me, like you, to submit to the meaning of this pain.

Crucifixion means undergoing a gathering of the powers of darkness against us, and in our frailty being unsure of the ultimate outcome.

This was what it was like for you, Lord Christ. Help me, like you, to submit to the meaning of this pain.

KAREN MAINS

NO GREATER BLESSING

GALATIANS 2:20 NIV
*I have been crucified with Christ and I no longer live, but
Christ lives in me. The life I live in the body, I live by faith
in the Son of God, who loved me and gave himself for me.*

If a single sin is so awful that you think it's safer not even
to aim for a holy life, how much more awful it is for an
entire life to practice sin, and remain absolutely ignorant of
the purer way! How can you, in your indulgent life, obey the
Crucified? . . . How can you obey Paul when he urges you
"to present your body a living sacrifice, holy, acceptable unto
God," when you are conformed to this world," and not
transformed by renewing your mind? How can you do this
when you aren't "walking" in this "newness of life," but still
pursue the routine of "the old man"? . . . Does all this seem
insignificant to you—being crucified with Christ, presenting
yourself as a sacrifice to God, becoming a priest to the most
high God, making yourself worthy for the Almighty to look
upon? What greater blessings can we imagine for you, if you
make light of the consequences of these things? For the con-
sequence of being crucified with Christ is that we will live
with Him, be glorified with Him, and reign with Him.

GREGORY OF NYSSA

LEAVE YOUR WORRIES *at the* CROSS

GALATIANS 5:24 NIV
Those who belong to Christ Jesus have crucified
the sinful nature with its passions and desires.

What do we do with these worries? Take your anxieties to the cross—literally. Next time you're worried about your health or house or finances or flights, take a mental trip up the hill. Spend a few moments looking again at the pieces of passion.

Run your thumb over the tip of the spear. Balance a spike in the palm of your hand. Read the wooden sign written in your own language. And as you do, touch the velvet dirt, moist with the blood of God.

Blood he bled for you.

The spear he took for you.

The nails he felt for you.

The sign he left for you.

He did all of this for you. Knowing this, knowing all he did for you there, don't you think he'll look out for you here?

MAX LUCADO

LIVING *on the* CROSS

GALATIANS 6:14 NRSV

*May I never boast of anything except the cross
of our Lord Jesus Christ, by which the world has
been crucified to me, and I to the world.*

I f we desire that there be no boasting except in the cross,
then we must live near the cross—indeed we must live on
the cross. This is shocking. But this is what Galatians 6:14 says:
"Far be it from me to boast except in the cross of our Lord
Jesus Christ, *by which the world has been crucified to me, and I to
the world.*" Boasting *in* the cross happens when you are *on* the
cross. Is that not what Paul says? "The world has been crucified to me, and I [have been crucified] to the world." The
world is dead to me, and I am dead to the world. Why?
Because I have been crucified. We learn to boast in the cross
and exult in the cross when we are on the cross. And until our
selves are crucified there, our boast will be in ourselves. . . .

When Christ died, we died. The glorious meaning of
the death of Christ is that when he died, all those who are his
died in him. The death that he died for us all becomes our
death when we are united to Christ by faith (Romans 6:5).

JOHN PIPER

WELCOME! SINNER, COME!

EPHESIANS 3:12 NLT

Because of Christ and our faith in him, we can now come fearlessly into God's presence, assured of his glad welcome.

From the cross uplifted high,
Where the Savior deigns to die,
What melodious sounds we hear,
Bursting on the ravished ear!
"Love's redeeming work is done—
Come and welcome! sinner, come!"

Sprinkled now with blood the throne;
Why beneath thy burdens groan?
On My piercèd body laid,
Justice owns the ransom paid:
Bow the knee, and kiss the Son,
Come and welcome, sinner, come. . . .

Soon the days of life shall end—
Lo, I come—your Savior, Friend!
Safe your spirit to convey
To the realms of endless day,
Up to My eternal home—
Come and welcome! sinner, come!

THOMAS HAWEIS

PRESS ON

PHILIPPIANS 2:8 NIV

And being found in appearance as a man, he humbled himself and became obedient to death—even death on a cross!

Our Savior was crucified for our sakes so that by His death He could give us life, train us, and motivate us to endure. I press on towards Him and to the Father and the Holy Spirit. I work hard to be found faithful and consider myself unworthy of worldly goods. . . . Think about all these things in your heart. Follow them with passion. As you have been commanded, fight for truth to the point of death. For Christ was "obedient" even "unto death." The Apostle Paul says, "Take heed lest there be in any of you an evil heart . . . in departing from the living God. But exhort one another . . . (and edify one another) while it is called to-day." Today means our entire lifetime. If you live like this, beloved, you will save yourself. You will make me glad and you will glorify God forever.

BASIL

THE SAVIOR BLEEDS

COLOSSIANS 1:14 NLT
God has purchased our freedom with
his blood and has forgiven all our sins.

Alas! And did my Savior bleed,
and did my sovereign die?
Would he devote that sacred head
for sinners such as I?

Was it for crimes that I have done,
he groaned upon the tree?
Amazing pity, grace unknown,
and love beyond degree!

Well might the sun in darkness hide,
and shut its glories in,
When Christ, and mighty Maker,
died for his own creature's sin.

Thus might I hide my blushing face
while his dear cross appears;
Dissolve my heart in thankfulness,
and melt mine eyes to tears.

Bur drops of grief can ne'er repay
the debt of love I owe;
Here, Lord, I give myself away;
'tis all that I can do.

ISAAC WATTS

UNFATHOMABLE MERCY

COLOSSIANS 1:22 NIV
*But now he has reconciled you by Christ's physical
body through death to present you holy in his sight,
without blemish and free from accusation.*

What we see, then, in the drama of the cross is not three actors but two, ourselves on the one hand and God on the other. Not God as he is in himself (the Father), but God nevertheless, God-made-man-in-Christ (the Son). Hence the importance of those New Testament passages which speak of the death of Christ as the death of God's Son: for example, "God so loved the world that he gave his one and only Son", "he . . . did not spare his own Son", and "we were reconciled to God through the death of his Son." For in giving his Son he was giving himself. This being so, it is the Judge himself who in holy love assumed the role of the innocent victim, for in and through the person of his Son he himself bore the penalty which he himself inflicted. As Dale put it, "the mysterious unity of the Father and the Son rendered it possible for God at once to endure and to inflict penal suffering." There is neither harsh injustice nor unprincipled love nor Christological heresy in that; there is only unfathomable mercy. For in order to save us in such a way as to satisfy himself, God through Christ substituted himself for us.

JOHN R. W. STOTT

NAILING DOWN REDEMPTION

COLOSSIANS 2:13–14 NIV

When you were dead in your sins and in the uncircumcision
of your sinful nature, God made you alive with Christ. He
forgave us all our sins, having canceled the written code,
with its regulations, that was against us and that stood
opposed to us; he took it away, nailing it to the cross.

Nothing was accidental about the cross of Christ. The
Son of God was not suddenly overcome by the wickedness of man and nailed to a cross. Quite the contrary, the cross
was the means by which the Son of God overcame the
wickedness of man. To secure the keys to the house of David
and open the door of salvation to all who would enter, God
drove His Son like a nail in a sure place. A firm place. An
enduring place.

As horrendous as the pounding hammer sounds to our
spiritual ears, Colossians 2:13–14 says that while we were
dead in our sins, God made us alive with Christ. . . .

I will never fully grasp how such human atrocities
occurred at the free will of humanity while God used them
to unfold His perfect, divine, and redemptive plan. Christ was
nailed to the cross as the one perfect human. He was the fulfillment of the law in every way. When God drove His Son
like a nail in a firm place, He took the written code, finally
fulfilled in His Son, and canceled our debt to it. With every
pound of the hammer, God was nailing down redemption.

BETH MOORE

THE THRONE *of* GRACE

HEBREWS 4:16 NIV
*Let us then approach the throne of grace with
confidence, so that we may receive mercy and find
grace to help us in our time of need.*

Because of who God is and what Jesus Christ has done in dying for us, changing the throne of judgment into a throne of grace, we who trust Christ are to draw near the throne of grace in confidence. If we came in our own merit, we could have no confidence at all. The throne of God would be a place of terror. But since God has done what was needed to take away all judgment for our sin, it is now sin for us to come in any other way but with confidence. If we come in confidence, we can come knowing that God will do exactly what the author of Hebrews says he will do and we will indeed "find grace to help us in our time of need."

Whatever our need may be! Do you seek forgiveness for sin? You will find God's grace forgiving you for every sin. Do you need strength for daily living? You will find the grace of God providing strength. Do you need comfort because of some great loss? God will provide comfort. Direction for some important decision? You will receive direction. Encouragement? You will receive encouragement. Wisdom? That too.

JAMES MONTGOMERY BOICE

SATISFACTION THROUGH SUBSTITUTION

HEBREWS 7:27 NRSV

Unlike the other high priests, he has no need to offer sacrifices day after day, first for his own sins, and then for those of the people; this he did once for all when he offered himself.

We strongly reject, therefore, every explanation of the death of Christ which does not have at its centre the principle of "satisfaction through substitution," indeed divine self-satisfaction through divine self-substitution. The cross was not a commercial bargain with the devil, let alone one which tricked and trapped him; nor an exact equivalent, a *quid pro quo* to satisfy a code of honour or technical point of law; nor a compulsory submission by God to some moral authority above him from which he could not otherwise escape; nor a punishment of a meek Christ by a harsh and punitive Father; nor a procurement of salvation by a loving Christ from a mean and reluctant Father; nor an action of the Father which bypassed Christ as Mediator. Instead, the righteous, loving Father humbled himself to become in and through his only Son flesh, sin and a curse for us, in order to redeem us without compromising his own character. The theological words "satisfaction" and "substitution" need to be carefully defined and safeguarded, but they cannot in any circumstances be given up. The biblical gospel of atonement is of God satisfying himself by substituting himself for us.

JOHN R. W. STOTT

THE NEED *for the* BLOOD

HEBREWS 9:22 NKJV
*And according to the law almost all things are purified with
blood, and without shedding of blood there is no remission.*

You must be saved by God's plan. It was love that prompt-
ed God to send His Son to save us and shed His blood.
That was the plan. And without the blood what hope have
you? There is not a sin from your childhood—from your cradle—up till now that can be forgiven, unless by the blood.
Let us take God at His word: "Without the shedding of
blood there is no remission of sins." Without the blood no
remission whatever. I don't see how a man can fail to comprehend this. That's what Christ died for; that's what Christ
died on Calvary for. If a man makes light of that blood what
hope has he? How are you going to get into the kingdom of
God? You cannot join in the song of the saints if you don't
go into Heaven that way. . . . You must accept the plan of
redemption and come in through it.

DWIGHT L. MOODY

THE DIVINE MYSTERY *of* THAT CROSS

1 PETER 2:24 NRSV
He himself bore our sins in his body on the cross,
so that, free from sins, we might live for righteousness;
by his wounds you have been healed.

O the divine mystery of that cross! Weakness hangs on it, power is freed by it, evil is nailed to it, and triumphal trophies are raised toward it. One saint said: "Pierce my flesh with nails for fear of Thee." He doesn't mean nails of iron, but of fear and faith. For the chains of righteousness are stronger than those of punishment. Peter's faith bound him when he followed the Lord as far as the high priest's hall. No person had bound him and punishment didn't free him since his faith bound him. Again, when Peter was bound by the Jews, prayer freed him. Punishment didn't hold him because he hadn't turned from Christ.

Do you also crucify sin so that you can die to sin? Those who die to sin live to God. Do you live for Him who didn't even spare His own Son so that He could crucify our sins in His body? For Christ died for us that we could live in His revived body. Therefore, our guilt and not our life died in Him who, it is said, "bare our sins in His own body on the tree; that being set free from our sins we might live in righteousness, by the wound of whose stripes we are healed."

AMBROSE

THE BURDEN GONE

1 PETER 2:24 NRSV
*He himself bore our sins in his body on the cross,
so that, free from sins, we might live for righteousness;
by his wounds you have been healed.*

Then I saw in my dream, that Christian asked him further if he could not help him off with his burden that was upon his back. For as yet he had not got rid thereof, nor could he by any means get it off without help.

He told him, "As to thy burden, be content to bear it until thou comest to the place of deliverance; for there it will fall from thy back of itself." . . .

Now I saw in my dream that the highway up which Christian was to go was fenced on either side with a wall that was called Salvation. Up this way, therefore, did burdened Christian run, but not without great difficulty, because of the load on his back.

He ran thus till he came to a place somewhat ascending; and upon that place stood a cross, and a little below, in the bottom, a sepulchre. So I saw in my dream, that just as Christian came up with the cross, his burden loosed from off his shoulders, and fell from off his back, and began to tumble, and so continued to do till it came to the mouth of the sepulchre, where it fell in, and I saw it no more.

JOHN BUNYAN

THE GATEWAY

REVELATION 13:8 KJV
The Lamb slain from the foundation of the world.

The Cross of Jesus is the revelation of God's judgment on sin. Never tolerate the idea of martyrdom about the Cross of Jesus Christ. The Cross was a superb triumph in which the foundations of hell were shaken. There is nothing more certain in Time or Eternity than what Jesus Christ did on the Cross: He switched the whole of the human race back into a right relationship with God. . . .

The Cross did not *happen* to Jesus: He came on purpose for it. He is "the Lamb slain from the foundation of the world." The whole meaning of the Incarnation is the Cross. . . .

The Cross is the exhibition of the nature of God, the gateway whereby any individual of the human race can enter into union with God. When we get to the Cross, we do not go through it; we abide in the life to which the Cross is the gateway.

The centre of salvation is the Cross of Jesus, and the reason it is so easy to obtain salvation is because it cost God so much. The Cross is the point where God and sinful man merge with a crash and the way to life is opened—but the crash is on the heart of God.

OSWALD CHAMBERS

SIX HOURS

MARK 15:42 NLT
*This all happened on Friday, the day of preparation,
the day before the Sabbath. As evening approached. . .*

Six hours on one Friday. Six hours that jut up on the plain of human history like Mount Everest in a desert. Six hours that have been deciphered, dissected, and debated for two thousand years.

What do these six hours signify? They claim to be the door in time through which eternity entered man's darkest caverns. They mark the moments that the Navigator descended into the deepest waters to leave anchor points for his followers.

What does that Friday mean?

For the life blackened with failure, that Friday means forgiveness.

For the heart scarred with futility, that Friday means purpose.

And for the soul looking into this side of the tunnel of death, that Friday means deliverance.

Six hours. One Friday.

What do *you* do with those six hours on that Friday?

MAX LUCADO

JESUS SPEAKS
from the CROSS

"It is finished."
JOHN 19:30 NIV

JESUS SPEAKS *from the* CROSS

Crucifixion was a lonely, painful, gruesome way to die. The method must have been designed in hell. It killed . . . slowly and with agony. In fact, it often prolonged life longer than pain could be felt. Victims would simply go into shock and remain barely alive, breathing by unconscious will. At this point, the executioners had an effective practice. They broke the legs of the condemned and swiftly caused them to die.

During those hours of excruciating suffering, Jesus made several statements. His words were brief. Certain physical aspects of crucifixion insured that no long speeches were made. Breathing was very difficult. Jesus' crucified companions quickly became silent. But He had some important things to say.

Most of us will agree that a person's comments at the door of eternity deserve special attention— how much more the final words of Jesus from the cross. Seven times He spoke. We will ponder each of those sayings.

STAND *at the* CROSS

LUKE 23:35 NLT
The crowd watched.

Where do you stand when you look at the cross? The impact of Jesus' final hours on our imagination depends on our perspective. Do we approach the cross in derision and doubt or do we come near to its base in humble adoration and gratitude? Do we stand back in fear or despair, sharing the incredulity of those who expected one thing from the Lord and got something else they didn't quite understand? Or do we stand back in awe, continually amazed by the significance of God the Son's suffering?

Deliberately changing our place of view can alter and improve our understanding of the cross. Drawing near or back can help us see the cross in new light. One dimension open to our imagination puts us above the cross, viewing events and people from God's perspective. We note, for instance, that Jesus' statements move out in concentric circles, beginning with the soldiers at his feet and moving outward to reach the finish line. Alter your position and you will alter your perspectives of the cross. This is literally crucial meditation and worship.

NEIL WILSON

FORGIVING YOUR ENEMIES

LUKE 23:34 NIV
*"Father, forgive them, for they
do not know what they are doing."*

We must remember the value of right belief. It is profitable for me to know that Christ bore my diseases and submitted Himself to my lusts for my sake. He became sin and a curse for me—for everyone, that is. He was humbled and became a servant for me. He is the Lamb, the Vine, the Rock, the Servant, and the Son of a handmaid for me. He doesn't know the Day of Judgment, but, for my sake, is ignorant of the day and hour. . . . What a glorious remedy—to have comfort in Christ! For He bore these things with enormous patience for our sakes—so we definitely can't bear them just for the glory of His name with common patience! Who wouldn't learn to forgive their enemies when they see that, even on the cross, Christ prayed for those who persecuted Him? Don't you see that the weaknesses of Christ's are your strength? So why do you ask Him about remedies for us? His tears wash us and His weeping cleanses us. . . . But if you begin to doubt, you will despair. For the greater the insult, the greater gratitude is due.

AMBROSE

Praying *for* Enemies

LUKE 23:34 KJV
Father, forgive them; for they know not what they do.

What is perfection of love? To love even our enemies and to love them so that they might become fellow Christians. For love shouldn't be fleshly. To wish people temporal, physical well-being is good. But when this fails, hope that their souls are safe. Do you wish life for your friend? You do well. Do you rejoice at your enemy's death? You do evil. However, even the life you wish for your friends may not be good for them. And the death of your enemies you rejoice over may have been for the good of them. It is uncertain whether this present life will be profitable or unprofitable for someone, but, without doubt, life with God is profitable. So love your enemies by wishing that they become Christians. Love your enemies so that they might fellowship with you. For Christ loved this way and, while hanging on the cross, said, "Father, forgive them, for they know not what they do." He didn't say, "Father, let them live long. Even though they kill Me, let them live." He was taking eternal death from them by His merciful prayer and by His supreme strength. . . . Therefore, if you have learned to pray for your enemy, you walk in the way of the Lord.

AUGUSTINE

REMEMBER HIM

LUKE 23:34 KJV
Father, forgive them; for they know not what they do.

Y ou have heard an insult, like the wind. You are like a wave.
When the wind blows, and the swells, the ship is then
endangered, the heart is in jeopardy, and the heart is tossed
back and forth. When you were insulted, you longed for
revenge. But if you have been avenged and so rejoice in the
person's pain, you have suffered shipwreck. Why is this?
Because Christ is asleep in you. What does it mean that Christ
is asleep in you? That you have forgotten Christ. Rouse Him
then. Call Christ to mind and let Him wake up in you. Pay
attention to Him. What do you want? Revenge. Have you
forgotten that, when He was being crucified, Christ said,
"Father, forgive them, for they know not what they do?" The
one who was sleeping in your heart didn't want revenge.
Wake Him up then. Remember Him. Remember Him
through His word, for He commands us to remember Him.
Then if Christ wakes up in you, you will say, "What kind of
person am I who wants revenge? Who am I to threaten other
people? I might die before I am avenged, . . . therefore, I will
restrain my anger and return to a calm heart." For when
Christ commanded the sea, peace was restored.

AUGUSTINE

SUCH LOVE

LUKE 23:34 NASB
*"Father, forgive them; for they
do not know what they are doing."*

Of all the scenes around the cross, this one angers me the
most. What kind of people, I ask myself, would mock
a dying man? . . .

The words thrown that day were meant to wound. And
there is nothing more painful than words meant to hurt. . . .

But I'm not telling you anything new. No doubt you've
had your share of words that wound. You've felt the sting of
a well-aimed gibe. Maybe you're still feeling it. Someone you
love or respect slams you to the floor with a slur or slip of
the tongue. And there you lie, wounded and bleeding.
Perhaps the words were intended to hurt you, perhaps not;
but that doesn't matter. The wound is deep. . . .

Did you see what Jesus did not do? He did not retaliate. . .

Did you see what Jesus did do? . . . He . . . spoke on their
defense. "Father, forgive them; for they do not know what
they are doing." . . .

Never, never have I seen such love.

MAX LUCADO

INCARNATE FORGIVENESS

LUKE 23:34 NASB
"Forgive them."

The cross tilted skyward and then slid into the worn hole in the rocky forehead called Calvary. The jolt sent fire through limbs just pierced. Further agony followed as the soldiers drove wedges between stone and timber to keep the crucifix upright.

With his first breath Jesus exhaled words we find incredible in that setting and hard to believe when we hear them applied to us. And yet, those words shouldn't surprise us. Jesus always looked through forgiving eyes. Confronted with a lame man dropped through a ceiling by desperate friends, Jesus responded with forgiveness, the deepest healing. Approached by his cross-companion with a helpless, humble plea, "Remember me," Jesus answered with assured forgiveness. Jesus is God's incarnate forgiveness. How could he not forgive and ask his Father to forgive those who unwittingly helped him accomplish forgiveness?

NEIL WILSON

YOUR VALUE

LUKE 23:43 NIV
"I tell you the truth, today you will be with me in paradise."

Now why did Jesus do that? What in the world did he have to gain by promising this desperado a place of honor at the banquet table? What in the world could this chiseling quisling ever offer in return? . . . Nothing!

That's the point. Listen closely. Jesus' love does not depend upon what we do for him. Not at all. In the eyes of the King, you have value simply because you are. You don't have to look nice or perform well. Your value is inborn.

Period.

Think about that for just a minute. You are valuable just because you exist. Not because of what you do or what you have done, but simply because you are. Remember that. Remember that the next time you are left bobbing in the wake of someone's steamboat of ambition. Remember that the next time some trickster tries to hang a bargain-basement price tag on your self-worth. The next time someone tries to pass you off as a cheap buy, just think about the way Jesus honors you . . . and smile.

MAX LUCADO

HOPE *of* PARADISE

LUKE 23:43 NASB
And He said to him, "Truly I say to you,
today you shall be with Me in Paradise."

What follows crucifixion? Paradise! Fellowship with the faithful of God, with those who have believed, who have persevered, who have held "fast the beginning of our assurance firm until the end" (Hebrews 3:14). Jesus' second statement from the cross was the promise of Paradise to one of the malefactors being crucified with Him. "And He said to him, 'Truly I say to you, today you shall be with Me in Paradise' " (Luke 23:43).

All suffering has an end. To those who believe on Jesus, it has a beginning and it has an end. It will not go on forever because it is controlled by the Alpha and the Omega. The end for every believer is Paradise, and Paradise belongs to God. It is the reward of those who overcome: "To him who overcomes, I will grant to eat of the tree of life, which is in the Paradise of God" (Revelation 2:7). Isn't that beautiful?

What do we need in the midst of suffering? Hope! The hope of glory, of life, of fellowship with Jesus! And what do we need to convey to others as we hang there suffering? We need to convey the reality and glory of the sure hope of heaven.

KAY ARTHUR

TODAY

LUKE 23:43 NLT
*And Jesus replied, "I assure you,
today you will be with me in paradise."*

Few of us get to know ahead of time the day we will pass from time into eternity. The thief on the cross received that privilege, and an infinitely greater gift of an unexpected destination—Paradise. While deathbed conversions aren't the norm and shouldn't be the plan, Jesus' assurance raises at least one large question: How was the thief transformed from a sinner on the way to eternal separation from God into a traveler destined for eternal fellowship with God? What did he do to be saved?

To ears accustomed to a very precise and measured (even canned) vocabulary of salvation, the thief's words may sound unsophisticated and incomplete: "Jesus, remember me when you come into your Kingdom." This is nothing like the traditional "sinner's prayer." Yet Jesus accepted it as repentance and faith. The man recognized his sinful condition and Jesus' unique role as King. He didn't assume forgiveness; he asked. Jesus responded with a wholehearted royal reprieve. The Lord commuted this sinner's sentence of eternal punishment onto his own impending death. Further interaction could wait until Paradise.

NEIL WILSON

HERE IS YOUR SON

JOHN 19:26 NIV
When Jesus saw his mother there, and the
disciple whom he loved standing nearby, he said
to his mother, "Dear woman, here is your son."

It was to this godly mother that Jesus turned in His dying hour. His last thoughts were of her, not with any thought of being comforted by her as she had often done when He was a child, but of her pain, and of her future once He was gone. His heart was a heart of flesh and His chivalrous manhood would not permit Him to forget the one who had brought Him into the world. Thus, "from the pulpit of the cross, Jesus preaches to all ages a sermon on the Fifth Commandment." . . .

In the midst of all Jesus was enduring in that dread hour He thought of her, who had been the guardian of His childhood and youth, and gave her as the inestimable legacy of love to His much-loved John. The injunction is to comfort widows in their affliction, and Mary was much afflicted as she stood by the cross—perhaps the only one of the family to witness the death of her son, she must have been greatly comforted as He makes every provision for her future security. The love, providing salvation by the cross was not unmindful of the material provision a bereaved widowed mother would need.

HERBERT LOCKYER

WHAT KIND *of* GOD?

JOHN 19:26–27 NLT
*When Jesus saw his mother standing there beside
the disciple he loved, he said to her, "Woman, he is your
son." And he said to this disciple, "She is your mother."
And from then on this disciple took her into his home.*

Mary is older now. The hair at her temples is gray.
Wrinkles have replaced her youthful skin. Her hands
are calloused. She has raised a houseful of children. And now
she beholds the crucifixion of her firstborn. . . .

Question: What kind of God would put people through
such agony? What kind of God would give you families and
then ask you to leave them? What kind of God would give
you friends and then ask you to say goodbye?

Answer: A God who knows that the deepest love is
built not on passion and romance but on a common mission
and sacrifice.

Answer: A God who knows that we are only pilgrims
and that eternity is so close that any "Goodbye" is in reality
a "See you tomorrow."

Answer: A God who did it himself.

John fastened his arm around Mary a little tighter. Jesus
was asking him to be the son that a mother needs and that
in some ways he never was.

Jesus looked at Mary. His ache was from a pain far
greater than that of the nails and thorns. In their silent glance
they again shared a secret. And he said goodbye.

MAX LUCADO

TAKE CARE *of* HER

JOHN 19:26–27 NASB
"Woman, behold, your son! . . . Behold, your mother!"

Jesus must have had many interesting conversations with his mother, but we are privy to only three of them. Each of these exchanges involved their unique relationship—he as eternal Son of God, she as mother of God. Their interaction was understandably complicated.

In Luke 2:50, Jesus gently corrected Mary's frantic declaration of concern by reminding her that she "should have known I would be in my Father's house." In the prelude of Jesus' first miracle during the wedding in Cana (John 2:1–12), Mary voiced a leading concern to Jesus, "They have no more wine." Jesus' response reminded his mother that her priorities were not necessarily his. Her agreement gave him the freedom to act.

Among Jesus' final tasks in life, he saw to his mother's care. He entrusted Mary and John to each other as mother-son. A sad tone of separation colors the term "woman" and highlights Jesus' loving transfer of his mother's allegiance from him to John, whom he also particularly loved. The universal effectiveness of Jesus' ministry as Messiah receives delightful confirmation in the way that he undertook for the common, human, and necessary duties of genuine living. His divinity shined clearly through matchless humanity.

NEIL WILSON

FAMILY *of* BELIEVERS

JOHN 19:26–27 NKJV

When Jesus therefore saw His mother, and the disciple whom
He loved standing by, He said to His mother, "Woman, behold
your son!" Then He said to the disciple, "Behold your mother!"
And from that hour that disciple took her to his own home.

Our Lord emphasized the human family, but even more He emphasized the spiritual *family* of God. The genuine and abiding relationship is not that of the flesh, but of the Spirit. As wonderful as earthly relationships are, there is a more intimate relationship between the children of God. John, as a believer, was a better choice to care for Jesus' mother than His brothers and sisters who did not believe.

Jesus brought into being the brotherhood of believers. He created a new society that is not segregated by race or nationality nor predicated upon social standing or economic power. It consists of those whose faith meets at the cross and whose experience of forgiveness flows from it. Jesus commended His own mother into the hands of a brother. At Golgotha that terrible day, Christ called upon a brother in the family of faith to minister to someone in need. That is still part of His call to those in God's family.

DAVID JEREMIAH

FORSAKEN

MATTHEW 27:46 NRSV
*And about three o'clock Jesus cried with a loud voice,
"Eli, Eli, lema sabachthani?" that is, "My God,
my God, why have you forsaken me?"*

Throned upon the awful tree,
Lamb of God, Your grief I see.
Darkness veils Your anguished face;
None its lines of woe can trace.
None can tell what pangs unknown
Hold You silent and alone.

Silent through those three dread hours,
Wrestling with the evil powers,
Left alone with human sin,
Gloom around You and within,
'Til the appointed time is nigh,
'Til the Lamb of God may die.

Hark, that cry that peals aloud
Upward through the whelming cloud!
You, the Father's only Son,
You, His own anointed One,
You are asking "can it be"
"Why have You forsaken Me?"

JOHN ELLERTON

THAT WE MIGHT NOT BE FORSAKEN

MARK 15:34 NRSV
At three o'clock Jesus cried out with a loud voice,
"Eloi, Eloi, lema sabachthani?" which means,
"My God, my God, why have you forsaken me?"

God had forsaken Jesus. It was not His imagination! God had actually abandoned His Son, leaving Him in the throes of sin's awful death. Jesus had no recourse; He had no aid. In that one inexplicably horrendous moment, the Father and the Holy Spirit were estranged from the Son. . . .

The cry had been recorded a thousand years earlier when His agony was prophetically penned by the psalmist in Psalm 22. Written by the Word and read countless times by the Word who had become flesh! Now it was fulfilled and screamed into the ears of the Holy God who had to punish sin, for He who knew no sin was at that moment made to be sin for us. . . .

The hour had come, the eternal hour of destiny. Never before, never again would there be a time like it when God the Father and God the Spirit would forsake God the Son for the sake of mankind, who for the most part could care less! Yet He did it that we, who were dead, estranged from God, might live, never to be forsaken by Him.

KAY ARTHUR

COMPLETELY QUALIFIED

MARK 15:34 KJV
Why hast thou forsaken me?

Jesus "learned obedience through what he suffered," as the writer to the Hebrews says, in the sense that by his suffering he learned the cost of his wholehearted obedience to his Father. His acceptance of the cross crowned his obedience, and he was never more pleasing to the Father than in this act of total devotion; yet that does not diminish the reality of his experience of being God-forsaken. But this reality has made him the more effective as the deliverer and supporter of his people. He is no visitant from another world, avoiding too much involvement with this world of ours; he has totally involved himself in the human lot. There is no depth of dereliction known to human beings which he has not plumbed; by this means he has been "made perfect"—that is to say, completely qualified to be his people's sympathizing helper in their most extreme need. If they feel like crying to God, "Why hast thou forsaken me?", they can reflect that that is what he cried. When they call out of the depths to God, he who called out of the depths on Good Friday knows what it feels like. But there is this difference: he is with them now to strengthen them—no one was there to strengthen him.

F. F. BRUCE

WORDS WE WON'T NEED *to* SAY

MATTHEW 27:46 NLT
At about three o'clock, Jesus called out with a loud voice,
"Eli, Eli, lema sabachthani?" which means,
"My God, my God, why have you forsaken me?"

Jesus began his first and last statements from the cross with the same word—Father. What a sharp contrast with this low, center point in the crisis of the cross, when Jesus experienced the full depth and distance of separation from God as he took on himself the sins of mankind. Fully human, Jesus called out from the enclosing darkness of God's withdrawal. He did not, in that moment, address God as Father, but simply as "My God, my God." Jesus' identification with and substitution for humanity reached its devastating climax.

The gospel writers, choked and humbled by the significance, seem to have been compelled to record the words in Jesus' native dialect, as if the Aramaic had a particular poignancy in conveying the Lord's dereliction. The expression is so dear it deserved to be heard and felt even before it was understood. They included a translation.

But the leering crowds gathered that day misunderstood. The linguistic diversity of Jerusalem at Passover resulted in a low roar of speculation, guessing that Jesus meant to call Elijah for help. The mixed reaction was wrong on all counts. We now know that Jesus cried out those words so that we would never have to say them.

NEIL WILSON

GOD COULD NOT LOOK

PSALM 22:1 NKJV

My God, My God, why have You forsaken Me? Why are You so far from helping Me, and from the words of My groaning?

As Jesus hung there stained, saturated, and sin-laden, the Father refused to look at His Son. Why? Christ was bearing every vile, degrading vice that depraved human beings had ever committed or would ever commit. His body and soul were completely immersed with man's abominations. He bore the disobedience of Adam, the murderous act of Cain, the adultery of David, and the murders of the Christians by Saul of Tarsus. He bore every sin committed since the inception of history and every sin which will be committed until the world disintegrates by fire. . . .

Never in the annals of history had so much sin been carried at one time, and it was all carried by the sinless One. It was all upon the sinless, holy, God-man, Christ Jesus, and this is why the Father turned away from the voice of His Son as Christ took our place (see Psalm 22:1). God could not look upon the scene. Truly, it was our sin, our wickedness, our transgressions, our iniquities, and our abominations that turned God's face from the heartbreaking event.

JACK VAN IMPE

HE KNOWS HOW WE FEEL

JOHN 19:28 NIV

*Later, knowing that all was now completed, and so that the
Scripture would be fulfilled, Jesus said, "I am thirsty."*

Just at the right time we are reminded that the one to
whom we pray knows our feelings. He knows temptation.
He has felt discouraged. He has been hungry and sleepy and
tired. He knows what we feel like when the alarm clock goes
off. He knows what we feel like when our children want different things at the same time. He nods in understanding
when we pray in anger. He is touched when we tell him
there is more to do than can ever be done. He smiles when
we confess our weariness. . . .

"I'm thirsty." . . .

He wants us to remember that he, too, was human. He
wants us to know that he, too, knew the drone of the humdrum
and the weariness that comes with long days. He wants us to
remember that our trailblazer didn't wear bulletproof vests or
rubber gloves or an impenetrable suit of armor. No, he pio-
neered our salvation through the world that you and I face daily.

He is the King of Kings, the Lord of Lords, and the Word
of Life. More than ever he is the Morning Star, the Horn of
Salvation, and the Prince of Peace.

But there are some hours when we are restored by
remembering that God became flesh and dwelt among us.
Our Master knew what it meant to be a crucified carpenter
who got thirsty.

MAX LUCADO

THIRSTY

JOHN 19:28 NLT
*Jesus knew that everything was now finished,
and to fulfill the Scriptures he said, "I am thirsty."*

The physical aspects of the work of salvation were now done. Jesus had experienced on our behalf the utter separation between God and humanity created by sin. All that remained was the final victory over death by dying. Jesus expressed his current condition without expectation of relief. He was simply stating the fact of his exhaustion and thirst. The word probably came out as a croak. His body could barely sustain the life that burned within him. The dampened sponge that touched his lips served no other purpose than to fuel his final two utterances.

In a special way, Jesus experienced on the cross the truth of the fourth beatitude, the one that describes those who reach the place where "they are hungry and thirsty for justice." Jesus lived with that thirst, as real and as overwhelming as his dry, swollen tongue and his parched throat in that moment. And in every sense of the word, he knew he was about to be satisfied.

NEIL WILSON

IT IS FINISHED

JOHN 19:30 KJV

When Jesus therefore had received the vinegar, he said, It is finished: and he bowed his head, and gave up the ghost.

Now this word, which Christ employs, well deserves our attention; for it shows that the whole accomplishment of our salvation, and all the parts of it, are contained in his death. His resurrection is not separated from his death, but Christ only intends to keep our faith fixed on himself alone and not to allow it to turn aside in any direction whatever. The meaning therefore, is that everything which contributes to the salvation of men is to be found in Christ and ought not to be sought anywhere else—or (which amounts to the same thing) that the perfection of salvation is contained in him. There is also an implied contrast, for Christ contrasts his death with the ancient sacrifices and with all the figures. It is as if he had said, "Of all that was practiced under the Law, there was nothing that had any power in itself to make atonement for sins, to appease the wrath of God, and to obtain justification; but now the true salvation is exhibited and manifested to the world."

JOHN CALVIN

DIVINE DECREE

JOHN 19:30 NKJV

So when Jesus had received the sour wine, He said, "It is finished!" And bowing His head, He gave up His spirit.

The death of Jesus Christ is the fulfillment in history of the very mind and intent of God. There is no place for seeing Jesus Christ as a martyr. His death was not something that happened *to* Him—something that might have been prevented. His death was the very reason He came.

Never build your case for forgiveness on the idea that God is our Father and He will forgive us because He loves us. That contradicts the revealed truth of God in Jesus Christ. It makes the Cross unnecessary, and the redemption "much ado about nothing." God forgives sin only because of the death of Christ. God could forgive people in no other way than by the death of His Son, and Jesus is exalted as Savior because of His death. . . . The greatest note of triumph ever sounded in the ears of a startled universe was that sounded on the Cross of Christ—"*It is finished!*" (John 19:30). That is the final word in the redemption of humankind. . . .

Jesus Christ became a curse for us by divine decree. Our part in realizing the tremendous meaning of His curse is the conviction of sin. Conviction is given to us as a gift of shame and repentance; it is the great mercy of God. Jesus Christ hates the sin in people, and Calvary is the measure of His hatred.

OSWALD CHAMBERS

PAID *in* FULL

When he had received the drink, Jesus said, "It is finished."
With that, he bowed his head and gave up his spirit.

After Christ's sacrifice there would be no more need to shed blood. He "once for all took blood into that inner room, the Holy of Holies, and sprinkled it on the mercy seat; but it was not the blood of goats and calves. No, he took his own blood, and with it he, by himself, made sure of our eternal salvation" (Hebrews 9:12 TLB).

The Son of God became the Lamb of God, the cross became the altar, and we were "made holy through the sacrifice Christ made in his body once and for all time" (Hebrews 10:10).

What needed to be paid was paid. What had to be done was done. Innocent blood was required. Innocent blood was offered, once and for all time. Bury those five words deep in your heart. *Once and for all time.*

MAX LUCADO

A CRY *of* VICTORY

JOHN 19:30 NLT
"It is finished!"

After the writer of Hebrews compiled his list of great examples of faith, recorded in Hebrews 11, he abruptly changed the paradigm by making the heroes of faith into a "huge crowd of witnesses" watching from the grandstand of history (Hebrews 12:1). Now the spotlight shifts to "us" who are preparing to run. How do we run? "We do this by keeping our eyes on Jesus, on whom our faith depends from start to finish" (12:2). The writer goes on to describe Jesus' work on the cross: "He was willing to die a shameful death on the cross because of the joy he knew would be his afterward" (12:2).

Seeing the end or visualizing the completed effort offers only a taste of the moment of completion. Jesus' victorious cry echoed through creation, forever turning the tables on evil's dominion. His work was done; his goal, reached; his challenge, met; his purpose, achieved; his great battle, won. We can add nothing to our salvation, not simply because we are unable, but because he has already declared it complete—finished!

NEIL WILSON

HE GAVE IT UP

LUKE 23:46 KJV
And when Jesus had cried with a loud voice,
he said, Father, into thy hands I commend my spirit:
and having said thus, he gave up the ghost.

His death was different. It was a victorious death. He brought His spoil with Him. It was a vicarious death. It had no personal claim upon Him except as the representative of sinners. He was doing man's dying for him. It was a voluntary death. No man took His life from Him; He laid it down of Himself. The Record plainly says that He cried with a loud voice and gave up His spirit. He did not yield to death in weakness; He summoned death to serve Him! It is significant that the inspired writer does not say, "He died," but "He gave up the ghost." That is, "He breathed out His life," clearly indicating the voluntary nature of the act. . . .

The Prophet of the Cross was speaking the language of *security* when He said, "Father, into thy hands I commend my spirit." For there is no security except as we commit all into the hands of God. The greatest demonstration of this is the Cross.

The security of the hollow of God's hand is the safety that every heart craves. It defies curses, crucifixions, crosses. And Jesus announced the fact before He breathed out His life.

RUSSELL BRADLEY JONES

The Finish Line

Luke 23:46 NLT

Then Jesus shouted, "Father, I entrust my spirit into your hands!" And with those words he breathed his last.

The moment of death represents the ultimate loss of control. Until the moment he exhaled this final prayer, Jesus was actively carrying out a plan designed by God for the salvation of humanity. As he crossed the finish line, Jesus entrusted himself to the Father for resurrection and restoration to his divine state. He had previously emptied himself (see Philippians 2:7) in order to take on full humanity. He had allowed the Father to insert him in the human race as a tiny, helpless baby. He had carried out all the implications of his mission for humanity, up to and including the cross (Philippians 2:8). Now he entrusted himself to the Father once more.

Believers throughout history, led by Christ himself, have set the bar high for dying well. What better statement of confidence and faith can we declare at the moment of death or inform our families and friends long before we die, that we intend to commit our spirit into our Heavenly Father's hands for safekeeping? Jesus confidently invaded death with that declaration. Can we who trust him do any less?

Neil Wilson

WHEN IT IS TIME

LUKE 23:46 NIV
*Jesus called out with a loud voice, "Father,
into your hands I commit my spirit." When
he had said this, he breathed his last.*

Even with His dying breath, Jesus was still King. The one
who said that no man could take His life from Him died
at the appointed time and in the appointed way. In the Old
Testament the literal statement for the moment when the
Passover Lamb was to be killed was "between the evenings,"
which according to Jewish tradition was somewhere between three in the afternoon and six in the evening . . . Jesus
was crucified on the exact day that the Passover lambs were
being killed (John 18:28). At 3:00 P.M. He cried His last, fulfilling His role as "the Lamb of God, Who takes away the sin
of the world" (John 1:29). . . .

Jesus died according to the purposes of Divine Providence, not the whims of cowardly men. Just so, you and I
will die, not according to the will of cancer, not according to
the will of an erratic drunk cruising along the highway, not
according to the will of a painful disease. We will die under the
good hand of God's providential care. We will pass through
the curtain according to God's clock, not the time-table of
random fate.

ERWIN LUTZER

THE DEPTHS *of* HIS LOVE

MARK 15:37 NIV
With a loud cry, Jesus breathed his last.

Several hundred feet beneath my chair is a lake, an underground cavern of crystalline water known as the Edwards Aquifer. We South Texans know much about this aquifer. We know its length (175 miles). We know its layout (west to east, except under San Antonio, where it runs north to south). . . . But for all the facts we do know, there is an essential one we don't. We don't know its size. The depth of the cavern? A mystery. Number of gallons? Unmeasured. No one knows the amount of water the aquifer contains. . . . We use it, depend upon it, would perish without it, but measure it? We can't. . . .

Who has plumbed the depths of God's love? Only God has. "Want to see the size of my love?" he invites. "Ascend the winding path outside of Jerusalem. Follow the dots of bloody dirt until you crest the hill. Before looking up, pause and hear me whisper, 'This is how much I love you.'"

Whip-ripped muscles drape his back. Blood rivulets over his face. His eyes and lips are swollen shut. Pain rages at wildfire intensity. As he sinks to relieve the agony of his legs, his airway closes. At the edge of suffocation, he shoves pierced muscles against the spike and inches up the cross. He does this for hours. Painfully up and down until his strength and our doubts are gone.

Does God love you? Behold the cross and behold your answer.

MAX LUCADO

JESUS RISES
from the DEAD

---

*"Why do you look for the living among the
dead? He is not here; he has risen!"*

LUKE 24:5–6 NIV

JESUS RISES *from the* DEAD

The stone was rolled away from the mouth of Jesus' tomb for only one purpose: to let observers see that it was empty. Jesus had already left the premises. Rocks, wood, and masonry no longer limited Him. Those who came to honor His body experienced the shock and joy of worshiping Him alive. He is risen, indeed.

The bodily resurrection of Jesus Christ is the foundation of Christianity and the pivotal event in history. If that tomb had not been empty, yours would never be, either. Everything that Jesus said and did before He died on the cross put Him in a very special category among religious founders and teachers throughout history. But His resurrection from the dead puts Him in a category by Himself.

That tomb remains empty. What we believe will not change its condition. But what we believe about the One who vacated the tomb will make all the difference for us in this life and the next. Allow yourself the wonder of experiencing Resurrection Sunday once again as you read the next pages.

SATURDAY

JOHN 19:42 NLT
*And so, because it was the day of preparation
before the Passover and since the tomb was
close at hand, they laid Jesus there.*

The disciples who lived through . . . Friday and Sunday, learned that when God seems most absent he may be closest of all; when God looks most powerless he may be most powerful; when God looks most dead he may be coming back to life. They learned never to count God out. . . .

Good Friday and Easter Sunday are perhaps the most significant days on the entire church calendar, and yet, in a real sense, we live our lives on Saturday, the day in between. Can we trust that God can make something holy and beautiful and good out of a world that includes Bosnia and Rwanda and inner-city ghettoes in the richest nation on earth? Human history grinds on, between the time of promise and fulfillment. It's Saturday on planet Earth; will Sunday ever come?

Perhaps that is why the authors of the Gospels devoted so much space to Jesus' last week than to the several weeks when he was making resurrection appearances. They knew that the history to follow would often resemble Saturday, the in-between day, more than Sunday, the day of rejoicing. It is a good thing to remember that in the cosmic drama, we live out our days on Saturday, the day with no name.

PHILIP YANCEY

JOSEPH'S PRIVILEGE

MARK 15:42–47 NRSV

When he learned from the centurion that he was dead,
he granted the body to Joseph.

We are here attending the burial of our Lord Jesus. Oh that we may by grace be planted in the likeness of it! Joseph of Arimathea was one who waited for the kingdom of God. Those who hope for a share in its privileges, must own Christ's cause, when it seems to be crushed. This man God raised up for his service. There was a special providence, that Pilate should be so strict in his inquiry, that there might be no pretence to say Jesus was alive. Pilate gave Joseph leave to take down the body, and do what he pleased with it. Some of the women beheld where Jesus was laid, that they might come after the Sabbath to anoint the dead body, because they had not time to do it before. Special notice was taken of Christ's sepulchre, because he was to rise again. And he will not forsake those who trust in him, and call upon him. Death, deprived of its sting, will soon end the believer's sorrows, as it ended those of the Saviour.

MATTHEW HENRY

GUARDS *in the* GARDEN

MATTHEW 27:64 NIV

"So give the order for the tomb to be made secure until the third day. Otherwise, his disciples may come and steal the body and tell the people that he has been raised from the dead. This last deception will be worse than the first."

Nicodemus and Joseph brought a sack of myrrh and aloes and, along with spices and strips of cloth, they wrapped Jesus' body in keeping with Jewish custom. But His enemies were nervous. They went to Pilate and asked to have a guard placed around the tomb because they feared the body would be stolen by His disciples who would then claim that He had risen from the dead, just as He had declared He would.

This I find startling. Utterly startling! Jesus' enemies evidently knew what Jesus meant better than His own followers did. The disciples were hiding in fear of being arrested and sharing in Jesus' fate. But His enemies evidently understood that Jesus had said that He would rise again from the dead after three days. Often, those who reject the message have greater fears that there might be a haunting truth to it than those who claim to believe it. They took extra precautions to guard against it. However, they could not permanently fight off God.

RAVI ZACHARIAS

SEEKING *the* SAVIOR

MATTHEW 28:1 KJV
*In the end of the sabbath, as it began to dawn toward
the first day of the week, came Mary Magdalene
and the other Mary to see the sepulchre.*

She sought the Saviour very early in the morning. If thou
canst wait for Christ, and be patient in the hope of having fellowship with Him at some distant season, thou wilt
never have fellowship at all; for the heart that is fitted for
communion is a hungering and a thirsting heart. She sought
Him also with very great boldness. Other disciples fled from
the sepulchre, for they trembled and were amazed; but Mary,
it is said, "stood." If you would have Christ with you, seek
Him boldly. Let nothing hold you back. Defy the world.
Press on where others flee. She sought the Saviour only.
What cared she for angels, she turned herself back from
them; her search was only for her Lord. If Christ be your one
and only love, if your heart has cast out all rivals, you will not
long lack the comfort of His presence. Mary Magdalene
sought thus because she loved much. Let us arouse ourselves
to the same intensity of affection; let our heart, like Mary's,
be full of Christ, and our love, like hers, will be satisfied with
nothing short of Himself.

CHARLES HADDON SPURGEON

JOYFUL SAVIOR

MATTHEW 28:1 NRSV

After the sabbath, as the first day of the week was dawning,
Mary Magdalene and the other Mary went to see the tomb.

When Christians speak of Jesus as a "Man of Sorrows" who is "acquainted with grief," they are not describing His inner spiritual nature. Grief was something thrust upon our Lord by His opposition. It was flung at Him along with blows and curses. He did not exchange His joy for sorrow; the sorrow came from without. The joy remained within. All the hostility that built up against Him, all the conspiring that resulted in His betrayal, arrest, imprisonment, trial, conviction, sentencing, flogging, and crucifixion, did not change Jesus. If He became acquainted with grief, it was only to endure it.

Perhaps it has occurred to you to question why the figure of our Savior is so seldom depicted with a benign or joyful expression on His face. Traditionally He appears solemn and sad, and often in a state of extreme agony, both in sculpture and on canvas. For centuries the principal representation of our Lord that the world has known is a man hanging on a cross. It should be remembered that as horrible as the crucifixion was, and as momentous for our salvation as it proved to be, it was followed by the resurrection, in which the heavenly Father turned death and seeming defeat and despair into glorious victory.

SHERWOOD ELIOT WIRT

THE THIRD DAY

MARK 16:3 NIV
They asked each other, "Who will roll the stone away from the entrance of the tomb?"

A strong Roman guard was posted at the tomb, with the opening sealed and the soldiers standing there with spears. No one could steal the body.

Early on Easter morning, the two women coming to the tomb were bearing spices for His body. A desperate desire to do something for the person who is no longer in his or her body, drives loved ones to bring flowers or do *something* near the remains of the person's so recently alive body. In those days the spices gave a satisfying fulfillment of this natural desire. With no thought of expectation, or feelings of hope, they dejectedly walked toward the tomb, only to find—empty! The stone was rolled away, the body was not there! It was two men in "shining garments"—obviously angels, sent as angels who had been sent to announce His coming to Mary thirty-three years before, who now told the women that the One for whom they were looking among the dead, was not dead, but *alive*. "He is not here, but is risen: remember how he spake unto you when ye was yet in Galilee, saying the Son of man must be delivered into the hands of sinful men, and be crucified, and the *third* day rise again."

Then they remembered.

EDITH SCHAEFFER

CHRIST HATH RISEN!

LUKE 24:2 NRSV
They found the stone rolled away from the tomb.

C hrist hath risen! Hallelujah!
Blessèd morn of life and light!
Lo, the grave is rent asunder,
Death is conquered through His might.

Christ is risen! Hallelujah!
Gladness fills the world today;
From the tomb that could not hold Him,
See, the stone is rolled away!

Christ hath risen! Hallelujah!
Friends of Jesus, dry your tears;
Through the veil of gloom and darkness,
Lo, the Son of God appears!

Christ hath risen! Hallelujah!
He hath risen, as He said;
He is now the King of glory,
And our great exalted Head.

FANNY CROSBY

DO YOU BELIEVE?

LUKE 24:5 NLT
*The women were terrified and bowed low before them.
Then the men asked, "Why are you looking
in a tomb for someone who is alive?"*

The women had planned to put spices on Jesus' body.
They had seen him die on the cross and be carried to a
tomb. They knew the spot. But Jesus was gone! In his place
stood two angels who reminded them of Jesus' prediction
that he would be crucified and then, on the third day, be
raised from the dead. Then the women remembered.

If they had listened, understood, and believed in the
first place, they would not have expected to find his body in
the tomb. But none of Jesus' followers had understood his
prediction; thus, they all were surprised by his resurrection.
Breathless with excitement, the women rushed back with
the wonderful news, but the eleven disciples and the others
didn't believe their report.

Do you believe? Because Christ rose from the dead, we
know that our world is heading for redemption, not disaster.
We know that death has been conquered and that we, too,
will be raised from the dead to live forever with Christ. We
know that Christ is alive and ruling his kingdom, and that
God's power that brought Jesus back from the dead is avail-
able to us so we can live for him in an evil world.

Do you believe? Then live with joy and hope and power.

DAVE VEERMAN

HE LIVES

LUKE 24:5 KJV
Why seek ye the living among the dead?

Come, see the place where Jesus lay,
And hear angelic watchers say,
"He lives, Who once was slain:
Why seek the Living midst the dead?
Remember how the Savior said
That He would rise again."

O joyful sound! O glorious hour,
When by His own almighty power
He rose and left the grave!
Now let our songs His triumph tell,
Who burst the bands of death and hell,
And ever lives to save.

The first begotten of the dead,
For us He rose, our glorious Head,
Immortal life to bring;
What though the saints like Him shall die,
They share their Leader's victory,
And triumph with their King.

THOMAS KELLY

CHRIST *the* LORD IS RISEN TODAY

MATTHEW 28:6 KJV
He is risen.

Christ, the Lord, is risen today, Alleluia!
Sons of men and angels say, Alleluia!
Raise your joys and triumphs high, Alleluia!
Sing, ye heavens, and earth, reply, Alleluia!

Lives again our glorious King, Alleluia!
Where, O death, is now thy sting? Alleluia!
Once He died our souls to save, Alleluia!
Where thy victory, O grave? Alleluia!

Soar we now where Christ hath led, Alleluia!
Following our exalted Head, Alleluia!
Made like Him, like Him we rise, Alleluia!
Ours the cross, the grave, the skies, Alleluia!

Hail, the Lord of earth and heaven, Alleluia!
Praise to Thee by both be given, Alleluia!
Thee we greet triumphant now, Alleluia!
Hail, the resurrection day, Alleluia!

CHARLES WESLEY

INFINITELY MORE

MARK 16:6 NLT

But the angel said, "Do not be so surprised. You are looking for Jesus, the Nazarene, who was crucified. He isn't here! He has been raised from the dead! Look, this is where they laid his body."

Practically everybody puts Jesus in the category of "best man who ever lived," many agree that he's "the greatest teacher the world has known," not a few insist he "showed us how we ought to live," and some believe he "demonstrated how to face death." But however true these opinions may be, they all fall short of what the Scriptures say about him. . . .

Even a moment's reflection will show that this series of events immediately lifts Jesus beyond the opinions mentioned above into a position that only he can occupy. He is infinitely more than revered teacher, glowing example, courageous facer of death, and unimpeachable role model. His resurrection is seen to be the Father's endorsement of all Jesus' claims and the seal of validation that his death takes away our sins. His life after death is a statement concerning the reality of eternal existence, and his conquering of death is a robust reminder that death need hold no fear for those who trust their eternal destiny to Jesus.

The bottom line is that approving opinions about Jesus' life miss the point unless married to joyous belief in his resurrection. Reverence, however sincere, for a dead Christ, however noble, will do nothing for a sinner headed toward a lost eternity. Only a personal experience of the risen Lord will suffice.

STUART BRISCOE

THE RISEN LORD

JOHN 20:16 NKJV

Jesus said to her, "Mary!" She turned and said to Him,
"Rabboni!" (which is to say, Teacher).

The title "Rabboni," is a term that carries the utmost respect, reverence, and love. It is a more emphatic and honored term than the more simple "rabbi."

Mary at the tomb made the grandest discovery of all—the risen Christ. The account reads she went to proclaim the glorious news, "I have seen the Lord!" At the tomb was the last time Christ was called by the term "Rabboni" or its near equivalents—"master," "teacher," "rabbi." From this momentous day, He would be the risen, triumphant, reigning Lord.

It is not enough that we ascribe to Christ those titles of respect and tradition. We too must know Him as our risen Lord. We too have a mandate and a mission to proclaim the Good News from personal experience, "I have seen the Lord." Only a vibrant encounter with the resurrected Christ and a recognition of His mighty power leads us to know Him as He truly is and to share His message with others. In that discovery is our destiny.

HENRY GARIEPY

THEY BELIEVED

JOHN 20:6–8 NLT

*Then Simon Peter arrived and went inside. He also noticed
the linen wrappings lying there, while the cloth that had covered Jesus' head was folded up and lying to the side. Then the
other disciple also went in, and he saw and believed.*

The grave-clothes lay like the shriveled, cracked shell of
a cocoon, left behind when the moth has emerged and
hoisted her bright sails in the sunshine. . . . Or, more accu-
rately, like a glove from which the hand has been removed,
the fingers of which still retain the shape of the hand.

In that manner, the grave-clothes were lying, collapsed
a little, slightly deflated—because there was between the rolls
of bandages a considerable weight of spices, but there lay the
linen cloth that had been wound 'round the body of Christ.

It was when they saw *that,* that the disciples believed.

The Greek word here for "see"—*theorei*—is not to
behold as one looks at a spectacle, not to see as the watch-
maker who peers through his magnifying glass.

It means to see with inner light that leads one to
conclusion.

It is perception
reflection
understanding—more than sight. . . .
They arrived at the conclusion
the unshakable, unassailable, certain conviction
that Jesus Christ had risen from the dead.

PETER MARSHALL

I Am *the* Resurrection

John 11:25 kjv

Jesus said unto her, I am the resurrection, and the life: he that believeth in me, though he were dead, yet shall he live.

In Jesus there are no sunsets; they are all sunrises. He is the "bright and morning star"—not the evening star. He heralds the dawn—not the dark. Rufus Moseley, a layman, called on to conduct a funeral, went to the New Testament to see how Jesus conducted a funeral and found that "Jesus did not conduct funerals. He conducted resurrections." This, that I have in Jesus, does not have the feel of a funeral upon it; it has the feel of a resurrection. . . . A noted New Testament scholar says the "the" can be omitted in both cases—"I am resurrection," not *"the* resurrection," his own resurrection. He was and is *"the* resurrection," his own, but he is more. He is the principle and power of resurrection. If you have Jesus, you have resurrection. He is resurrecting your mind, your body, your spirit, your hopes, your outlook, your everything. In him you are resurrected now. I shall salute the resurrection of my body as an old friend: "I've known you all my life. For life has been one long glorious resurrection. Welcome, friend, I knew you would come."

E. Stanley Jones

THE RESURRECTION *and the* LIFE

JOHN 11:25 NRSV
*Jesus said to her, "I am the resurrection and the life. Those
who believe in me, even though they die, will live."*

It is no wonder that Jesus is named after many good things
in the Gospel. If we look at the names by which the Son of
God is called, we will understand how many of these good
things He is. The feet of those who preach His name are beautiful. One good thing is life. Jesus is the Life. Another good
thing is the light of the world (when it is true light that
enlightens people). And the Son of God is said to be all these
things. Another good thing, in addition to life and light, is the
truth. A fourth is the way that leads to truth. Our Savior teaches us that He is all these things. He says: "I am the Way and the
Truth and the Life." Ah, isn't it good that the Lord shook off
earth and mortality to rise again? And we have obtained this
benefit from the Lord: that He is the Resurrection. He says, "I
am the Resurrection." The door through which one enters
into the greatest joy is also good. And Christ says, "I am the
door." . . . We must not neglect mentioning the Word, who is
God after the Father of all. For this is another good, no less
than the others. Happy, then, are those who accept these goods
and receive them from those who announce their blessings,
those whose feet are beautiful.

ORIGEN

NOTHING BUT *the* TRUTH

LUKE 24:46–47 NKJV

Then He said to them, "Thus it is written, and thus it was necessary for the Christ to suffer and to rise from the dead the third day, and that repentance and remission of sins should be preached in His name to all nations, beginning at Jerusalem."

History is replete with those who have had delusions of grandeur about themselves. Some have even been willing to die for their cause. But, like all men, they were defeated by death. If we dug up their graves, we'd find their dead bodies. But that's what makes Jesus unique. He predicted His death, predicted His burial, and prophesied that one day He would come out of the grave victorious over death. Three days after His death, He did just that.

The Scriptures record it. All who have tried to disprove it have been defeated. Scientists, determined to destroy the Christian faith, have been unable, and many skeptics and atheists have been brought to faith after studying the death and resurrection of Jesus Christ. It is one of the most thoroughly documented events in the world's history.

Through His death we are redeemed, and through His blood our sin atoned, but all of that is meaningless if he did not come out of the grave. Christ's resurrection validated what He did on the cross.

DAVID JEREMIAH

WE SHALL LIVE AGAIN

JOB 14:14 NKJV

*If a man dies, shall he live again? All the days of
my hard service I will wait, Till my change comes.*

Four hundred years before Christ's birth, the Greek
philosopher Socrates lay dying from poison. He was considered the wisest teacher in the world, but when his friends
asked, "Shall we live again?" he could only answer, "I hope
so, but no man can know."

In Job 14:14, another man asked the same question. "If
a man dies, shall he live again?" It's an age-old question. It
haunts many people and tests every religious persuasion—
the most crucial question of the ages. In Hebrews 2:15 we
find that some men live all their lives in bondage to the fear
of death. Many are afraid that death will catch up with them.
Without some assurance of life after death, death becomes a
terrifying proposition. But that is exactly why we can celebrate Easter: The resurrection of Jesus Christ answers that
age-old question once and for all. The Resurrection takes
Christianity out of the realm of philosophy and turns it into
a fact of history. It proves that there is life beyond this life.

DAVID JEREMIAH

Die *for a* Lie?

ACTS 12:2 NLT
He had the apostle James (John's brother) killed with a sword.

One area often overlooked in challenges to Christianity is the transformation of Jesus' apostles. Their changed lives provide solid testimony for the validity of his claims . . . I can trust the apostles' testimonies because, of those men, eleven died martyrs' deaths on the basis of two things: the resurrection of Christ, and their belief in him as the Son of God. . . .

The response that is usually chorused back is this: "Why, a lot of people have died for a lie; so what does it prove?"

Yes, a lot of people have died for a lie, but they thought it was the truth. Now if the resurrection didn't take place (i.e., was false), the disciples knew it. I find no way to demonstrate that they could have been deceived. Therefore these eleven men not only died for a lie—here is the catch—but they knew it was a lie. It would be hard to find eleven people in history who died for a lie, knowing it was a lie.

JOSH MCDOWELL

OUR ASSURANCE

ROMANS 4:25 NIV
*He was delivered over to death for our sins
and was raised to life for our justification.*

The Resurrection also gives us assurance about our own salvation. Jesus was indeed "raised to life for our justification" (Romans 4:25). Our salvation does not depend on our achievements but on Christ's achievement, which we know is complete. This is one of the great attractions of Christianity to the non-Christian. In Islam there is no such assurance. Muslims faithfully perform their rituals, hoping that God will have mercy on them, but having no assurance of God's acceptance. The Jehovah's Witnesses, despite the confidence with which they proclaim their understanding of the Scriptures, do not have such an assurance.

To the Buddhists and Hindus the path to liberation is a long and dreary climb spanning countless numbers of lives, with no assurance of when they will be able to offset all the bad karma they have gathered along the way. What good news it can be to such pilgrims, weary of toiling for their salvation, when they hear the words of Paul: "Therefore, there is now no condemnation for those who are in Christ Jesus, because through Christ Jesus the law of the Spirit of life set me free from the law of sin and death" (Romans 8:1-2).

AJITH FERNANDO

FREE, BUT NOT CHEAP

ROMANS 6:23 NIV

*For the wages of sin is death, but the gift of God is eternal
life in Christ Jesus our Lord.*

Grace is a wonderful word. It means the free, unmerited favor of God. It's His remedy for sin . . . for the sinner.

Grace is free. But not cheap.

It's the costliest gift ever offered.

It cost the Son of God His life. He, the "Friend of sinners," came into history to make an infinite sacrifice for the sins of all mankind, from the first human being to the last one ever to live. He was the "Lamb of God who takes away the sin of the world." Born to be crucified. Suffered our death that we might receive His life. Bore our sin that we might be made righteous in His perfection. Became poor that we might have His riches.

His gift of grace is free for the asking, free for the taking. . . .

In His mercy, God doesn't give us what we deserve: judgment. In His grace He gives us what we do not deserve: justification.

If we acknowledge that we are sinners—if we confess our sin—if we desire His forgiveness, cleansing, renewal, *life* — if we ask God for forgiveness . . .

He will respond in grace.

RICHARD HALVERSON

UTMOST CONFIDENCE

1 CORINTHIANS 15:17 NLT
And if Christ has not been raised, then your faith is useless,
and you are still under condemnation for your sins.

Why is it so important to believe in the Resurrection? "If Christ is not risen, then is our faith vain," and if Christ is not risen, our loved ones who have already died are lost. If Jesus Christ is not raised from the dead, "we are of all men most pitiable." If Christ is risen from the dead, "He is the firstfruits of those who believe." The picture Paul gives us is of the firstfruits of a harvest, the promise of what is to come. He is the firstfruits of God's harvest of souls—and we are the rest of the harvest.

Paul says the hope of the Resurrection is the reason he is willing to go through intense suffering for Christ. What would be the point he asks, if Christ were not truly alive? By far the biggest problem in life is death. . . . But for the Christian the stone has been rolled away from the tomb of death. It's empty! Death for the Christian is the gateway into life. Christ has gone before to tell us there is a new world ahead of us and we can face the grave with utmost confidence in that promise.

JILL BRISCOE

NO MORE STING

1 CORINTHIANS 15:54–55 KJV
Death is swallowed up in victory. O death,
where is thy sting? O grave, where is thy victory?

Hail! victorious Jesus, hail!
On Thy cloud of glory sail
In long triumph through the sky,
Up to waiting worlds on high.

Heaven unfolds its portals wide,
Glorious Hero, through them ride:
King of glory mount Thy throne,
Thy great Father's, and Thine own.

Praise Him all ye heavenly choirs,
Raptured, sweep your sounding lyres
Sons of men, in humbler strain,
Sing your mighty Savior's reign.

Every note with wonder swell;
Sin o'erthrown, and captived hell!
Where is now, O death! thy sting?
Where thy terrors, vanquished king!

THOMAS SCOTT

HIS TRIUMPH

ROMANS 6:9 NLT
We are sure of this because Christ rose from the dead, and he will never die again. Death no longer has any power over him.

Jesus Christ has come to invade every form of death and to infuse it with His life. He is capable of doing that because in His own dying He absorbed all the power of death in Himself.

In His body, death was swallowed up. In submitting to the torment of Calvary, He mastered the Tormentor. He bore in Himself the full stroke of the blade of death and received into Himself all the bitter fruit due to the sinners of the world. Somehow, in one mighty transference, all of the delinquent accounts of the history of human sin and failure were paid by His sinless Person. He received the agony of our penalty and provided the ecstasy of our deliverance.

It is because of His own sinlessness that He was capable of doing this. Only the magnitude of an unencroached-upon, untainted soul could absorb the awesome dimension of sin that Christ encountered on the cross. The sins of the entire human race engulfed Him, but death could not hold Him. In God's Son was found a sinlessness that could take on the guilt of all humanity and still survive an encounter with divine justice. Christ exhausts the power of sin, breaks the power of death, and comes through in triumph.

JACK HAYFORD

NO MORE DEATH

I CORINTHIANS 15:56–57 NLT

For sin is the sting that results in death, and the law gives sin its power. How we thank God, who gives us victory over sin and death through Jesus Christ our Lord!

Death is destroyed. The cross has triumphed over it. It no longer has any power but is truly dead. This is why all of Christ's disciples despise death and no longer fear it. They take the offensive against it. And by the sign of the cross and by faith in Christ they trample it down as dead. Before the Savior came, death was terrible to the saints. Everyone wept for the dead as though they perished. But now that the Savior has risen, death isn't terrible anymore. For everyone who believes in Christ tramples over death. They would rather die than deny their faith in Christ. For they know that when they die they aren't destroyed, but actually begin to live. Through the Resurrection they become incorruptible. For the devil, who once maliciously rejoiced in death, is the only one truly dead now that we are relieved of death's pains. As proof of this, people are cowards and terrified of death before they believe Christ. But when they have turned to Christ's faith and teaching, they despise death so much that they even eagerly rush up to it. They testify of Christ's victorious Resurrection.

ATHANASIUS

IT HAPPENED *to* YOU

GALATIANS 2:20 NASB

I have been crucified with Christ; and it is no longer
I who live, but Christ lives in me; and the life which
I now live in the flesh I live by faith in the Son of God,
who loved me, and delivered Himself up for me.

Our salvation takes care of our eternal security, and our identification takes care of our daily walk of victory. By identification, I mean that Christ's life is now mine and mine His. "It is no longer I who live, but Christ lives in me" (Galatians 2:20). What happened to Christ at Calvary happened to me. Christ was crucified, I was crucified. Christ was buried, I was buried. Christ was raised, I was raised. Identification is the theme song of Romans 6. When we are identified with Him and have accepted that by faith sin's power is broken, we are free to walk in the Spirit, liberated to become the persons God wants us to be. It is Christ Jesus living His life in us and through us as individuals. Our relationship to Him is that we are saved, we are forgiven, we are accepted, we are children of God. We are secure in the Cross. We can have the peace and assurance that our daily walk is pleasing and honorable to Him. . . .

One who is safe and secure in the love of God and sustained by His grace no longer hears from a distant God. He now listens to Someone who loves him enough to bring him to a personal relationship, and that makes all the difference.

CHARLES STANLEY

OUR TRUE HOME

EPHESIANS 2:19 NKJV
*Now, therefore, you are no longer strangers
and foreigners, but fellow citizens with the saints
and members of the household of God.*

Always remember that we have renounced the world and are living here as guests and strangers in the meantime. Anticipate the day assigned to each of us for our home-coming. This day will snatch us up, set us free from the snares of the world, and return us to Paradise and the kingdom. Who, in foreign lands, wouldn't hurry to return to their own country? Who, when rushing to return to his friends, wouldn't eagerly want the winds at his back so that he could embrace those dear to him sooner? We consider paradise as our country. We already consider the patriarchs as our parents. Why don't we hurry and run, so that we can see our country and greet our parents? A great number of our dear ones are waiting for us there. A dense crowd of parents, brothers, and children is longing for us, already assured of their own safety and eager for our salvation. . . . Beloved, let us hurry to these people eagerly. Let us long to be with them and to come to Christ quickly. May God see our eager desire. May the Lord Jesus Christ look at the purpose of our mind and faith. He will give the larger rewards of His glory to those with a greater desire for Him!

CYPRIAN

HIS PASSION

DEATH *to* SELF

PHILIPPIANS 2:5, 8 NIV
Your attitude should be the same as that of Christ Jesus:
. . . he humbled himself and became obedient to death.

To be a Christian is to be a subject—subject to a king—that is, to welcome the rule of God in one's life. Jesus Himself became subject to the Father—"Lo, I come to do Thy will, O God" (Hebrews 10:7 Amp.). This meant that He had come to this world, not to gain, but to lose; not to get, but to give; not to be served, but to serve; not to obtain bread but to *be* bread, the Bread of heaven, broken for the life of the world.

"Let this mind be in you which was also in Christ Jesus. . . . He humbled Himself" (Philippians 2:5–8 Amp.).

That puts it in very simple terms. If you want to be a Christian, see that your mind is made up as his was: be humble, be subject, be obedient—even to *death*. It will mean death. Be sure of that. Death to some of your desires and plans at least. Death to *yourself*. But never forget—Jesus' death was what opened the way for his own exaltation and our everlasting *Life*. Our death to selfishness is the shining gateway into the glories of the palace of the King. Is it so hard to be his subject? Is the price too high?

ELISABETH ELLIOT

New Life

Colossians 2:12 NLT

With him you were raised to a new life because you trusted the mighty power of God, who raised Christ from the dead.

Let this, therefore, be fixed in our minds: that Christ has stretched out his hand to us, that he may not desert us in the midst of the course, but that, relying on his goodness, we may boldly raise our eyes to the last day. . . . For in what respect do believers differ from wicked men, but that, overwhelmed with afflictions and like sheep destined for the slaughter (Romans 8:36), they have always one foot in the grave and, indeed, are not far from being continually swallowed up by death? Thus there remains no other support of our faith and patience but this: that we keep out of view the condition of the present life, and apply our minds and our senses to the last day, and pass through the obstructions of the world—until the fruit of our faith at length appear.

John Calvin

OUR MEDIATOR

HEBREWS 9:15 NIV
*For this reason Christ is the mediator of a new covenant, that
those who are called may receive the promised eternal inheri-
tance—now that he has died as a ransom to set them free
from the sins committed under the first covenant.*

How tremendously great is the remission and redemption
of sins through Jesus Christ!

Many Christians do not sufficiently realize the work
which Jesus Christ is doing for us at this very moment. Many
of us believe that He died for our sins. We believe in His death
and resurrection, but we forget that after His resurrection, He
ascended into heaven and sat down on the right hand of the
Father and began to live for us as truly as He died for us.

The devil makes accusations against us day and night.
But Jesus is our Advocate. In Him we are the righteousness
of God (2 Corinthians 5:21).

If, after having been forgiven for a sin, we are still worrying about it, even for five minutes more, we are robbing
both Him and ourselves of much joy.

"Resist the devil, and he will flee from you" (James 4:7).
No better weapon could be found to use against him than
this text.

The consciousness of sin may degenerate into defeatism,
"It's too bad, but that's the way I am." The devil rejoices when
we are defeated, but is afraid of the consciousness of victory.

The devil makes us conscious of sin. The spirit of God
makes us conscious of sin, and then conscious of victory.

CORRIE TEN BOOM

FELLOWSHIP FOREVER

REVELATION 21:3 NKJV

*And I heard a loud voice from heaven saying, "Behold,
the tabernacle of God is with men, and He will dwell with
them, and they shall be His people. God Himself
will be with them and be their God."*

There will be no sanctuary or tabernacle or temple in
heaven—and no churches. Revelation 21:22 says that
"the Lord God Almighty and the Lamb are its temple." Because God will be dwelling in the midst of His people, just
as He started off doing in the Garden of Eden, there will be
no need for a sanctuary for Him to dwell in.

We incorrectly call our churches "sanctuaries" today
because they are where we draw together once a week to
worship God and hear His Word proclaimed. But God does
not dwell in buildings in this age; He dwells in His people.
At present, we cannot "see" His presence as we will be able
to in heaven. Instead of dwelling "in" us in heaven, He will
dwell "among" us, in our very presence.

The same Jesus who healed the sick, raised the dead, fed
the multitudes, died on Calvary, was raised from the dead,
and who ascended into heaven will be walking among us in
heaven. We will have unbroken, personal fellowship with
Him forever.

DAVID JEREMIAH

OUR HOPE

PHILIPPIANS 3:21–22 NKJV

For our citizenship is in heaven, from which we also
eagerly wait for the Savior, the Lord Jesus Christ, who will
transform our lowly body that it may be conformed to His
glorious body, according to the working by which
He is able even to subdue all things to Himself.

While we don't know exactly how our bodies are going to be changed in that glorious day, we do know that the limitations and pain and suffering and death will be forever gone! To the Corinthians Paul said that our bodies will be buried in decay and raised without decay; they will be sown in humiliation and raised in splendor; they will be sown in weakness and raised in strength; they will be sown a physical body and raised a spiritual body (1 Corinthians 15).

Our new bodies will be like the glorious body of our Lord Jesus Christ. Apart from the resurrection of Jesus Himself, there are only three resurrections recorded in the Gospels: the son of the widow of Nain, the daughter of Jairus, and Lazarus. All of these situations began in mourning until Jesus came; then that sorrow was turned into joy and gladness. Jesus said of Himself, "I am the resurrection and the life." Whenever the life of Jesus means death, death is always defeated. When He comes again, death will be dealt its final blow. As Paul said to the Corinthians, "Death is swallowed up in victory" (15:54).

DAVID JEREMIAH

FREED *from* DEATH

---

1 PETER 1:23 NLT

*For you have been born again. Your new life did not come
from your earthly parents because the life they gave you will
end in death. But this new life will last forever because it
comes from the eternal, living word of God.*

Christ is the life . . . because he never permits the life
which he has once bestowed to be lost, but preserves it
to the end. For since flesh is so frail, what would become of
men if, after having once obtained life, they were afterwards
left to themselves? The perpetuity of the life must, therefore,
be founded on the power of Christ himself, that he may
complete what he has begun.

The reason why it is said that believers never die is that
their souls, being born again of incorruptible seed (1 Peter
1:23), have Christ dwelling in them, from whom they derive
perpetual vigor. For though the body be subject to death on
account of sin, yet the spirit is life on account of righteousness
(Romans 8:10). That the outward man daily decays in them is
so far from taking anything away from their true life, that it
aids the progress of it, because the inward man is renewed
from day to day (2 Corinthians 4:16). What is still more, death
itself is a sort of emancipation from the bondage of death.

JOHN CALVIN

FOR SURE

1 JOHN 1:1 KJV

That which was from the beginning, which we have heard,
which we have seen with our eyes, which we have looked
upon, and our hands have handled, of the Word of life.

Jerusalem had been anything but impressed with the way
Christ's disciples had conducted themselves during the
arrest and trial of the Nazarene. His followers had certainly
not been courageous. In fact, they had all either fled to save
their own lives or followed at a great distance. Peter was so
fearful that he had even denied having known the Nazarene.

Then after their Master's death, the band of disciples
had stayed in hiding with the doors locked—"for the fear of
the Jews."

Yet after that first Easter morning, we find these same men
timid
frightened
ineffective
preaching openly, with no fear of anyone.

Their personal conviction rings like a bell through the
pages of the New Testament . . . steady and strong. . . .

"That which we have heard with our own ears, seen
with our own eyes, handled with our own hands, declare we
unto you."

And of what were they so sure?

That Jesus Christ was alive.

PETER MARSHALL

A UNIQUE SAVIOR

1 CORINTHIANS 15:12–14 NIV

But if it is preached that Christ has been raised from the dead, how can some of you say that there is no resurrection of the dead? If there is no resurrection of the dead, then not even Christ has been raised. And if Christ has not been raised, our preaching is useless and so is your faith.

Without the Resurrection, Christianity would have been stillborn. You can't have a living faith if all you have is a dead savior. Without the Resurrection, the Christian faith might be a commendable way of life, but Jesus would be just another great teacher who lived His life and returned to dust. Christianity would not be the truth from God if Jesus did not rise from the dead.

The Resurrection places Jesus Christ in a class by Himself. It makes Him unique. Other religious can compete with Christianity on some things. They can say, for example, "Your founder gave you a holy book? Our founder gave us a holy book. Your founder has a large following? So does ours. You have buildings where people come to worship your God? We have buildings where people come to worship our god."

But Christians can say, "All of that may be true, but our Founder rose from the dead!" End of conversation.

TONY EVANS

JESUS APPEARS *to* HIS FOLLOWERS

―

*He said to them, "This is what I told
you while I was still with you: Everything
must be fulfilled that is written about me in
the Law of Moses, the Prophets and the
Psalms." Then he opened their minds
so they could understand the Scriptures.*

LUKE 24:44–45 NIV

JESUS APPEARS *to* HIS FOLLOWERS

Many different people spent time with Jesus after the Resurrection. Most of them doubted in one way or another. Thomas may have been the most vocal in his reluctance to believe Jesus was alive, but all of them displayed a certain amount of shock because they didn't expect Jesus to rise from the grave. In spite of His promises, they were surprised.

Jesus' post-resurrection appearances had a common result. Doubters became convinced. Many of those who testified to His resurrection maintained their witness even in the face of painful death. Their lives and their message carry the ring of truth that continues to reverberate in history.

As you think about the varied appearances of Jesus in this section, take some time to reflect on the way their witness has affected your life and the ways in which Jesus has demonstrated Himself alive for you.

WHO ARE YOU LOOKING FOR?

JOHN 20:15 NIV
"Woman," he said, "why are you crying?
Who is it you are looking for?"

Why are you crying? Who is it you are looking for?" That was the question asked of Mary when she went to the garden where the body of Jesus had been laid in a tomb. During the few short years that the disciples had with Jesus, their conversations had abounded with questions. There is, therefore, a tender note of indictment when this question is asked of *them*. This actually has overtones of a question He had asked them on more than one occasion. To His earliest followers, He had asked, "What do you want?" He had asked the same of the disciples of John the Baptizer—"What did you go out to see?" One has to presume that He repeatedly stopped them to ask of themselves what it was that they wanted God to be in order to merit their approval.

During their years with Him, their inability to grasp so much of what He said wins both our sympathy and our bewilderment. Indeed, they were with One who was like no other, and therefore, their tentative posture every step of the way is understandable. But how much more specific did He have to be before they were clear as to who He was?

RAVI ZACHARIAS

I WILL NEVER LET YOU GO

JOHN 20:17 NIV

Jesus said, "Do not hold on to me, for I have not yet returned to the Father. Go instead to my brothers and tell them, 'I am returning to my Father and your Father, to my God and your God.'"

One of the postresurrection images of Christ I love most is when He has to tell Mary Magdalene to peel herself from Him so that each of them can be released to do what God had called them to do (see John 20:17). The moment she recognized Jesus, she obviously latched on to Him for dear life as if to say, "Now that I've found you, I will never let you go!" Although you and I have never seen Christ face-to-face, we're not altogether different. We sometimes receive a fresh revelation of Christ in a moment of crisis. Then we may not want to budge from it for the rest of our days.

Christ seems to say to us, "Yes, this revelation is a gift to you, but be careful not to get stuck here. Don't cling to your sightings of Me. Let those moments be fuel for your future. Walk by faith and not by sight. There's work to be done! Rest assured I'll always be with you because now that I've found you, I will never let you go."

BETH MOORE

DAY 329

IT HAD *to* BE DONE

LUKE 24:26 NLT
*"Wasn't it clearly predicted by the prophets
that the Messiah would have to suffer all these
things before entering his time of glory?"*

If thou willingly bear the Cross, it will bear thee, and will
bring thee to the end which thou seekest, even where
there shall be the end of suffering; though it shall not be
here. If thou bear it unwillingly, thou makest a burden for
thyself and greatly increaseth thy load, and yet thou must
bear it. If thou cast away one cross, without doubt thou shalt
find another and perchance a heavier.

Thinkest thou to escape what no mortal hath been able
to avoid? Which of the saints in the world hath been without
the cross and tribulation? For not even Jesus Christ our Lord
was one hour without the anguish of His Passion, so long as
He lived. *It behooved,* He said, *Christ to suffer and to rise from the
dead, and so enter into his glory.* And how dost thou seek another way than this royal way, which is the way of the Holy Cross?

THOMAS À KEMPIS

STUDY *and* PRAY

LUKE 24:32 NKJV
*And they said to one another, "Did not our heart
burn within us while He talked with us on the road, and
while He opened the Scriptures to us?"*

The word *burn* means exactly what you think it does: "to make to burn, . . . flaming . . . to consume with fire." . . . Your heart means far more to Christ than anything. That your heart is utterly taken with Christ is more important than any amount of service you could render or rules you could keep. . . . God wants to completely captivate your heart and cause it to burn with passion for Him. It is His absolute priority for you according to Mark 12:30; joy and satisfaction will elude you in its absence. Two immutable keys exist that turn our spiritual ignition and inflame godly passion. Both are tucked like rubies in the embers of Luke 24:32. "'Were not our hearts burning within us while he [1] talked with us on the road and [2] opened the Scriptures to us?'"

To me, "talked with us on the road" is a wonderfully personal and tender representation of prayer and "opened the Scriptures to us" is a perfect representation of Bible study. Beloved, we may do many other things to fan the flame of our spiritual passion for Christ, but all other efforts are in vain without the two sticks of prayer and Bible study rubbed together to ignite a fire.

BETH MOORE

PEACE *to* YOU

JOHN 20:19 KJV

Then the same day at evening, being the first day of the
week, when the doors were shut where the disciples were
assembled for fear of the Jews, came Jesus and stood in the
midst, and saith unto them, Peace be unto you.

I s it not always so? Does He not come just when He is
needed most, and is not His first word always, Peace be
unto you? "Jesus Christ the same yesterday, and to-day, and
for ever."

I wonder if He showed them His hands and His side,
and His feet, too, not only that they might recognize Him
in their ill-lighted room, but that always on to the end they
might remember this: I, Whom you follow, suffered; if you
would follow Me you cannot avoid suffering; you must not
be surprised at any suffering. "Think it not strange," "Count
it all joy." More even than that (for His call all along had been
to take up the cross and carry it), it seems to me that by His
showing of hands and side and feet, He was impressing this
great truth upon their minds: "Verily, verily, I say unto you,
Except a corn of wheat fall into the ground and die, it abideth alone: but if it die, it bringeth forth much fruit." "There
is no life except by death." But first He said, "Peace be unto
you."

AMY CARMICHAEL

A CHOICE *of the* WILL

JOHN 20:25 NLT

They told him, "We have seen the Lord!" But he replied, "I won't believe it unless I see the nail wounds in his hands, put my fingers into them, and place my hand into the wound in his side."

When most of the disciples first saw Jesus alive after his crucifixion, Thomas had not been with them. When the other disciples told him about the fact of the Resurrection, Thomas replied, "I won't believe it unless I see" (John 20:25). Some of us are skeptical like Thomas was. We find it very easy to doubt what we cannot see or touch. . . . Thomas finally did see the risen Christ, who said to him, "Don't be faithless any longer. Believe!" (John 20:27). When Jesus called Thomas to believe, he appealed to Thomas's will. . . .

Choosing to believe in the resurrection of Jesus Christ leads to joy, peace, and the experience of his risen life in us. The living Christ is the biggest reason we tell others about our faith. Paul, writing to the Corinthians, said, "If Christ has not been raised, then your faith is useless" (1 Corinthians 15:17). No other religion in the worlds boasts that its founder was actually God who became a man, was killed, yet rose again from the dead. Such claims should certainly be investigated! Even if you are skeptical by nature, like Thomas was, it is safe to investigate your doubts by taking them directly to Christ. Let him help you choose to believe!

JILL BRISCOE

HAUNTED *by the* MEMORY

JOHN 21:9–10 NLT

When they got there, they saw that a charcoal fire was burning and fish were frying over it, and there was bread. "Bring some of the fish you've just caught," Jesus said.

After his resurrection, Jesus appeared to his disciples on a beach, having made a charcoal fire and cooked their breakfast (John 21:9). Of all of them, Peter must have caught his breath as he smelled the acrid smoke. It surely surrounded him with memories of an awful night not too long before when he had stood shivering as he warmed himself by another charcoal fire (John 18:18). . . .

Now, on a beach, the resurrected Jesus was cooking breakfast for Peter and the others over a charcoal fire. After that meal, the Lord asked Peter three times, "Do you love me?" Can you imagine how that question triggered by his recent failure, must have pierced Peter's soul? . . . Yet Jesus let Peter know that, in spite of his failure, Peter could be forgiven. What's more, the resurrected Lord told him that he had special work for Peter to do. . . .

Peter allowed Jesus Christ to forgive him, cleanse him from his sins, and fill him with the Holy Spirit so that he could serve his Lord powerfully. We can do the same.

JILL BRISCOE

TAKE CARE *of the* SHEEP

JOHN 21:16 NIV

Again Jesus said, "Simon son of John, do you truly love me?"
He answered, "Yes, Lord, you know that I love you."
Jesus said, "Take care of my sheep."

What could be greater than to be seen doing the things of Christ declared to be proofs of love for Him? He said, addressing the leader of the apostles, "Peter, lovest thou Me?" When Peter confessed that he did, the Lord added, "if thou lovest Me tend my sheep." The Master didn't ask the disciple if he loved Him in order to get information (why would He when He already knows everyone's heart?), but to teach us how great an interest He has in the care of these sheep. Clearly, then, those who labor for these sheep that Christ values so highly will receive a great reward. For when we see anyone caring for members of our household, or our flocks, we consider that person's zeal for them to be a sign of love towards ourselves. Yet all these things can be bought with money. Imagine, then, how great a gift Christ will give to those who tend the flock He purchased, not with money nor anything of that kind, but by His own death. For He gave His own life to pay for the herd.

CHRYSOSTOM

PIERCING QUESTIONS

JOHN 21:17 KJV
He saith unto him the third time, Simon, son of Jonas,
lovest thou me? Peter was grieved because he said unto him
the third time, Lovest thou me? And he said unto him, Lord,
thou knowest all things; thou knowest that I love thee.
Jesus saith unto him, Feed my sheep.

[Peter] was awakening to the fact that in the real true centre of his personal life he was devoted to Jesus, and he
began to see what the patient questioning meant. There was
not the slightest strand of delusion left in Peter's mind, he
never could be deluded again. There was no room for pas-
sionate utterance, no room for exhilaration or sentiment. It
was a revelation to him to realize how much he did love the
Lord, and with amazement he said—"Lord, Thou knowest
all things." Peter began to see how much he did love Jesus;
but he did not say—"Look at this or that to confirm it."
Peter was beginning to discover to himself how much he did
love the Lord, that there was no one in heaven above or
upon earth beneath beside Jesus Christ; but he did not know
it until the probing, hurting questions of the Lord came. The
Lord's questions always reveal me to myself.

The patient directness and skill of Jesus Christ with
Peter! Our Lord never asks questions until the right time.
Rarely, but probably once, He will get us into a corner
where He will hurt us with His undeviating questions, and
we will realize that we do love Him far more deeply than
any profession can ever show.

OSWALD CHAMBERS

UTTERLY CHANGED

JOHN 21:17 NKJV
Jesus said to him, "Feed My sheep."

Dear friend, I beseech you, look at Peter utterly changed —the self-pleasing, the self-trusting, the self-seeking Peter, full of sin, continually getting into trouble, foolish and impetuous, but now filled with the Spirit and the life of Jesus. Christ had done it for him by the Holy Ghost. . . .

That story must be the history of every believer who is really to be made a blessing by God. That story is a prophecy of what everyone can receive from God in Heaven. . . .

How was it that Peter, the carnal Peter, self-willed Peter, Peter with the strong self-love, ever became a man of Pentecost and the writer of his epistle? It was because Christ had him in charge, and Christ watched over him, and Christ taught and blessed him. The warnings that Christ had given him were part of the training; and last of all there came that look of love. In His suffering Christ did not forget him, but turned round and looked upon him, and "Peter went out and wept bitterly." And the Christ who led Peter to Pentecost is waiting today to take charge of every heart that is willing to surrender itself to Him.

ANDREW MURRAY

HIS SUFFERING WAS UNDERSTOOD

JOHN 21:18–19 NRSV

"Very truly, I tell you, when you were younger, you used to fasten your own belt and to go wherever you wished. But when you grow old, you will stretch out your hands, and someone else will fasten a belt around you and take you where you do not wish to go." (He said this to indicate the kind of death by which he would glorify God.)

Among many other saints, the blessed apostle Peter was condemned to death, and crucified, as some do write, at Rome. Hegesippus saith that Nero sought matter against Peter to put him to death; which, when the people perceived, they entreated Peter with much speech that he would leave the city. Peter, through their importunity at length persuaded, prepared himself to avoid. But, coming to the gate, he saw the Lord Christ come to meet him, to whom he, worshipping, said, "Lord, whither dost Thou go?" To whom He answered and said, "I am come again to be crucified." By this, Peter, perceiving his suffering to be understood, returned into the city. Jerome saith that he was crucified, his head being down and his feet upward, himself so requiring, because he was (he said) unworthy to be crucified after the same form and manner as the Lord was.

FOXE'S BOOK OF MARTYRS

What About Him?

JOHN 21:21-22 NLT
Peter asked Jesus, "What about him, Lord?"
Jesus replied, "If I want him to remain alive until
I return, what is that to you? You follow me."

Jesus had told Peter, rather enigmatically, "When you are old you will stretch out your hands, and others will direct you and take you where you don't want to go" (John 21:18). Peter then noticed John standing nearby and said, "What about him, Lord?" (21:21). . . .

The answer Jesus gave was straight to the point. . . . In simple language, that meant that what Jesus decided to do with John was none of Peter's business! John's future was strictly between Jesus and John. In the same way, Peter's future lay in Jesus' hands and was therefore only of concern to Jesus and Peter. What Jesus had told Peter about his own future was all that Peter needed to know.

Jesus added, "You follow me!" (21:22). In light of the future that Peter was being called to live, he could not afford to allow any distractions from the fundamental and all-consuming call to follow Jesus. That was what he had been challenged to do years earlier beside the lake, and his call had not been rescinded or altered.

Trying to understand God's ways of dealing with other people can be confusing. We may become disgruntled, but one thing will help. We should let Jesus do his job, which is to lead, and we should do ours, which is to follow. That will keep us on track.

STUART BRISCOE

JESUS GIVES *the* GREAT COMMISSION

"Therefore, go and make disciples of all the nations, baptizing them in the name of the Father and the Son and the Holy Spirit."
MATTHEW 28:19 NLT

JESUS GIVES *the* GREAT COMMISSION

The Resurrection got the disciples' full attention, and the Great Commission gave them
direction. Jesus originally promised He would
make them into fishers of people. When He sent
out His disciples the last time, He declared open
season on the world. Jesus announced that people
from every nation are candidates for discipleship.
Every person ought to hear the gospel.

The parameters of the mission were global;
the time frame, "until the end of the age;" the
message: Become a disciple of Jesus and "obey all
the commands I have given you."

No aspect of Jesus' commission has been
rescinded. Believers live under standing orders. If
all the power and passion of Jesus' life and ministry
were poured into His final words, then our failure
to carry out that command in our lives may be a
symptom of disobedience or unbelief. The challenge of the Great Commission is serious and
personal; consider once again to what degree it
reflects the way you spend your days.

JOYFUL WORSHIPERS

MATTHEW 28:16–17 NLT
Then the eleven disciples left for Galilee,
going to the mountain where Jesus had told them to go.
When they saw him, they worshiped him.

Happy are they who have reached the end of the road we seek to tread, who are astonished to discover the by no means self-evident truth that grace is costly just because it is the grace of God in Jesus Christ. Happy are the simple followers of Jesus Christ who have been overcome by his grace, and are able to sing the praises of the all-sufficient grace of Christ with humbleness of heart. Happy are they who, knowing that grace, can live in the world without being of it, who, by following Jesus Christ, are so assured of their heavenly citizenship that they are truly free to live their lives in this world. Happy are they who know that discipleship simply means the life which springs from grace, and that grace simply means discipleship. Happy are they who have become Christians in this sense of the word. For them the word of grace has proved a fount of mercy.

DIETRICH BONHOEFFER

A STORY *to* TELL

MATTHEW 28:19 NASB
"Go therefore and make disciples of all the nations."

We've a story to tell to the nations,
    That shall turn their hearts to the right,
A story of truth and mercy,
A story of peace and light,
A story of peace and light.

We've a message to give to the nations,
That the Lord who reigns up above
Has sent us His Son to save us,
And show us that God is love,
And show us that God is love.

We've a Savior to show to the nations,
Who the path of sorrow has trod,
That all of the world's great peoples
Might come to the truth of God,
Might come to the truth of God.

H. ERNEST NICHOL

EVERY NATION

MATTHEW 28:19 NRSV
"Go therefore and make disciples of all nations."

O Church of God, arise!
  Reach out thy helping hand,
And like a trumpet let thy voice
Go forth to ev'ry land;
Lay not thine armor down,
Nor cease by day or night,
To lift the sword of Gospel truth,
And wield it for the right.

O Church of God, arise!
Thy borders wide extend,
And o'er the earth's remotest bounds
Thy heralds quickly send;
Thine armies now are great,
But greater they must be,
For ev'ry nation, ev'ry clime
Shall yet rejoice in thee.

FANNY CROSBY

GRANT US WORDS

MATTHEW 28:20 NLT
*"Teach these new disciples to obey all the
commands I have given you. And be sure of this:
I am with you always, even to the end of the age."*

We pray that words may be given to us, as it is written in
the book of Jeremiah, "The Lord said to the prophet:
'Behold, I have put My words in thy mouth as fire. See, I have
set thee this day over the nations, and over the kingdoms, to
root out and to pull down, and to destroy, and to throw down,
and to build and to plant.'" For we need words now that will
root out of every wounded soul the disgraces spoken against
the truth. . . . We also need thoughts that will pull down all edi-
fices based on false opinions. . . . And we require a wisdom
that will throw down all high things that rise against the
knowledge of God. Just as we must not stop rooting out and
pulling down the hindrances that have just been mentioned,
we must, in place of what has been rooted out, plant the plants
of God's field. In place of what has been pulled down, we must
raise the building of God and the temple of His glory. For that
reason, we must also pray to the Lord who gave the gifts
named in the book of Jeremiah. Pray that He may grant us
words for building up the temple of Christ, for planting the
spiritual law, and for teaching others to do the same.

ORIGEN

MISSIONARIES

JOHN 20:21 NIV
Again Jesus said, "Peace be with you!
As the Father has sent me, I am sending you."

Jesus said salvation must be preached "to the ends of the earth." No place is to be missed, no one left out. He didn't say only the good nations, the western nations, or the eastern nations. He didn't say tell only those who are willing to listen to you, or those you like, or those who won't persecute you. He said all nations.

When Jesus gave his disciples their marching orders, he told them to begin at Jerusalem, the place of their worst experiences and greatest failure. They were then to go on to Judea, the place where their neighbors and Jewish relatives lived and knew the worst about them. After that, they were to go on to Samaria, the place of their worst prejudices. From there they were to go to the ends of the earth. . . .

Actually, it is often easier to go to the farthest parts before attending to the nearest. We feel we are too well known in our "Jerusalem," so we fear that people won't believe us. But we need to start there.

JILL BRISCOE

THE BIG PICTURE

ACTS 1:8 NIV

"But you will receive power when the Holy Spirit comes on you; and you will be my witnesses in Jerusalem, and in all Judea and Samaria, and to the ends of the earth."

This is the big picture. Christ came and died and rose again in order to gather a joyful, countless company for his name from all the peoples of the world. This is what every Christian should dream about.... It is crucial that millions of Christians fulfill their life calling in secular jobs, just as it is crucial that during wartime the entire fabric of life and culture not unravel. But during wartime, even the millions of civilians love to get news from the front lines. They love to hear of the triumphs of the troops. They dream about the day when war will be no more. So it is with Christians. All of us should dream about this. We should love to hear how the advance of King Jesus is faring. We should love to hear of gospel triumphs as Christ plants his church among peoples held for centuries by alien powers of darkness.

JOHN PIPER

THE GREATER MINISTRY

MATTHEW 24:14 NKJV
*"And this gospel of the kingdom will be preached
in all the world as a witness to all the nations,
and then the end will come."*

I remember when television first came out. Many Christians shunned it, believing it was run by the prince of the power of the air. The evil one certainly had his influence in that medium (and still does), but why not use television as a means to proclaim the good news? Why not use radio? Why not use print? Why not use the Internet? Why not use any means at hand to take the message of the gospel and spread it throughout the whole world? The farther the better. The faster the better. The sooner the better. Until He comes!

What Jesus was saying to His disciples was this: "While I was on this earth, I was localized. I could only touch individual men and women in My travels and speak to a few local audiences. But believe Me, after I am gone and the Holy Spirit comes to fill and empower My sons and daughters, then My ministry will be as far spread as Christians are."

So wherever there is a Christian, there is Christ. Wherever there is a believer, there is ministry.

DAVID JEREMIAH

GIVE IT AWAY

ACTS 1:8 NKJV

"But you shall receive power when the Holy Spirit has come upon you; and you shall be witnesses to Me in Jerusalem, and in all Judea and Samaria, and to the end of the earth."

God never gives us anything to keep for ourselves. Whether it is money, insight, or truth, it has to be shared. Jesus said in His great command in Matthew 28:19–20, "Go therefore and make disciples of all the nations, baptizing them in the name of the Father and of the Son and of the Holy Spirit, teaching them to observe all things that I have commanded you." To those who witnessed His Ascension He declared in Acts 1:8, "But you shall receive power when the Holy Spirit has come upon you; and you shall be witnesses to Me in Jerusalem, and in all Judea and Samaria, and to the end of the earth." Jesus very clearly let His disciples know that the truth He had taught them during the past three years was not to be kept in a personal reservoir of knowledge. They were to give away everything they had received.

CHARLES STANLEY

OUR COMMISSION

ACTS 1:8 NRSV

"But you will receive power when the Holy Spirit has come upon you; and you will be my witnesses in Jerusalem, in all Judea and Samaria, and to the ends of the earth."

This is the commission that still holds for today. This is not given only to a corporate body, to the church as a body; it is not a corporate commission. This is a very personal command to each believer—personally, privately. This was given to these men even before the Holy Spirit had come and formed the church. It is a direct command for you and for me today. It is our business to get the Word of God out to the world. We can't say that it is up to the church to send missionaries and to give out the gospel, and then sit back and let others do it. The all-important question is whether *you* are getting out the Word of God. Have you gone to the ends of the earth as a witness to the gospel? Or do you support a missionary or a radio program that does? Are you personally involved? Today there are a great many people who want to talk about the times and seasons of His coming, but they don't want to get involved in getting out the Word of God. But that is His commission—not only to the apostles—that is His commission to you and me. . . . He wants people to be saved. This is our commission.

J. VERNON MCGEE

WHAT IS YOUR WITNESS?

ACTS 1:8 KJV

*But ye shall receive power, after that the Holy Ghost
is come upon you: and ye shall be witnesses unto me both in
Jerusalem, and in all Judaea, and in Samaria,
and unto the uttermost part of the earth.*

"In Jerusalem," which applied to us means our hometown,
there should be a witness to Christ. "All Judaea" is equivalent to our community; "Samaria" represents the other side of
the tracks, the folk we don't associate with. Although we may
not meet with these people socially, we are to take the gospel
to them. Of course we can't associate with everybody. We can
select our friends as everyone else does. That is part of the freedom which we have. There are folk who wouldn't want to
associate with us. There are lots of folk who wouldn't want me
around; I would crimp their style. But we have both the privilege and the responsibility to get the Word of God out to folk
whether or not we associate with them socially.

Finally, this witness to Christ is to go to the uttermost
part of the earth. We never should lose sight of the fact that
this is the Lord's intention. He has told us if we love Him
to keep His commandments. His command is personal. We
can't pass this off on the crowd, and say "The church is doing
it; so I don't need to get involved." How much are you involved, friend? What is your witness to Christ?

J. VERNON MCGEE

YOU ARE *the* STORY

ACTS 1:8 NLT

"But when the Holy Spirit has come upon you, you will receive power and will tell people about me everywhere—in Jerusalem, throughout Judea, in Samaria, and to the ends of the earth."

The heart of Christ's strategy for telling the world of God's love is something different: He witnesses through each of His followers wherever they are, day in, day out.

Which makes every believer indispensable. Each follower of Christ spends much of his or her time where the professionals do not: in touch with the unbelievers. And love works only on contact!

Which is the point of Pentecost (Acts 2). The Holy Spirit was given to every disciple there (120), not just to the apostles (12). Subsequently, He also came upon the three thousand who responded to their witness. Pentecost fulfilled the amazing promise of Christ in His last discourse: "Anyone who has faith in me will do what I have been doing. He will do even greater things than these" (John 14:12).

What Jesus began in His incarnation—in His own body—was now to be continued through the bodies of every believer, simultaneously, wherever they are. Jesus began something during His brief ministry on earth which was to continue through His body, the Church, after He ascended.

The book of Acts is the record of that continuation.

And the book of Acts is *still being written!*

RICHARD HALVERSON

RIVERS *of* LIVING WATER

JOHN 7:38 NKJV
*"He who believes in Me, as the Scripture has said,
out of his heart will flow rivers of living water."*

Jesus was hung on the cross, He was pierced, He died. Though He cried out from Calvary, "My God, my God, why hast thou forsaken me?" this was not His last word. Rather, He said, "It is finished" and turned to the Father: "Father, into thy hands I commend my spirit." The work is done, and since Pentecost every person who believes on Jesus as his Savior has the Holy Spirit, the Spirit of Christ, the Spirit of truth—all these are words for the same Person—living within him. The Holy Spirit, not some inner strength or psychological integratedness, is the source of the overflowing rivers of living water. There are to be living waters, a watered garden in the time of drought. The Holy Spirit lives within!

Not only are these rivers to be copious, they are also to be diffused; the "rivers of living water" are to *flow,* flow out to others. The Holy Spirit is not to be kept selfishly within myself, like a treasure clutched in a small child's fist. The waters are not to be dammed up until they become a stagnant pool. They are to be a flowing, flowing, flowing river.

FRANCIS SCHAEFFER

GIVE YOURSELF

JOHN 7:38 NLT
*"If you believe in me, come and drink! For the Scriptures
declare that rivers of living water will flow out from within."*

The more I understand and contemplate Jesus' surrender
of Himself for me, the more do I give myself again to
Him. The surrender is a mutual one: the love comes from
both sides. His giving of Himself makes such an impression
on my heart, that my heart with the self-same love and joy
becomes entirely His. Through giving Himself to me, He of
Himself takes possession of me; He becomes mine and I His.
I know that I have Jesus wholly for me, and that He has me
wholly for Him. . . .

And how come I then to the full enjoyment of this
blessed life? . . . Through faith I reflect upon and contemplate
His surrender to me as sure and glorious. Through faith I
appropriate it. Through faith I trust in Jesus to confirm this
surrender, to communicate Himself to me and reveal Himself
within me. Through faith I await with certainty the full experience of salvation which arises from having Jesus as mine, to
do all, all for me. Through faith, I live in this Jesus who loved
me and gave Himself for me.

ANDREW MURRAY

THE PROOFS *of* HIS PRESENCE

ROMANS 8:36 NIV

*As it is written: "For your sake we face death all day long;
we are considered as sheep to be slaughtered."*

When a great king sends an emissary to a rebellious
people, you expect a mission of ruthless power and
terror. But when God sent his Son to us rebels, he sent him
in gentleness and humility, although he was a King sending
a son who was also a King.

He sent Jesus as God, but he also sent him as a Man to
men. He sent him on an errand of mercy, of persuasion, not
of *force*. Force is foreign to the nature of God. Jesus came to
invite men, not to drive them to repentance. And God's
motive in sending him was love, not judgment . . . though
one day he *will* send him in judgment, and "who will abide
the day of his coming?"

How do we know that he came, the Son of God, the
Son of Man? We know as we see the results of his coming—
as we see his followers refuse to deny him, even though they
are flung to wild beasts or tortured; as we see their numbers
increase as persecution increases; as we see that nothing can
conquer their faith in the Lord. Such things are not the work
of mortal man. They are evidence of the power of God. They
are the proofs of Christ's presence.

EPISTLE OF DIOGNETUS

THE HEART *of the* GOSPEL

ROMANS 3:25–26 KJV
*Whom God hath set forth to be a propitiation through faith
in his blood, to declare his righteousness for the remission of
sins that are past, through the forbearance of God; To declare,
I say, at this time his righteousness: that he might be just,
and the justifier of him which believeth in Jesus.*

The gospel tells us that our Creator has become our
Redeemer. It announces that the Son of God has
become man "for us men and for our salvation," and has died
on the cross to save us from eternal judgment. The basic
description of the saving death of Christ in the Bible is as a
propitiation, that is, as that which quenched God's wrath
against us by obliterating our sins from His sight. God's wrath
is His righteousness reacting against unrighteousness; it shows
itself in retributive justice. But Jesus Christ has shielded us
from the nightmare prospect of retributive justice by becoming our representative substitute, in obedience to His Father's
will, and receiving the wages of our sin in our place. By this
means justice has been done, for the sins of all that will ever
be pardoned were judged and punished in the person of God
the Son, and it is on this basis that pardon is now offered to
us offenders. Redeeming love and retributive justice joined
hands, so to speak, at Calvary, for there God showed Himself
to be "just, and the justifier of him that hath faith in Jesus."

Do you understand this? If you do, you are now seeing
to the very heart of the Christian gospel.

J. I. PACKER

THE GOOD NEWS

JOHN 1:12 NIV

Yet to all who received him, to those who believed in his name, he gave the right to become children of God.

It was impossible that Our lives, which were alienated from God, could return to the high and heavenly place through our own power. . . . He freed us from the curse by taking our curse on Himself as His own. . . . Having become what we were, He again united humanity to God through Himself. Through purity He brought our new selves, created after God's image, into a close relationship with the Father of our nature. All of God's fulness physically dwelt in Him. He drew everything that shares in His body and is similar to Him into the same grace. And He proclaims good news . . . to everyone who became a disciple of the Word up until today. The good news is that people are no longer condemned or cast out of the kingdom of God. But they are children again and returned to the position God assigned to them. . . . For our sakes He took part in flesh and blood and saved us. He brought us back to the place from which we strayed, becoming mere flesh and blood by sin. And so He from whom we were formerly alienated through our revolt has become our Father and our God.

GREGORY OF NYSSA

SHARING *in* HIS SUFFERINGS

PHILIPPIANS 3:10 NIV
*I want to know Christ and the power of his
resurrection and the fellowship of sharing in his
sufferings, becoming like him in his death.*

When I get to heaven in my new resurrected body, this is what I hope to do. It may be theologically incorrect, but I hope I can take my old wheelchair with me. Not my streamlined travel model, but my old Sherman tank that I use in Southern California—my old clunky, dusty wheelchair. That's what I want beside me when I'm standing before Jesus, because then I'll be able to say, "Lord Jesus, do You see this thing? Well, before You send it to hell, there's something I want to tell You. I was in this thing for more than three decades and You were right, in this world I did have trouble. But the more troublesome life was in that wheelchair, the more I leaned on You. And the more I leaned on You, Lord, the stronger I discovered You to be. The affliction was light and momentary compared to the privilege it was to share in the fellowship of Your sufferings. You died for sin, I died to sin, and that's how I became like You in Your death. And if I had not been paralyzed, I don't think I would have cared about such stuff. But Lord, in the process of sharing in Your suffering, I became much closer to You. I felt Your strength. I was able to reveal to others your smile, and miraculously, my heart beat in rhythm to Yours."

JONI EARECKSON TADA

OUR OBSESSION

HEBREWS 12:1 NIV

*Therefore, since we are surrounded by such a great
cloud of witnesses, let us throw off everything that hinders
and the sin that so easily entangles, and let us run with
perseverance the race marked out for us.*

The power of the indwelling Christ is what keeps dynamic Christians alive and excited about life. . . .

As we walk in the power of the indwelling Christ, eternity's values become more important to us. Lost people become our obsession because lost people are God's obsession. Although we still hold jobs, earn a living, and pay bills, these things no longer are the focus of our lives. Although we work to keep ourselves attractive, we are not engrossed in clothes, hairstyles, or shoes. Our primary purpose and source of excitement is to reach out to the lost. . . .

When the life of Jesus is at work in us, enabling us to communicate the Gospel naturally as we go through life, we will be renewed day by day.

LUIS PALAU

JESUS ASCENDS
into HEAVEN

---

*They said, "Men of Galilee, why are
you standing here staring at the sky?
Jesus has been taken away from you
into heaven. And someday, just as
you saw him go, he will return!"*
ACTS 1:11 NLT

JESUS ASCENDS *into* HEAVEN

When God visited earth, the modes of His arrival and departure were completely unexpected. He came as a baby—hidden, humble, and absolutely surprising in its commonness. He came like everyone because He had something for everyone. When He left, Jesus did so in plain sight. He didn't vanish; He ascended. He was gone, but in such a way that His imminent return has been a daily possibility, just as He promised.

The ascension of Jesus was not nearly so much an end as a beginning. When He disappeared in the clouds, the anticipation began. God intended it to be an active, adventurous, meaningful anticipation. He directed us to watch and wait—busily. When we focus too much on watching, we don't carry out His commands. When we lean too much on the waiting, we begin to lose sight of His promise to return. Those first disciples stood there for a while staring at the sky. Apparently, they were immobilized by yet another surprising turn of events. An angel had to remind them that there was work to do before Jesus would come again in the same way that He had left.

This section deals with the in-between time, when we watch and wait. Jesus has prepared a place. He will return. Will you be ready?

CHOOSE YOUR SIDE

MATTHEW 28:17 NLT
When they saw him, they worshiped him—
but some of them still doubted!

Everybody has an opinion. Everyone is choosing a side.
You can't be neutral on an issue like this one. Apathy?
Not this time. It's one side or the other. All have to choose.

And choose they did.

For every cunning Caiaphas there was a daring Nico-
demus. For every cynical Herod there was a questioning Pilate.
For every pot-mouthed thief there was a truth-seeking one.
For every turncoat Judas there was a faithful John.

There was something about the crucifixion that made
every witness either step toward it or away from it. It simultaneously compelled and repelled.

And today, two thousand years later, the same is true. It's
the watershed. It's the Continental Divide. It's Normandy.
And you are either on one side or the other. A choice is demanded. We can do what we want with the cross. We can
examine its history. We can study its theology. We can reflect
upon its prophecies. Yet the one thing we can't do is walk
away in neutral. No fence-sitting is permitted. The cross, its
absurd splendor, doesn't allow that. That is one luxury that
God, in his awful mercy, doesn't permit.

On which side are you?

MAX LUCADO

OUT *of* SIGHT

ACTS 1:9 NASB

And after He had said these things,
He was lifted up while they were looking on,
and a cloud received Him out of their sight.

He is gone—a cloud of light
Has received Him from our sight;
High in heav'n, where eye of men
Follows not, nor angels' ken;
Through the veils of time and space,
Passed into the holiest place;
All the toil, the sorrow done,
All the battle fought and won.

He is gone—but not in vain,
Wait until He comes again:
He is risen, He is not here,
Far above this earthly sphere;
Evermore in heart and mind
There our peace in Him we find:
To our own eternal Friend,
Thitherward let us ascend.

ARTHUR P. STANLEY

THE OPEN DOOR

LUKE 24:51 KJV
And it came to pass, while he blessed them,
he was parted from them, and carried up into heaven.

By His Ascension Our Lord enters heaven and keeps the door open for humanity.

On the Mount of Ascension the Transfiguration is completed. If Jesus had gone to heaven from the Mount of Transfiguration, He would have gone alone; He would have been nothing more to us than a glorious Figure. But He turned His back on the glory, and came down from the Mount to identify Himself with fallen humanity.

The Ascension is the consummation of the Transfiguration. Our Lord does now go back into His primal glory; but He does not go back simply as Son of God; He goes back to God as *Son of Man* as well as Son of God. There is now freedom of access for anyone straight to the very throne of God by the Ascension of the Son of Man. As Son of Man Jesus Christ deliberately limited omnipotence, omnipresence and omniscience in Himself. Now they are His in absolute full power. As Son of Man Jesus Christ has all power at the throne of God. He is King of kings and Lord of lords from the day of His Ascension until now.

OSWALD CHAMBERS

THE CLOUD *of* GLORY

ACTS 1:9 NKJV

Now when He had spoken these things, while they watched,
He was taken up, and a cloud received Him out of their sight.

There was a cloud to receive Him. What kind of a cloud was that? Was it a moisture cloud? No, this was the same *shekinah* glory cloud that had filled the tabernacle. In His high priestly prayer He had prayed: "And now, O Father, glorify thou me with thine own self with the glory which I had with thee before the world was" (John 17:5). When He was born into this world, He was wrapped in swaddling clothes. When He left this earth, He was wrapped in glory clouds. This is the way He returned to the Father's right hand. . . .

It is the glorified Jesus who went up into heaven. This same Jesus, the glorified Jesus, will return in like manner and to the same place. Zechariah 14:4 tells us: "And his feet shall stand in that day upon the mount of Olives, which is before Jerusalem on the east, and the mount of Olives shall cleave in the midst thereof toward the east and toward the west, and there shall be a very great valley; and half of the mountain shall remove toward the north, and half of it toward the south." He took off at that place, and He will come back to that place.

J. VERNON MCGEE

HAIL! VICTORIOUS JESUS!

ACTS 1:9 KJV

And when he had spoken these things, while they beheld, he
was taken up; and a cloud received him out of their sight.

Hail! victorious Jesus, hail!
On Thy cloud of glory sail
In long triumph through the sky,
Up to waiting worlds on high.

Heaven unfolds its portals wide,
Glorious Hero, through them ride:
King of glory mount Thy throne,
Thy great Father's, and Thine own.

Praise Him all ye heavenly choirs,
Raptured, sweep your sounding lyres
Sons of men, in humbler strain,
Sing your mighty Savior's reign.

Every note with wonder swell;
Sin o'erthrown, and captived hell!
Where is now, O death! thy sting?
Where thy terrors, vanquished king!

THOMAS GIBBONS

HE WILL RETURN

ACTS 1:11 NLT
*They said, "Men of Galilee, why are you standing
here staring at the sky? Jesus has been taken away
from you into heaven. And someday, just as
you saw him go, he will return!"*

The all-merciful and giving Father has tenderness toward those that fear Him and kindly and lovingly gives good things to those who come to Him with a trusting mind. Therefore, let us not be double-minded; neither let our souls be proud on account of His exceedingly great and glorious gifts. It is written, "Wretched are they who are of a double mind and of a doubting heart, who say, These things we have heard even in the times of our fathers; but, behold, we have grown old, and none of them has happened unto us." Far be it from us, you foolish ones! Instead, compare yourselves to a tree: for instance, the vine. First of all, it sheds its leaves, then it buds, next it puts forth leaves, and then it flowers; after that comes the sour grape, and then follows the ripened fruit. You see how in a little time the fruit of a tree comes to maturity. So shall God's will be accomplished, soon and suddenly, as the Scripture also bears witness saying, "Speedily will He come, and will not tarry," and "The Lord shall suddenly come to His temple, even the Holy One, for whom ye look."

CLEMENT OF ROME

HIS KINGDOM WILL COME

MICAH 4:3 NLT

*The LORD will settle international disputes. All the nations will
beat their swords into plowshares and their spears into pruning
hooks. All wars will stop, and military training will come to an end.*

In the time of Jesus the people of Israel were still looking
forward to this restoration. Before Jesus' crucifixion, his disciples were confident that Jesus would go about fulfilling
Micah's prophecy by ridding Israel of the Roman occupation
and bringing them peace and prosperity. But their hopes
were dashed when he died. However, after his resurrection
from the dead, the disciples quickly resorted to their earlier
hopes and asked Jesus, "Lord, are you going to free Israel now
and restore our kingdom?" (Acts 1:6). Jesus made it clear in
his response that his kingdom was not that kind of kingdom.
Instead, he indicated that Micah's prophecy would be fulfilled
when his eternal kingdom, populated by the redeemed, is
established.

This is the kingdom for which Christians pray repeatedly, "May your kingdom come soon" (Matthew 6:10) and
about which Jesus said, "My Kingdom is not of this world"
(John 18:36). Wars will cease one day, but only when Christ's
eternal kingdom comes. Until then, Paul's words speak loud-
ly: "Do your part to live in peace with everybody, as much as
possible" (Romans 12:18). We may not be able to stop wars.
But by God's grace we can obey this command and, "as much
as possible," live in peace with others.

STUART BRISCOE

AT *the* RIGHT HAND *of* GOD

———

ROMANS 8:34 NIV

Who is he that condemns? Christ Jesus, who died—
more than that, who was raised to life—is at the
right hand of God and is also interceding for us.

To Him the ascension came as *the culminating divine assurance* that the work He had come to do had been completed to the entire satisfaction of the Father, to whose right hand He had now been exalted. "The right hand of God" is metaphorical language for divine omnipotence. "Sitting" does not imply that He is resting, but reigning as King and exercising divine omnipotence. The doctrine of the ascension is therefore the divine affirmation of the absolute sovereignty of Christ over the whole universe. . . .

For the believer, our Lord's ascension has blessed implications for us. Though physically remote, He is always spiritually near. Now free from earthly limitations, His life above is both the promise and the guarantee of ours. "Because I live, ye shall live also," He assured His disciples (John 14:19). His ascension anticipates our glorification and leaves us the assurance that He has gone to prepare a place for us (John 14:2). . . .

It brings Him very near to us as we remember that He carried His humanity back with Him to heaven (Hebrews 2:14–18; 4:14–16).

"He led captivity captive" (Ephesians 4:8). His ascension was His triumphant return to heaven and indicated that the tyrannical reign of sin is ended.

J. OSWALD SANDERS

HIS PASSION

ABUNDANT LIFE!

———

JOHN 10:10 NRSV

"I came that they may have life, and have it abundantly."

The one great work of God's love for us is, He gives us His Son. In Him we have all. Hence the one great work of our heart must be to receive this Jesus who has been given to us, to consider Him and use Him as ours. I must begin every day anew with the thought, I have Jesus to do all for me. . . . In all weakness or darkness or danger, in the case of every desire or need, let your first thought always be, I have Jesus to make everything right for me, for God has given Him to me. Whether your need be forgiveness or consolation or confirmation, whether you have fallen, or are tempted to fall, into danger, whether you know not what the will of God is in one or another matter, or know that you have not the courage and the strength to do this will, let this always be your first thought, the Father has given me Jesus to care for me. . . . For this purpose, reckon upon this gift of God every day as yours. . . . Take Him, and hold Him fast in the love of your heart.

ANDREW MURRAY

SOURCES

✦ Arthur, Kay. Excerpts taken from: *Beloved*. Copyright © 1994 by Kay Arthur. Published by Harvest House Publishers, Eugene, OR. Used by Permission.

✦ Begg, Alistair. *What the Angels Wish They Knew*. Chicago: Moody Publishers, 1998.

✦ Blackaby, Henry and Claude King. *Experiencing God workbook*. Nashville: LifeWay, 1990.

✦ Boice, James Montgomery. *Amazing Grace*. Wheaton, Ill.: Tyndale House Publishers, 1993.

✦ Bonhoeffer, Dietrich. *The Cost of Discipleshp*. New York: The Macmillan Co., 1967.

✦ Bright, Bill. *God: Discover His Character*. Orlando, Fla.: NewLife Publications, 1999.

✦ Briscoe, Jill. *Daily Study Bible for Women*. Wheaton: Tyndale House Publishers, 1999.

✦ Briscoe, Jill. *The Heartbeat of Jesus*. Wheaton, Ill.: Scripture Press, Victor Books, 1984.

✦ Briscoe, Stuart. *The One Year Book of Devotions for Men*. Wheaton, Ill.: Tyndale House Publishers, 2000.

✦ Bruce, F. F. Quotations taken from *Hard Sayings of Jesus* by F. F. Bruce. ©1983 F. F. Bruce. Used by permission of InterVarsity Press, P.O. Box 1400, Downers Grove, IL 60515. www.ivpress.com.

✦ Campolo, Anthony. *The Power Delusion*. Wheaton, Ill.: Victor Books, 1984.

✦ Carmichael, Amy. *Edges of His Ways*. Fort Washington, Penna.: Christian Literature Crusade, 1955.

✦ Chambers, Oswald. *My Utmost for His Highest*. New York.: Dodd, Mead, and Company, 1935.

✢ Chesterton, G. K. *The Everlasting Man*. Garden City, New York: Image Books, Doubleday & Co., 1955.

✢ Colson, Charles W. *Born Again*. Old Tappan, New Jersey: Fleming H. Revell, a division of Baker Book House Company, 1976.

✢ Curtis, Brent and John Eldredge. Reprinted by permission of Thomas Nelson Inc., Nashville, TN., from the book entitled *The Sacred Romance,* copyright date 1997 by Thomas Nelson Publishers. All rights reserved.

✢ DeMoss, Nancy Leigh. *Lies Women Believe*. Chicago: Moody Publishers, 2001.

✢ Edersheim, Alfred. *The Life and Times of Jesus the Messiah*. McLean, Virginia: MacDonald Publishing Company, n.d.

✢ Elliot, Elisabeth. From *A Lamp for My Feet* by Elisabeth Elliot © 1985 by Elisabeth Elliot. Published by Servant Publications, P.O. Box 8617, Ann Arbor, Michigan, 48107. Used with permission.

✢ Evans, Anthony T. *Who is This King of Glory?* Chicago: Moody Publishers, 1999.

✢ Fernando, Ajith. *The Supremacy of Christ*. Wheaton, Ill.: Crossway Books, 1995.

✢ Foster, Richard J. *Prayer*. San Francisco: HarperSanFrancisco, a division of HarperCollins Publishers, 1992.

✢ *Foxe's Book of Martyrs*. Old Tappan, New Jersey: Fleming H. Revell, 1989.

✢ Gariepy, Henry. *100 Portraits of Christ*. Wheaton, Ill.: Victor Books, 1987.

✢ Gire, Ken. *The Divine Embrace*. Wheaton, Ill.: Tyndale House Publishers, 2003.

✢ Graham, Billy. *Angels: God's Secret Agents*. New York: Pocket Books, a division of Simon & Schuster, 1975.

✢ Guinness, Os. Reprinted by permission. *The Call,* Os Guinness, 1998, W. Publishing, Nashville, Tennessee. All rights reserved.

✦ Halverson, Richard C. *No Greater Power*. Portland: Multnomah Press, 1986.

✦ Hayford, Jack. *The Visitor*. Wheaton, Ill.: Tyndale House Publishers, 1986.

✦ Jeremiah, David. Excerpted from *God in You*. ©1998 by David Jeremiah. Used by permission of Multnomah Publishers, Inc.

✦ Jeremiah, David. *Life Wide Open*. Nashville: Integrity Publishers, 2003.

✦ Jeremiah, David. *My Heart's Desire*. Nashville: Integrity Publishers, 2002.

✦ Jeremiah, David. *Sanctuary*. Nashville: Integrity Publishers, 2002.

✦ Jones, E. Stanley. *A Song of Ascents*. Nashville: Abingdon Press, 1968. Used by permission.

✦ Jones, Russell Bradley. *Gold From Golgotha,* 1945. © Impact Christian Books, 332 Leffingwell Ave., Kirkwood, MO 36122. www.impactchristianbooks.com.

✦ Keller, W. Phillip. *Rabboni*. Old Tappan, New Jersey: Fleming H. Revell Company, 1977.

✦ L'Engle, Madeleine. Reprinted from *Penguins & Golden Calves*. Copyright ©1996 by Crosswicks, Inc. Used by permission of WaterBrook Press, Colorado Springs, CO. All rights reserved.

✦ L'Engle, Madeleine. Reprinted from *The Rock That Is Higher*. Copyright © 1993 by Crosswicks, Inc. Used by permission of WaterBrook Press, Colorado Springs, CO. All rights reserved.

✦ Laurie, Greg. *Breakfast with Jesus*. Wheaton, Ill.: Tyndale House Publishers, 2003.

✦ *Life Application Study Bible*. Quotation taken from Personality Profile of Judas. *Life Application Study Bible* copyright ©1988, 1989, 1990, 1991, 1993, 1996 by Tyndale House Publishers, Inc., Wheaton, IL 60189. All rights reserved.

✦ Lockyer, Herbert. *Seven Words of Love*. Waco, Tex.: Word Books, 1975.

✢ Lotz, Anne Graham. Reprinted by permission. *God's Story.* Anne Graham Lotz, 1999, W. Publishing, Nashville, Tennessee. All rights reserved.

✢ Lucado, Max. Reprinted by permission. *He Chose the Nails,* Max Lucado, 2000, W. Publishing, Nashville, Tennessee. All rights reserved.

✢ Lucado, Max. *It's Not About Me.* Nashville: Integrity Publishers, 2003.

✢ Lucado, Max. *No Wonder They Call Him the Savior.* Portland, Ore.: Multnomah Press, 1986.

✢ Lucado, Max. *Six Hours One Friday.* Carmel, New York: Guideposts, 1989.

✢ Lucado, Max. Reprinted by permission. *When Christ Comes,* Max Lucado, 2000, W. Publishing, Nashville, Tennessee. All rights reserved.

✢ Lutzer, Erwin. *Cries from the Cross.* Chicago: Moody Publishers, 2002.

✢ MacArthur, John. *Truth for Today* by John MacArthur. Copyright 2001 by John MacArthur. Used by permission of J. Countryman, a division of Thomas Nelson, Inc.

✢ Mains, David. *8 Survival Skills for Changing Times.* Wheaton, Ill.: Chariot Victor Books, 1993.

✢ Mains, Karen. Reprinted by permission of Thomas Nelson Inc., Nashville, TN., from the book entitled *Comforting One Another,* copyright date 1997 by Karen Mains. All rights reserved.

✢ Marshall, Catherine. Reprinted by permission. *The Helper,* Catherine Marshall, 1978, W. Publishing, Nashville, Tennessee. All rights reserved.

✢ Marshall, Peter. *The First Easter.* Old Tappan, New Jersey: Chosen Books, Fleming H. Revell, a division of Baker Book House Company, 1959.

✢ McDowell, Josh. *More Than a Carpenter.* Wheaton, Ill.: Tyndale House Publishers, 1977.

✢ McGee, J. Vernon. *Acts: Chapters 1–14* in the *Thru the Bible Commentary Series.* Nashville: Thomas Nelson Publishers, 1991. Used by permission of Thomas Nelson, Inc.

✢ Meyer, Joyce. *Battlefield of the Mind.* New York: Warner Faith, a division of Warner Books, 2002.

✢ Meyer, Joyce. *Knowing God Intimately.* New York: Warner Faith, 2003.

✢ Miller, Calvin. *Into the Depths of God.* Minneapolis: Bethany House Publishers, a division of Baker Book House Company, 2000.

✢ Moore, Beth. *Beloved Disciple* workbook. Nashville: LifeWay Press, 2002.

✢ Moore, Beth. *Jesus, The One and Only.* Nashville: Broadman & Holman Publishers, 2002.

✢ Osborne, Grant and Philip Comfort, eds. *John.* In the *Life Application Bible Commentary Series.* Wheaton, Ill.: Tyndale House Publishers, Inc., 1993.

✢ Osborne, Grant and Philip Comfort, eds. *Mark.* In the *Life Application Bible Commentary Series.* Wheaton, Ill.: Tyndale House Publishers, Inc., 1994.

✢ Osborne, Grant and Philip Comfort, eds. *Matthew.* In the *Life Application Bible Commentary Series.* Wheaton, Ill.: Tyndale House Publishers, Inc., 1996.

✢ Packer, J. I. *I Want to be a Christian.* Wheaton, Ill.: Tyndale House Publishers, 1987.

✢ Packer, J. I. Quotations taken from *Knowing God* by J. I. Packer. ©1973 J. I. Packer. Used by permission of InterVarsity Press, P.O. Box 1400, Downers Grove, IL 60515. www.ivpress.com.

✢ Palau, Luis. *Stop Pretending.* Colorado Springs: Nexgen, an imprint of Cook Communications, 2003. Cook Communications Ministries, Colorado Springs, CO 80918.

✢ Pink, Arthur W. *Gleanings in the Godhead.* Chicago: Moody Publishers, 1975. (Now published under the title *The Nature of God.*)

✢ Piper, John, *Don't Waste Your Life.* Wheaton, Ill.: Crossway Books, 2001.

✢ Pippert, Rebecca Manley. Quotations taken from *Out of the Salt Shaker and Into the World* by Rebecca Manley Pippert. ©1999 by Rebecca Manley Pippert. Used by permission of InterVarsity Press, P.O. Box 1400, Downers Grove, IL 60515. www.ivpress.com.

✢ Pollock, John. *The Master.* Wheaton, Ill.: Victor Books, 1985.

✢ Sanders, J. Oswald. *The Incomparable Christ.* Chicago: Moody Publishers, 1952.

✢ Sauer, Erich. *The Triumph of the Crucified,* translated by G. H. Lang. Grand Rapids: Wm. B. Eerdmans Publishing Company, 1957.

✢ Sayers, Dorothy. *The Whimsical Christian, "The Greatest Drama Ever Staged."* New York: Collier Books, Macmillan Publishing Company, 1978.

✢ Schaeffer, Edith. *Christianity is Jewish.* Wheaton, Ill.: Tyndale House Publishers, 1975.

✢ Schaeffer, Francis A. *No Little People,* Wheaton, Ill.: Crossway Books, 1974, 2003.

✢ Smedes, Lewis B. Reprinted from *How Can It Be All Right When Everything Is All Wrong?* Copyright © 1999 by Lewis B. Smedes. Used by permission of WaterBrook Press, Colorado Springs, CO. All rights reserved.

✢ Sproul, R. C. *The Holiness of God.* Wheaton, Ill.: Tyndale House Publishers, Inc., 1998.

✢ Stanley, Charles. Reprinted by permission of Thomas Nelson Inc., Nashville, TN., from the book entitled *How to Listen to God* copyright date 1985 by Oliver Nelson Books. All rights reserved.

✢ Stott, John R. W. Quotations taken from *The Cross of Christ* by John R. W. Stott. ©1986 John R. W. Stott. Used by permission of InterVarsity Press, P.O. Box 1400, Downers Grove, IL 60515. www.ivpress.com.

✦ Stowell, Joseph M. *Why It's Hard to Love Jesus.* Chicago: Moody Publishers, 2003.

✦ Swindoll, Charles R. *Rise and Shine.* Portland, Ore.: Multnomah Press, 1989.

✦ Tada, Joni Eareckson. Quotations taken from *Praying Through Life's Problems.* Nashville: Integrity Publishers. Copyright ©2003 by the American Association of Christian Counselors.

✦ Ten Boom, Corrie. *Amazing Love.* Fort Washington, Penna.: Christian Literature Crusade, 1953.

✦ Tozer, A. W. Reprinted from *The Pursuit of God* by A. W. Tozer, copyright ©1982, 1993 by Christian Publications, Inc. Used by permission of Christian Publications, Inc., 800.233.4443, www.christianpublications.com.

✦ Van Impe, Jack. *Great Salvation Themes.* Troy, Mich.: Jack Van Impe Ministries, 1991.

✦ Veerman, David. *Beside Still Waters.* Wheaton, Ill.: Tyndale House Publishers, 1996.

✦ Veerman David. *On Eagles' Wings.* Wheaton, Ill.: Tyndale House Publishers, 1995.

✦ Wiersbe, Warren W. *Meet Your King.* Wheaton, Ill.: Victor Books, 1980.

✦ Wirt, Sherwood Eliot. *Jesus Man of Joy.* Eugene, Ore.: Harvest House Publishers, 1999.

✦ Yancey, Philip. Quotation first appeared in the June 17, 1996 issue of Christianity Today Magazine. Used by permission of Christianity Today International. www.CTLibrary.com.

✦ Zacharias, Ravi. Reprinted by permission. *Jesus Among Other Gods,* Ravi Zacharias, copyright date 2000, W. Publishing, Nashville, Tennessee. All rights reserved.

✦ Zacharias, Ravi. *Recapture the Wonder.* Nashville: Integrity Publishers, 2003.